SECRET LOCHS AND SPECIAL PLACES

Secret Lochs and Special Places

An Angling Memoir

Bruce Sandison

BLACK & WHITE PUBLISHING

First published 2015
by Black & White Publishing Ltd
29 Ocean Drive, Edinburgh EH6 6JL

1 3 5 7 9 10 8 6 4 2   15 16 17 18

ISBN   978 1 84502 786 5

Typeset by RefineCatch Limited, Bungay, Suffolk
Printed and bound by ScandBook, Sweden

For Ann

In my love
Is love for me
And by that light
She leads me.
Rest weary soul
Upon her breast,
For in her eyes
I see the kindness
Of all ages.

CONTENTS

CONTENTS

FOREWORD

Many years ago, a friend and I were fishing the River Helmsdale on the east coast of Scotland. Day after wet, windy day we caught nothing and were having a seriously bad time. We were advised to seek advice from the widely recognised guru and oracle of hill-loch fishing, Bruce Sandison. So, nervously, I rang his number.

Bruce lived up to his reputation and opened up to us his encyclopedic knowledge of Caithness and Sutherland lochs and lochans; which ones had the largest fish, where to get a permit, the most successful flies and how to fish them, and their locations. His knowledge and prodigious memory gave us an unforgettable week; good fishing every day in a beautiful landscape surrounded by the best that nature has to offer.

Secret Lochs and Special Places is Bruce's fourteenth book. His books are not travel books. They are written with passion by a man in love with his chosen environment, about his family and friends and about his native land; as seen through the eyes of a fisherman, naturalist, walker, historian and storyteller.

After several years of army life and 'responsible' jobs, he seems to have had a 'Road to Damascus' experience that directed him to up sticks and move his family to the far north of Scotland, close to the Caithness Flow Country – not such strange surroundings for me, I come from the edge of the Cambridgeshire Fens

– proving that it is always important to follow one's natural instincts. The move encouraged him to write, bring up a wonderful family, and to fish and hill walk.

His stories of picnics, outings and walks (trudges) with his wife Ann and their children are not only entertaining but also instructive on how to keep a wet, windblown and midge-bitten group happy. Bruce's books are also wonderful guides and histories of Scotland's myriad lochs, mountains, hills, rivers and islands, and the archaeological remains to be found in these stunning surroundings. His books aren't for tourists: they are for those who wish to share his enjoyment of all his homeland has to offer. There are few paths in Scotland which haven't had the imprint of Bruce's size 11 walking boots. Oh, and he also takes some excellent photographs.

All this information is spiced with accounts of family outings, adventures and disasters, stories of big fish, Viking marauders, clan quarrels and murderous giants hurling rocks at one another. He tells of the best and most beautiful lochs, where they are and how to fish them. They are all, of course, home to huge, solitary brown trout lurking as sirens to tempt the optimistic to failure.

There is another, less well-known side to Bruce. Sandison, the Campaigner. He has, and does, speak out against the vested interests of corporate and financial activities that are disastrous to the fragile ecology in this unique part of the world: the fiscally advantageous forestry planting in Caithness that ruined many of its special places by introducing the non-indigenous Sitka spruce; the poisoning of sea lochs and estuaries by the salmon farming industry that has damaged the wild salmon and sea-trout stocks on the west coast and in the islands. Many may know of '*Old Trout*', *Private Eye*'s fishing correspondent. That was Bruce, and we should be grateful to him for exposing to public view what was happening.

Making a success of living in a wild place, far from shopping malls, supermarkets and motorways, may perhaps seem simple.

It's not; it's complicated and needs a glue to cement it together. For Bruce and Ann, I am sure the glue has been fly-fishing. Catching fish by this demanding method doesn't need to be evaluated by the number and weight of what is caught, but rather by the sheer pleasure and contentment of time spent in outstanding places, and the conversation of like-minded friends.

Success or failure, either way, there is always the all-encompassing variety of the scenery, as rich and wide-reaching as Bach Cello Suites; the 'wow' of a kingfisher streaking by; seeing otters, stoats, rabbits, wildflowers, trees, birds, deer, falcons, harriers, owls, mountains, hills, moors, rivers, lochs, lakes and ponds. And for both Bruce and me there is the enjoyment and passion of living at the furthest points of the British Isles: he, to look north to Iceland, whilst I stare south to Africa. A shared delight of the magic of the periphery.

Peter Fluck
Cadgwith, Cornwall
August 2015

PREFACE

This book tells the story of some seventy years' fly-fishing in Scotland. Along the way, it also tells the story of my growing up, getting married and raising a family, all of whom were to become fly-fishers. My belief is that introducing little ones to that gentle art is far better than giving them money; money comes and goes, but a love of fly-fishing brings them a lifetime's joy. My wife, Ann, began her journey as an angler around the same time as me, guddling trout from small Border streams near Hawick. When we met, we immediately found common ground, as well as a shared love for J. S. Bach, Beethoven, Mozart, classical music, art and literature; and we have argued about these subjects throughout our fifty-four years of marriage. When they were young, our four children – Blair, Lewis-Ann, Charles and Jean – were constantly exposed, not only to fishing but also to the arts and the great outdoors.

Ann and I married in 1961. I had always wanted to be a writer and Ann's first love was art, but as young adults, trying to make our way, we were always busy; Ann as a dental surgeon, whilst I worked in sales management and public relations in the building industry and, for a few uncomfortable and ultimately unsuccessful years, as a poultry farmer in egg production in Northumberland. There wasn't really much time for writing or art, let alone fishing, until we moved north to live in Wick in Caithness. Ann continued as a dentist and I found employment in agriculture as the manager of a land drainage company. Prior to that, I had written a humorous piece that was published in *Punch* in 1970 and had begun to write for the fishing magazine *Trout and Salmon*. Thus, in 1981, I decided to become a full-time writer. This would have been impossible had it not been for Ann agreeing to support the family whilst I tried to establish myself, based upon the publication of my first book, *Trout Lochs of Scotland*, the promise of regular work from *Trout and Salmon*, and being appointed angling correspondent for the *Scotsman* newspaper.

This is why my new book is all about fishing in the far north, where we have now lived for almost forty years. The book features Caithness; Sutherland; Orkney and Shetland; and Benbecula, the Uists and the Western Isles. It is essentially about the outstanding wild brown trout fishing to be found there, as well as some exciting salmon and sea-trout fishing. When we arrived in Caithness, Clan Sandison amounted to six in number, but by the year 2000 we numbered twenty, including ten grandchildren and, more recently, a great-granddaughter. Collectively I call them 'the enemy', but these have been wonderful years. Yes, times of turmoil and disappointments as well, but largely years of great joy and happiness. Two of our family moved north as well and live nearby: Blair and his wife Barbara, and their children – Blair retired after a career in the oil and gas industry; and Jean, with Jessica and Jake, who's married to Ian Smart, the head stalker on Ben Loyal Estate. Charles, an artist who has carved himself an international reputation, is married to Nanna, who is also an artist, and they live in Finland. Lewis-Ann is a teacher, and she and her daughter live in Dumfriesshire with her partner, Clark, an amazingly talented restorer of vintage vehicles.

As you might expect, they all fish and appear in the pages of my book, along with their cousins. I am enormously proud of them and honoured that I may call them friends. I have no doubt that there will be errors in the text of my book. Neither do I doubt that the members of Clan Sandison will be quick to point them out and put me right. I would expect nothing else. But if some of my words bring an occasional smile to the face of the reader, then I think that my work will have been worthwhile and will be well satisfied. Thank you.

Bruce Sandison
Hysbackie, August 2015

CAITHNESS

Hid disna matter far a be,
There's things mean chist wan place til me –
A flag-fenced county 'side 'e sea,
Ma ain dear Kaitness.

— Alexander Miller (1905–45)

When we first came to live in Caithness in 1975, I happened to mention to a workmate that my paternal grandfather had been born in the small fishing village of Staxigoe a few miles distant from the county town of Wick. 'If I were you,' he replied, 'I would keep quiet about that.' Apparently, it was alleged, Staxigoe was a noted den of scoundrels. Grandfather, a painter to trade, eventually moved his family to Edinburgh in search of work. However, as a young man, my father, John Sandison, used to spend his long summer holidays staying with his uncle, George Reay, at Elzy Farm on the outskirts of Staxigoe, which is how one of the best-attended Caithness boxing matches came to be arranged.

In the 1920s the Wick school truant officer, known as the 'wheeper-in', was also named John Sandison and he had a formidable fighting reputation. A bunch of worthies thought it would be a great idea to arrange a match between the two Johns. The fight took place in a farm building overlooking Staxigoe harbour. The ring was formed out of bales of straw. Wagers were placed and spirits high. Happily for my father his opponent's spirits were even higher because, being certain of victory, the 'wheeper-in' had taken considerable refreshment prior to the off. Father won.

During the 1800s Wick was the most prosperous herring fishing port in Europe and father told me that, as a boy, he remembered the quayside still busy with curing stations and Wick Bay bustling with boats. A less likely place for such an explosion of effort is hard to imagine: it boasted the most dangerous harbour along the east coast. In spite of these disadvantages hundreds of boats fished from Wick and the industry employed more than 5,000 people.

During the sixteen-week summer season tens of millions of herring were caught, cured and exported. But herring fishing was thirsty work. More than 800 gallons of whisky were drunk each week. Local ministers complained bitterly that whilst it was hard to get people into church for evening service, 'for a wedding you could get six pipers at a stroke, and not a teetotaller amongst them'.

Whether angler or not, you will always find a warm welcome in Caithness, Scotland's Lowlands beyond the Highlands; a land of fine golden-sand beaches, spectacular cliffs and ruined castles, ancient monuments and modern visitor facilities; a county where non-angling members of your tribe will find plenty to do whilst you get on with a man's proper function in life, the removal of fish from their natural habit.

The county is perfect bucket-and-spade country, with magnificent beaches at Reiss to the north of Wick, and at Dunnet Bay near Castletown. Dramatic ruined castles cling to black-scarred clifftops, the most stunning of which are Sinclair and Girnigoe Castles near Noss Head by Wick. There are dramatic Neolithic sites to be explored: the Grey Cairns of Camster; marvellously preserved 5,000-year-old burial cairns to the south of Watten; the standing stones of Rangag at Loch Stemster by the A895 Latheron/Thurso road.

The country also has some of the finest trout fishing in Scotland and excellent salmon fishing on the rivers Thurso, Wick and Forss. Sea-trout may be found in the Loch of Wester, which drains into Sinclair Bay, and in the sea at the mouth of that river. The most important point of contact for anglers is in the tackle shop in Wick High Street, an Aladdin's cave of piscatorial pleasure. Presiding here is Hugo Ross, *Mr Caithness Angling*. Hugo will direct your fishing efforts, advising where to fish, when to fish, permission and prices, boats, flies and tactics. My family and I have known Hugo for more years that I care to remember and have benefitted mightily from his kindness and endless courtesy.

The first Caithness loch I fished was Watten and it became a very special place for me and for other members of Clan Sandison. After a few years' living in Wick, we found a house at Ruther on a hill looking south over Loch Watten to the Caithness mountains – the Scarabens (2,022ft), Maiden Pap (1,475ft), Morven (2,316ft) and Small Mount (1479ft) – and the magnificent peatland wilderness of the Caithness Flow Country, an area that was to become a well-loved and frequently visited family destination.

Loch Watten is some three miles long by a half-mile wide and contains brown trout of the highest quality; perfectly shaped fish with small heads and deep bodies, silvery with salmon-pink flesh. They fight with extraordinary strength and even a modest-sized trout will bend your rod and tax your skill. When we first fished Watten, it was unusual to see more than half a dozen boats on the water. Today, it is busier, but I still often pass by and need only one hand to count the number of boats afloat.

The loch was not always its present size. A Caithness farmer, Charlie Alexander from Camster, told me that his father remembered seeing women washing clothes at the north-east end of the loch, chatting to women, similarly employed, on the opposite shore. The water level was raised when a stem was installed at the Watten end, where the loch drains out to join the Wick River. The late Sinclair Swanson of Banks Lodge said that his grandfather netted the loch during the 1920s and introduced trout from Loch Leven to improve the quality of fish. Others aver that the reverse was true, that stock from Loch Watten was used to improve the quality of Loch Leven trout.

Whatever the truth, there do seem to be two strains of trout in the loch. I have always thought that this was a consequence of the loch being linked to the Wick River. In high-water levels and after heavy rain, salmon and sea-trout can enter Watten from the Wick River. When the water level drops, they are trapped. Thus, whilst trout at the north end have the appearance of classically sculpted wild brown trout, the fish at the south end of the loch are often as silvery as sea-trout. However, I know of no instance of a fish being positively identified as a sea-trout, although there are anecdotal records of salmon being taken; one, a fresh-run fish weighing 7lb, fell to a Black Pennell being fished by Sandy Meiklejohn; Sandy used to have a tackle shop in Wick and he told me the story himself.

The loch is evenly shallow, about ten feet at its deepest point, with a marl bottom which gives a pH in the order of 8.5, a marvellous habitat that provides excellent feeding for its adipose-finned residents. Extensive weed patches, more extensive as the season advances, produce abundant fly life as well as giving good cover for the predatory trout, which feed upon these insects. Fishing is by fly only, and boat fishing is the most productive fishing method. Bank fishing is possible, but it is generally uncomfortable due to the rocky nature of most of the margins.

After nearly forty years fishing this wonderful loch, I have to confess that there is probably no one area better than another, although, of course, we all have our favourite drifts. A lot depends upon the time of year, weather and water conditions, and the 101 other excuses we anglers love to trot out to explain our lack of success. For many years, at the start of the season, which is 1 May on Loch Watten, my son Blair and I would go afloat for our first outing about the 7th or 8th of that month. Generally, it could be savage, cold entertainment for little reward but, uncannily, more often than not, we had two fish whilst rowing back to the harbour at the Watten Village end of the loch.

Well, to be precise, I caught the fish using the old Scottish method, the 'turning flee', as Blair rowed the boat past the broken fence post that comes down to the water at the north end of Factor's Bay. Each trout weighed about 1lb 8oz. Blair, to this day, hotly disputes my claim, saying the only reason the fish rose was because of his skill at judging forward speed of the boat and its relationship to the shore; as the boat is rowed along, the angler casts at right angles to its forward motion, leaving his flies on the water and allowing the speed of the craft to turn them. If a fish is going to take, it does just as the flies begin to turn.

Blair was fourteen years old when we first fished Watten together and I generally acted as gillie and guide, fitting on the outboard motor and completing other essential pre-getting-afloat tasks. I was, therefore, very pleased one afternoon a few years later when Blair insisted that he did the work. 'You have done this for me so often that it is about time that I returned the compliment. All you will have to do is select the flies you want on your cast. I will put up your rod and make up your cast and attach the flies. Relax and let me get on with it,' he said.

I did, and, once afloat, he motored to the island, where we started our first drift. Conditions were just about perfect and Blair was soon into a fish. 'Well done, Blair,' I said. A moment later I felt a tug, saw a considerable splash, but the trout was gone. Meanwhile, Blair hooked, played and successfully landed his second fish. Nothing I seemed to do could hook the fish that came to my flies. I was muttering curses, despairingly, and Blair commiserated, 'I guess that it happens to us all, eventually, as we get older.'

5

'What happens?' I asked.

'We just can't react quickly enough,' he replied.

I decided that the only solution was to change my flies and reeled in to do so, whilst Blair landed his third trout. My usual early season Watten cast was a Ke-He on the 'bob', a March Brown in the middle and a Silver Butcher on the tail, and I pulled out my fly box to look for alternatives, which was when I discovered the real cause of my misfortune, and the real reason for Blair's seemingly noble decision to prepare my rod and tie on my flies. He had surreptitiously and wickedly cut the hooks from each of my flies. I roared with laughter, whilst at the same time making a mental note to fully repay my son's kindness at a later date.

It was whilst on Loch Watten that Blair and I developed our 'Theory of Thoughtless Fishing', a method absolutely guaranteed to catch fish. We were out one day when conditions were perfect: a south-west breeze gently ruffled the surface, a cloudless sky, not too bright after recent rain. With mounting hope, we launched the boat and tied up our casts. Every fly had caught fish before: Ke-He, Black Pennell, Silver Butcher, Woodcock & Hare-lug, Invicta and Soldier Palmer. Fish were rising, and obviously this was going to be a day to remember.

With consummate skill, Blair and I applied ourselves to our task. Lines shot out straight-arrow straight; flies settled gossamer-like on the waves and were worked expertly across the surface. Boat handling was of the highest order, each succeeding drift perfectly positioned. We fished the shallows, the deep, the island, the weeds, Shearer's Pool, Sandy Point, Lynegar Bay, Factor's Bay, down the middle, round the sides, everywhere, without so much as touching a trout. I fished with the same flies, being too dejected to change; Blair broke records changing casts, going through every pattern in his box and in mine.

We rehearsed the well-tried clichés. What would be the point if you caught fish every time you went out? What fun would that be? Catching fish isn't all that important anyway; simply being out, communing with nature, is sufficient, enjoying the beauty of the countryside. Try explaining that to the cats when they're wrapping themselves round your leg and Ann is sharpening the filleting knife. The meowing dies away to a reproachful croak and the expression on Ann's face turns from one of expectation to cynical tolerance.

Blair and I were exhausted. About the only thing we had not thrown at the fish were the remains of an egg and tomato sandwich. Like the Ancient Mariner, we drifted over the loch, flies trailing behind the boat, exhausted. We exchanged a disconsolate look and Blair took the oars. Without a word, he began the long haul home. It was somewhere near the island at the entrance to Factor's Bay that it happened. My flies were trailing behind the boat and I thought that I saw the silver flash of a trout dash at them. Suddenly it came to me, the 'Theory of Thoughtless Fishing', the answer to our problem. Have you ever asked yourself when most of the fish take? The answer is simple. It is when you are looking the other way, when you are not concentrating. Nine times out of ten, in my experience, trout rise when you are watching a black-throated diver, lighting a cigarette, pouring a dram, changing a cast or, more often than not, when you are fankled. This indisputable fact is the cornerstone of my theory.

Blair must have sensed my excitement, but completely misjudged the cause.

'Come on, Dad,' he said. 'It's not as bad as that. No need to jump overboard quite yet.'

'Watch this, Blair,' I announced confidently. I yawned and, left-handed, flicked the flies out. They fell on the water in an undisciplined heap. 'Anything good on telly tonight, Blair?' I asked. Almost instantly there was an almighty splash as a trout took my tail fly. I dived for the rod and, three minutes later, had a splendid 1lb fish safely in the net. I flicked the flies out again. 'You know,'

I continued casually, 'I really think that we should make a start on digging over the garden when we get home. What do you think?' Another fish rose, was landed and despatched.

'That was lucky, Dad,' exclaimed Blair.

'Luck be damned,' I replied, and explained my theory to Blair.

A look of utter disbelief grew on his face, quickly followed by hysterical laughter. 'You expect me to believe that,' he roared. 'I knew it had to happen – you've finally gone off your trolley.'

As we were speaking, Blair had cast a long line out to starboard and had ignored it completely whilst wading into me. When the fish took, he got such a fright that he toppled over backwards into the bow, his reel screaming in protest. He struggled upright and turned to face the action, his face aglow with pleasure. 'Perhaps you might just have something after all, Dad!' he cried joyfully. For the rest of the afternoon, we experimented: dipping the point of the rod under the water and leaving the flies to look after themselves, considering the play of sunlight on the water and the beauty of nature. We discussed politics, religion, literature, art, music and sport, the only interruption to our discourse being when we were otherwise engaged, landing trout.

One evening, being a thoughtful father, I drove down to the mooring-bay to collect Blair, who had been on the loch with a couple of his friends. As I waited, a boat came ashore and I watched as the angler gathered his stuff together: rod, bag, landing net – which looked suspiciously dry – outboard motor, petrol tank and so on. As he passed, he glowered at me and noisily dumped his gear into the boot of his car. Once de-wadered and shod, he came over to speak to me.

'You don't happen to know where Bruce Sandison lives, do you?' he asked.

Cautiously, I replied, 'I think he lives round here, but I'm not sure where.'

'If I could lay my hands on the blighter, I'd tell him a thing or six – the only reason I fished the loch was because of what I read in one of his books. They are lies, all lies; I never saw a damn fish all day!'

Some allege that the most productive area on the loch is known as the 'Golden Triangle'. Draw an imaginary line from the Oldhall boathouse on the west shore, across the loch to Sandy Point, an obvious headland on the far shore. Extend the line north for a few hundred yards and join it up again with the boathouse. This is the Golden Triangle. The north end of Watten is known as Shearer's Pool, where the burn bustles in from adjacent Loch Scarmclate. Fish tend to be smaller here. However, the water is deeper close to the north-east bank, where the railway line runs, and larger trout can lie there, particularly towards the end of the season. If all else fails, set the boat to drift down the middle of the loch, north to south, and cast with confidence. There are fish everywhere.

Having said which, in my case, the Watten end is always more kind to me than the north end. Fishing from Factor's Bay at the Watten Village end of the loch, there is a small island where a pair of mute swans and a colony of Arctic terns used to nest. The bay which this island guards is an ideal place to spend an hour or so in pursuit of breakfast; then north again along what is known locally as the Whin Bank. The end of this bank, before the loch swings closer to the railway line which parallels the north shore, is also a likely spot; I have caught magnificent trout here, very close to the bank, in barely two feet of water.

If the wind is right, another good drift is from the island, south across the middle of the loch to the Targets, the remains of a Second World War firing range. In contrary winds, exploring the shore here, about 10 yards out, can also be useful; I once had a superb specimen of 3lb 2oz in weight on a warm June evening a few yards from the boathouse at Oldhall. I also lost my fishing rod in this area when fishing with my friend, the late Sandy Bremner from Brabsterdorran; Sandy was having good sport and I was kept busy landing his fish. After a particularly lively trout I returned to my seat in the stern to recommence fishing. No rod. Stupidly, I searched the boat, expecting to see it somewhere, then realised that I must have knocked it overboard when attending to Sandy's trout.

It was like losing an old friend. The rod had been made for me by a former Hardy's of Alnwick rod-builder; cane, with a butt-extension attachment for sea-trout and grilse. Although I carefully noted the place where the rod had gone down, I did not have much hope of ever seeing it again, until, that is, Ann, who was a dental surgeon, had a patient who was a diver. When Ann explained what had happened, he volunteered to try to find my rod.

We set out on a windy afternoon. When we reached the area where I was sure my rod lay, the diver went over the side. I rowed the boat forward and back over the area, with the diver surfacing now and again to follow my direction, much to the consternation of a couple of other boats fishing nearby. My benefactor told me in advance that he would be able to maintain the search for thirty minutes and, as that time limit came ever closer, I began to despair. Suddenly, like King Arthur's sword 'Excalibur' rising from the waves, the tip of my rod appeared, followed by the arm of the diver. I would love to pretend that there was a 4lb trout attached to the tail fly, but that would be a lie and, as everyone knows, anglers never tell lies.

Both my mother and father loved fly-fishing and in their later years they used to stay with us in Caithness. My father's final outing, when he was very frail, was on Loch Watten. It was late June and one of those precious, good-to-be-alive days: a gentle south-west wind, warm, bright but not too bright; the sort of day when you just knew that you were going to catch fish. Blair was with me and, together, we got father safely into the boat and made him comfortable. We motored out of Factor's Bay and set up a drift from close to the island over towards the far shore. I held the oars and Blair fished. He hooked a good trout and passed the rod to his granddad. With a quiet smile, father played the fish and brought it to the net. It was his last trout.

I taught my parents to fish and my two brothers, Ian and Fergus, and a whole host of grandchildren, nephews and nieces and their multitudinous friends. Mother, particularly, was always amazingly successful. Her last outing, again on Watten, was unforgettable. She had spotted a large trout in our freezer and was suggesting that it would be nice to take a fish home to cook for her friends. I resisted her none-too-delicate demands, since the fish in question was a trout of over 4lb in weight that I prized highly and had caught on Loch Heilen, the largest trout that I ever caught there. Finally, I announced that if she wanted to take a few fish home with her, then she should catch them herself. Thus it was agreed that we would fish Watten the following day.

It was not the best of days, mid-May, raining on and off, cold and quite windy. I had packed appropriate wet-weather gear and at the mooring-bay suggested to her that it was better to be warm and comfortable than cold and miserable. 'If you think that I am going to put that lot on, then you had better think again,' she said. 'I will look ridiculous.' Patiently, I tried to persuade her, but to no avail. Driven to near distraction, a not entirely unknown state of affairs when involved in a disagreement with Mima Sandison, I declared, 'Well, in that case we are not launching the boat, and that is my last word. If you really want to go back to Edinburgh with trout, get dressed.'

Much to my surprise, and relief, she agreed and I helped her into waterproofs, attached the outboard motor, put up the rods, made the casts and, eventually, got her into the boat. I started the engine and headed for the area where Blair and I had taken my father on his last outing. Turning into the drift, I cut the engine and reached for the rods. No rods to be seen. I had left them on the bank. I said nothing, but restarted the outboard and headed back to the mooring-bay.

'Where are you going?' mother asked. 'I'm not cold and we

11

haven't even started fishing. I know, you have forgotten your cigarettes. Your father and I have told you for years that you should stop smoking, but oh no, you just go your own way . . .'

I could feel my blood-pressure rising rapidly, again. Leaping ashore, I picked up the rods and returned to the boat to find mother helpless with laughter.

Back on the drift, with the weather improved, I got some line out for mother and handed her a rod. 'There we are, fishing at last.'

I turned my back to raise the outboard engine and heard mother shout, 'I've got one!' And she had. The trout was, I am sure, as much surprised as mother was and it set off like a rocket leaping and dancing on the surface, sending the reel screaming. Mother was delighted and she played the trout perfectly. As I judged it time to get the net ready, I bent down to pick it up – when a trout of about 2lb landed at my feet. The fish, in a final leap, had jumped into the boat by itself. Mother looked at me and began to laugh again. 'You know, Bruce, if you had told me that story I would never have believed you.'

North of Watten is little Loch Scarmclate, also known locally as Stemster, a nursery for Loch Watten and joined to it by a narrow stream. Scarmclate has the same high-quality trout as Watten and this is the ideal loch to introduce a newcomer to the gentle art of fly-fishing. It is best to launch your attack during the early months of the season because as autumn approaches Scarmclate becomes heavily weeded. The loch is also very shallow and, in days gone by, farmers used to extract marl from it to use as fertiliser. Therefore, bank fishing is not advisable since there are sudden, unexpected holes.

Scarmclate is an important resting and breeding place for wild-fowl and often, in winter, the loch is covered with graceful Icelandic whooper swans. During summer months, Scandinavian fieldfare, redwing and buntings flit and feed in the well-cultivated fields that surround Scarmclate and a pair of binoculars is almost as important as a fishing rod when afloat. Fish average 8oz, although there are larger trout. Catch them anywhere on the loch, but the best area is at the east end; inch down the shore and into the bay where the burn tumbles out to Watten. Water is deep here and I have taken fish of over 1lb there on small, size 16 flies.

Much as I love lochs Watten and Scarmclate, I am obsessed with its near neighbour, Loch Heilen. I believe that it is one of the most difficult trout lochs in the north of Scotland. In fact, I am sure that the word 'dour', which means hard, stern, stiff, sulky, sullen, stubborn and unyielding, was especially invented to describe Loch Heilen; I have thrashed Heilen for three decades and, more often than not, gone home empty-handed. Some days – indeed, most days – you would swear that the loch was completely devoid of fish. Nothing could be further from the truth, which is why I suspect that I keep going back for more punishment. Heilen contains utterly outstanding trout, fish of up to and over 11lb in weight; classic fish, designed, I am sure, by Leonardo da Vinci, supremely lovely and amazingly strong. It's just catching them, or rather being unable to do so, that bothers me.

On a few never-to-be forgotten evenings, I have seen the whole surface of the loch alive with eagerly feeding fish and the air thick with hatching flies. One such evening, I was rewarded with four trout, all of them over 2lb in weight, two of which I kept. Another time, fishing from the boat, I landed my best-ever fish, a trout of 4lb 8oz. I should confess, however, that the trout took me, rather than the other way round. The boat was a few yards out from the shore and I was sitting in the stern, wondering why on earth I continued to torture myself fishing the loch. A cup of coffee was beside me, as I pondered over which flies to try next. My rod was resting sideways across the boat, unattended, the flies trailing in the water, although we were practically stationary at the time.

And yes, that is exactly when the fish took. The first thing I knew about it was when my rod began to disappear over the side of the boat. I dropped my cup, spilling hot coffee down my shirt

13

front and scalding my chest, tossed a half-smoked cigarette into the loch and lunged for the rod. My companion, in the bow, was speechless and we both watched in astonishment as the trout took off like an express train for the middle of the loch. At the end of a seemingly never-ending run, the fish leapt clear of the water. I dropped the point of the rod and began to work the trout back towards me. After several more runs and moments of high tension in the boat, the fish was brought to the net and landed. It had taken a size 14 Silver Butcher. I shall never forget its entirely unexpected arrival or the enormous fight it gave.

Loch Heilen lies to the north of Loch Watten and is surrounded by heather moorland and fertile fields. Consequently, high winds, which are not entirely unknown in these airts, can stir up the bottom and make the loch unfishable for days at a time. Given that the loch is at its most productive in May and early June, a time that is synonymous with unsettled weather – in Caithness this period is known as the May Gobs – striking it right on Heilen is very much a matter of chance. For residents, this is not a problem; they just wait it out until the loch is back to normal. For visitors, however, whose time is limited, it can be frustrating. Thinking further about it, I suppose this same applies to other shallow Caithness waters, including Watten, St John's and Toftingall. But being shallow makes them what they are: outstanding natural fisheries. So my best advice on this subject is just to grin and bear it. We now live in North Sutherland and on the last three occasions when I booked the boat on Heilen, the loch was unfishable.

Loch Heilen is about 170 acres in extent, with an average depth of little more than four feet. Therefore, you may launch your attack from either boat or bank. I prefer fishing from the bank, particularly along the south shore in the vicinity of the small fishing hut. In my early days it was the site of a Second World War concrete shelter and in a ruinous state. This was also the site of the old mooring-bay. Wading is safe and easy along this bank, and it is possible to cover a vast area from the shore. The west end and the east end are more troublesome, and care is required because the bottom is soft and squelchy. Wading here is a dangerous, boot-trapping business. I have never caught anything in these areas, either from bank or boat, and they become virtually unfishable because of weed growth as the season advances.

The north shore may also be waded, but it is very much rock-and-stumble country. A boat is a more convenient means of fishing this bank. A word of warning here: although the loch is shallow, the boat mooring-bay has been vigorously excavated and the water here is chest high. Don't wade in to attach the outboard engine or you will almost certainly take a ducking. Step from dry land straight into the boat. Indeed, it is best to leave your tackle at the car parking place and row the boat back there to set up the boat, reversing the process at the end of the day.

There is another, less expected but very welcome advantage to the loch being so shallow – as a visiting angler discovered, when he asked me to arrange a gillie for him for his day out. He was a novice angler, recovering, I believe, from the effects of an addiction and had been advised to take up fishing for the sake of his health. It was clear from his tackle that no expense had been spared, from the top of his tweed cap to the lightweight trout rod with the cellophane still wrapped round the butt, pristine, unmarked fishing bag and fingerless gloves. The boat on the loch at that time was a narrow, unfriendly affair, much given to wobbling about a bit. The angler had insisted on sitting in the bow and as the gillie, a strong, young lad, rowed up the loch to begin a drift, the forward speed and the weight of the pair of them up front caused the bow to dip under the water like a diving submarine, leaving them both floundering on the surface. Happily, they could stand up and wade ashore, but that was, I think, the end of the poor man's piscatorial adventures.

As there is more to fishing than catching fish, so it is with Loch Heilen. Apart from the beauty of the trout in the loch, along its banks and amongst the heath is an astonishing array of wild flowers: wild pansy, lady's bedstraw, angelica, marsh marigold, yellow flag, the unique Scottish primrose (*primula scotica*) and many more. In winter months, the loch plays host to statuesque Arctic whooper swans and greylag geese. Spring and summer is loud with the cry of golden plover and curlew. One memorable spring morning I watched a snow-white, peregrine-shaped bird swoop by and I'm sure that it was a rare Greenland falcon. If you love the countryside, as most anglers I know do, then you will find it hard to be sad at Heilen, regardless of what the weather brings, or the trout do or do not do.

Plan your visit in May or June when most of the specimen trout for which the loch is famous are taken; as the season advances so does weed growth and this makes fishing hazardous. You might well hook a trout, but there is no guarantee that you are going to land it. Invariably, it dives for the weeds from the word go. Consequently, use no less than 61b breaking nylon to avoid send- ing the fish off with your cast in its mouth. Local experts tend to use one fly, often a dry fly pattern, and this is perhaps the most productive fishing method. In spite of its dour reputation, to visit Caithness and not fish Loch Heilen would be an unforgivable angling crime. After all, why should I be the only one to suffer?

It was with that last statement in mind that I remember fishing Heilen along with a less-than-willing companion on a cold, wet afternoon. We have all been there. As the prospect of fish, like our body temperature, diminished, our thoughts began to turn to a warm dram or three followed by a hot bath. The only reason my friend had agreed to the expedition was because of what he had read about it in one of my books; an explanation that he men- tioned several times, as the rain continued to pour and his spirits continued to plummet. Just as I was about to admit defeat and hoist the white flag, I heard him shout. There he was, rain drip- ping off his nose, the rod bent double and the reeling howling. He had hooked a good fish. I netted the trout for him and, before returning it to fight another day, we both agreed that it was closer to 6lb than 5lb.

'Well done!' I said. 'Now, what about a quick exit to the nearest pub?'

'If you don't mind, Bruce,' he replied, 'I wouldn't mind another half hour or so.'

A few miles north from Loch Heilen lies Loch St John's, a well-managed fishery, circular in shape and of about the same size as its dour neighbour. The local angling club, the St John's Loch Improvement Association, formed in the 1960s, stock their water and in the late 1970s I was a committee member of the association, taking my turn on hatchery duty where the trays were cleansed with Malachite Green, a chemical now banned because it presents a significant risk to human health. The loch was in trouble then: catches were falling, fewer fish and fewer anglers. It had once been the premier trout fishery in Caithness, renowned for the size and quality of its trout and revered throughout Scotland.

The association was determined to reverse that. A few members had suggested, as a stop-gap measure, the introduction of rainbow trout and some were placed in the loch, but had been fished out; I remember a very heated discussion about a proposal to stock more rainbow trout, which was, happily in my view, soundly defeated. It was agreed instead to renew efforts to restock the loch with roe and sperm from native fish, stripped from them on their spawning beds during October and November. St John's is about the same size as Heilen and almost as shallow, and one of the problems we faced in the hatchery then was water quality; it was, invariably, plagued by the persistent presence of fine particles of peat, which chocked the development of the fish in the hatchery.

The committee was fortunate then to have as members Harry Officer, principal officer at the Thurso Department of Agriculture; Adam Black, a biology teacher at Thurso High School; and old

Donnie Mackay from Dunnet, all now fishing that great trout loch in the sky. Harry and Adam determined that the best way to tackle the clean-water problem in the hatchery was two-fold: firstly, to draw the water that fed the hatchery from much further out in the loch. And secondly, to construct a filter made up of different grades of sand and gravel through which the water would flow before entering the hatchery.

The local quarrying company, Sutherland Bros., gifted the sand, and Harry and I, plus trailer and shovels, visited their site at Westerdale to collect the material. A work party was formed and a series of posts dug into the bed of the loch to support the pipe to the hatchery, suspended a foot or so from the bottom of the loch. At that time I looked after an agricultural land-drainage company, Ray Holt Ltd, and we donated a length of 80mm fibre-covered drainage pipe. Getting the fish safely to the loch presented its own problems, primarily how to oxygenate the plastic sacks of fish on their journey from hatchery to loch. This was solved by Messrs Erridge & Sandison of the Wick Dental Practice, who, at not inconsiderable inconvenience, provided the oxygen cylinders and the means of getting it into the containers.

Looking back, I guess that I spent more time stumbling about in St John's hammering in posts than I did fishing the loch, but these were happy times. Today, the association is far more professionally organised and it operates a modern, fully equipped and efficient hatchery; although I did raise an eyebrow when I read on the association website that the new hatchery replaced '. . . a rather basic outdoor facility used in previous years'. It was the best we could do, guys, given financial constraints, and it was done with the best interests of the loch at heart.

The loch is now stocked with between 8,000 and 10,000 fingerings, all produced from native stock. Scottish Natural Heritage and the government's Freshwater Fisheries Research Laboratory in Pitlochry advise the association on stocking policy and it is estimated that, because of the superlative abundance of food, trout stocked at 2oz to 3oz reach a weight of between 10oz to 12oz within their first year. A primary source of that food is the loch's spectacular mayfly hatch. These delicate insects fill the air throughout June and into July, the UK mainland's most northerly mayfly hatch. The loch also contains freshwater shrimps, caddis and snails, along with a wide range of other insects much beloved of trout.

I think that boat fishing brings the best results, although there are areas were bank fishing is allowed. The trout average in the order of 1lb, but large fish are taken regularly, with specimen trout of over 3lb in weight. The classic drift on St John's is from the mouth of the spawning burn, in the north and close to the angling club mooring-bay, down the west shoreline to the old mooring-bay on the south shore; keep the boat about 25 yards out from the bank and look out for action. However, the south-west shore has been kind to me as well, and, I suppose, the truth of the matter is that you may catch fish almost anywhere on the loch.

The loch-side facilities provided are without equal to any-thing that I know north of the Great Glen and are a credit to the energy and enterprise of the association. A splendid new boat-house has been constructed and the mooring-bay makes getting afloat a pleasure, rather than the usual gut-busting heaving and hauling that I associate with getting afloat on many Highland waters. Most recently, my eldest grandson, Brodie, and I fish St John's in the late spring. Even then it can be savage entertain-ment, cold and windy, but we invariably are rewarded with a trout or two. Well, to be honest and accurate, Brodie is. He is an excellent rod – after all, I taught him to fish, so I would say that, wouldn't I?

My wife, Ann, and I have had some memorable evenings on the loch. Not so much from the point of fishing but rather because of the magic spell the loch seems to cast over all who know it. One quiet evening, towards the end of June, we were surrounded by the haunting call of oyster-catchers. The setting sun set the loch ablaze, and gold and silver bars sparkled and shone across the surface. It was as though we were in a different world, a world of serenity and ever-lasting peace. There is an old story about St John's. It records the fact that the special quality of the water banished fear and cleared burdened minds. If the sufferer came to the loch, walked round it, drank from the loch and left without looking back, he would be cured of all ills. Fancy perhaps, but not, I feel, too far-fetched.

For more traditional fishing, visit Loch Calder to the west of the village of Halkirk. This is the source of Caithness's and much of North Sutherland's domestic water supply, which can make the margins unstable. The loch drops to 120 feet in depth at the north end and has a reputation of holding huge ferox trout, although they are rarely caught. If you wish, fish for them using the old Scottish method of trawling: fish a bait-lure sunk to a depth of some thirty feet trailed behind a slowly moving boat. Calder is the only loch in Caithness where bait-fishing is allowed; the others are fly-only.

Calder can be a cheerless, dangerous place to fish, particularly if the wind gets up. Be aware of these dangers and always wear a life jacket. Also, the margins shelve quickly into deep water. I discovered this to my cost when we beached the bow of the boat on the shore near Buolloch. I stepped out of the stern into five feet of icy-cold water. Fortunately, I am 6ft 4in. so I survived, otherwise it could have been much more serious.

Anyway, the boat makes it easier to reach the best fishing areas. These are, primarily, along the south-west shore and in the finger-like west extension of the loch towards Brawlbin Mains farm. The wide bay to the north, at Rubha Gar, can also be highly productive. Calder trout are not large, averaging about 8oz in weight, but there is no doubt that the loch does contain some monsters that rarely rise to surface flies; the largest fish taken from Calder weighed 7lb. The loch also contains Arctic char, as far as I am aware the only Caithness loch to do so, but, as with ferox, they are rarely caught.

South from Calder is another dour Caithness water, Loch Olginey, stocked in days past by that great Caithness angler, the late Dan Murray. Olginey can be a nightmare and one will often swear that it is entirely fishless. Until it produces a trout of over 5lb, then all is forgiven. Olginey is easy of access and best fished from the bank. The loch is full of huge underwater boulders, ready to catch the boat-fisher unawares. It is just as easy to spend a day catching nothing from the bank as it is from a boat and a lot safer.

One of the great advantages, if you are inflicted with the incurable disease of angling, of living in Caithness is that you are surrounded by first-class trout lochs, all of which are easily accessible. This makes it tempting to try to catch that most magical aspect of fishing, the dawn rise. However, our first attempt at doing so was rather less than magical and more maniacal. The loch in question was one of our favourites, Ruard, a short walk west from the A895 Latheron/Thurso road, near Achavanich. There is a good track from the road out to an old farm building at Acharaskill. From there a sheep path that follows the banks of the outlet burn up to the loch. Keep to the track, although it might seem to be a less direct way to the loch, which is a nightmare hike through the heather.

The sheep track is a naturalist's delight: myriad wild flowers, bog asphodel, tormentil, bugle, eyebright, primrose, wonderful clumps of yellow flag, and many more. The surrounding moorlands host golden plover, dunlin, greenshank, meadow pipit, lark, curlew, hen harrier and the occasional golden eagle. Otters fish both the stream and loch, and wildcat hunt amidst the heather. Ruard is a stunning setting, surrounded by glorious moorlands, including magnificent Blar nam Faoileag, 'the sparkling place'; a Site of Special Scientific Interest and a growing, living peat bog, red-tipped sphagnum decked, and summer white with cotton grass and alive with the hum of insects. Ann and I have spent happy hours there, sometimes hardly bothering to cast a fly, although in all the years we fished Ruard, we never returned without something for breakfast the following day.

Another of Ruard's attractions is the fact that there is an excellent boathouse close to the water's edge, and it seemed to be the perfect place to spend a night, prior to addressing the dawn rise. It was mid-May when we decided to do a bit of dawn fishing and we set off on a Friday evening full of hope and good intentions. Ann had packed a small portable cooker. I packed the hip flasks.

'Don't worry about taking too much food, Ann,' I announced grandly. 'We will eat the trout we catch.'

'Are you sure, Bruce?' Ann replied.

Spring in the Highlands, we thought, the first blink of warm sun, soft, zephyr-like breezes, curlew calling down the hill. Everything went well, at first. The walk out was wonderful and by early evening a brace of trout were cooking on the stove. Content, we unrolled the sleeping bags and settled in for the night, full of anticipation of the coming dawn's delights.

It started snowing at about 9.30 p.m. and half an hour later the wind had reached gale force. Waves, blown from the loch, lashed the side of the boathouse with unremitting fury. We huddled in our sleeping bags, numb with cold, shivering miserably, like twin Calibans locked in riven oaks. Frequent resort to hip flasks did little or nothing to bring back feeling, but through sheer exhaustion we finally managed to fall asleep. And slept soundly until 8.30 the following morning, missing the dawn rise, if any fish had been misguided enough to put a snout above the fractious surface, which I very much doubted.

There is a small, narrow dark loch, the Dubh Loch, a step from the south-east shore of Ruard. It is possible to cover the whole surface area of the loch from the shore, which I have done, on several occasions, and never caught a fish, let alone seen one rise.

I think that the loch is probably fishless, but, there again, who knows? One thing that I do know is that further south from Ruard are two little waters near Coire na Beinne (735ft), Lochan Coire na Bienne and Loch a' Cheracher; a former head keeper of the estate told me that they were well worth a visit and contained specimen trout of a considerable size. But getting there is only for the fit and hardy; a two-and-a-half-mile tramp from roadside Loch Rangag over trackless, difficult terrain to reach Coire na Bienne, and a further mile to find a' Cheracher.

There are two other notable lochs close to Achavanich, road-side waters and very easily accessible, Stemster and Rangag. In the Middle Ages, Rangag was reputed to be the site of monstrous robber Grey Steel. He had a castle by the loch and made his living by waylaying travellers on the Ord of Caithness, the eastern border between Caithness and Sutherland where the road by the sea clings to the edge of sheer cliffs. Grey Steel demanded pay-ment before the travellers could pass through his territory. Those either unable or unwilling to do so were hurled to their deaths over the cliff. For anglers, Rangag is a beginner's paradise; it is full of bright little trout that are not particular about which flies they take. When he was four years old, I introduced my first grandson, Brodie, to fly-fishing on the loch. Twenty-seven years later he now takes me out.

Loch Stemster is as well known for its famous standing stones as it is for the quality of the trout it contains. The stones, by the south shore of the loch, form the shape of an irregular oval and were erected some 4,000 years ago in the Bronze Age. Thirty-six stones remain and the tallest is 6ft 6in. in height. It is thought that the original site contained fifty-four stones. There is a burial mound nearby that is probably more than 5,000 years old. Much of the site has been vandalised over the years and as recently as 2003 the site narrowly escaped further turmoil: in an embarrass-ing error, the Highland Council came close to covering part of the site with tarmac to make a layby. Happily, before any damage

23

was done, local people alerted the authorities and the work was stopped.

Loch Stemster was always one of the first lochs we fished at the start of the season; even in March the loch gave good sport. Another attraction of Stemster is that it is almost circular in shape, meaning that no matter from which direction the wind blew, or indeed howled, there was always an area where you could comfortably fish. There used to be a boat on the loch, but we always fished from the bank and I have caught trout from all round the shoreline. It is rarely necessary to wade, and in some areas it is inadvisable to do so because of the nature of the bed of the loch: uneven, and littered with difficult rocks and sudden depths.

However, at the south end, there are three 'fingers' of rock and from these it is possible to wade out a considerable distance, thus opening up an extensive area to your well-presented flies. I remember one April afternoon fishing from the west finger when I hooked and landed two fish, each weighing around 1lb, on the same cast. The average weight of trout in the loch seems to be about 10oz and if there are larger fish, then I never managed to tempt them to rise. But Stemster is a joy to fish and the perfect place for a family picnic; there is a good vehicle access on the west shore and this allows you to be extravagant in what you decide to bring along for lunch, including, as far as we were concerned, friends we wanted to persuade that fly-fishing could be civilised fun.

One of our favourite Caithness destinations was a group of lochs in the Flow Country, near Altnabreac railway station; a request 'stop' on the line from Wick/Thurso to Inverness. The lochs are accessed by a rough road from Westerdale, past Loch More and on to Dalnawhillan Lodge by the upper reaches of the Thurso River. Hang a right at the lodge and three miles later you are confronted by the gaunt, intimidating grey bulk of Lochdubh Hotel. The building was still operating as a hotel when we first passed that way; indeed, Ann and I once dined there – excellent food, but it also cost a new exhaust system for our car due to the potholed state of the road. Continue on from Lochdubh to reach Altnabreac Station. Turn right there, and follow an even worse track for a mile and a half and park overlooking little Loch Caise; a long, tortuous journey, but well worth the effort involved in getting there.

There are four lochs here: Caise and, to its east, Garbh Loch; then cross the railway line at Caise and follow a track north to the boathouse at Coal Loch, and a mile to the west of Coal is Skyline Loch. All of these lochs drain south through Sleach Water and Loch More and into the Thurso River; for many years brown trout were taken from the Thurso to stock them and other lochs in the area. Unless you had seen these lochs before the factory tree-farmers moved in during the 1980s, it would be hard to appreciate fully the enormous damage that the planting has done. They once lay like silver gems amidst the heather, virtually untouched by the hand of man for thousands of years.

Now, much of these moorlands have gone, ripped up by deep forestry ploughing. New roads scar this wilderness, deer fences and locked gates bar the way. Some might argue that the new forest roads have made access easier. I do not count myself amongst that number. For me, a wonderful treasure has been ruined by sheer greed and commercialism. We were lucky to have known these waters before the foresters moved in, and, in any case, since the planting stopped these roads have deteriorated terribly.

Caise is full of 6oz trout that make it a paradise for those new to fly-fishing. It was also a paradise for midges, that Highland curse. I remember one hot summer day . . . I intended to fish Loch Garbh, a mile away over the moor, so I quickly unloaded the car and carried everything down to Caise: fishing tackle, rugs, picnic basket, binoculars, books, toys, papers, paints – just the essentials for a day out with Charles and Jean, who was eighteen months old at the time. With the family comfortably ensconced, Ann larding out the suntan lotion and Charlie's first cast scaring every trout for several acres, I left them to it and set off over the moor.

On my return, I saw that they had abandoned the boat and were gathering up the picnic gear as rapidly as they could. As I got to them, I discovered the reason: they were in the midst of a vast cloud of midges that seemed to be intent on eating them alive. Little Jean was crying, pitifully, and I swept her into my arms and made for the car, with Ann and Charles hot on my heels. Ever since that day Jean has reacted furiously at the first hint of a midge attack.

Strangely, for some reason I can't remember ever being troubled by midges at any of the other waters here and after that incident we generally gave Caise a miss. There is a fifth loch here, marked but unnamed on the OS Map, between Caise and Garbh, but I have never seen any water in it. Garbh, however, was always a delight to fish and one of my 'special' places, not only because of the beauty of its surroundings but also because of the fact that it held some really excellent wild brown trout. The average weight of fish was in the order of 8oz, but there were reputed to be some monsters; fish of over 4lb had been caught.

There used to be a punt on Garbh, and Ann and I once made the mistake of taking it out. It seemed like a good idea at the time, but halfway down the loch we realised that we had made a grave error. The damn thing began to leak like a sieve. Being flat-bottomed didn't help matters, as when I moved to row, the water slushed ominously around feet. Our fishing bags were already soaked and I seriously expected that we would shortly be joining them, except that it would most probably be in the loch rather than in the wretched punt. In retrospect, we could have both drowned, but somehow I managed to get the punt back into shallow water and we scampered ashore. I learned a lesson that day, the hard way, that fishing is a dangerous pastime. Be prepared and aware of the hazards.

One morning, when Blair and I were fishing Garbh, from the

bank, I hooked one of the loch's legendary trout. It was a nasty day, raining, and Blair had retired, hurt, to the shelter of the old tin boathouse by a small, sandy bay at the north end; this structure has long since been scattered across the moor by wind, but even then it provided only a minimum degree of shelter, being largely open to the elements through age and infirmity. Nevertheless, it gave at least a sense of protection and I saw him watching me as I inched along the bank in search of sport. 'Fair-weather fisherman,' I yelled.

My starboard wader was half full because I had become over-excited, trying to cover a particularly promising rise, but there are times when you just know that something large is about to take. This was one of these times. So when the trout grabbed, the force of it almost wrenched the rod from my hand and I let out a triumphant roar – 'Got him!' – as the reel screamed. Blair jumped up and came towards me, landing-net poised. I caught a brief glimpse of a huge, sail-like tail above the surface before my cast broke. 'What did you say, Dad?' said Blair.

Caol Loch, across the railway, was always kind to us. It is shaped like a pearl, narrow in its beginning, opening out to the north. We have had many happy family days on Caol. It is best fished from the boat, as wading is uncomfortable, and there seemed to be an imaginary line across Caol, drawn west to east, where, as the loch broadened, most trout were caught. As ever, getting the boat afloat was often a challenge, particularly if you were first there at the beginning of the season. I remember one such occasion when Ann and I struggled mightily for half an hour and eventually managed to float the boat, whereupon it almost immediately began to sink. Hauling the hulk ashore again, I examined the problem: a small hole at the bottom of the transom. I jest not, but the hole ended up being plugged, successfully, by my underpants.

Neither do I jest when I tell you that once, when fishing Caol, looking east towards the ridge of a hill, I thought I saw the ground moving. It was raining and I wiped my eyes and looked again. It was a most strange experience, but I was not mistaken; a series of four mushroom-shaped humps were moving slowly along the ridge. I watched for several minutes before the answer became clear; the mushrooms grew in size until I could make out five people walking in line astern, each carrying an umbrella. They came towards the loch and I was able to make out that under each umbrella, perched on the arm of the walkers, was a bird of prey. They were hawkers, and I discovered later that it is important to keep the bird's wings dry.

Caol trout were not large, 8oz–10oz, with a 1lb trout being remarkable. But they were very pretty, and rose and fought with great dash and spirit, and it was very rare to have a blank day. If you are looking for something a bit larger, then you might consider hiking north from the end of Caol Loch to examine Lochan Losgann, a tiny dot on the moorland and easily missed if you wander too far either left or right. Use a compass to make sure that you don't. This is trackless country and the going is stiff to ankle-breaking, but my information is that it does, or most certainly used to, hold trout exceeding 4lb in weight. It probably still does because it rarely sees an angler from one season to the next.

However, of all these lochs, Skyline is perhaps the most exciting. Until the 1970s it had been fished by a private syndicate and was rarely available to the general public, but by the time Clan Sandison arrived in Caithness permission to fish could be obtained through the Ulbster Arms Hotel in Halkirk. The loch is half a mile in extent from north to south, barely 150 yards wide and is fished from the bank. Every time Ann and I fished Skyline we were greeted upon arrival by a pair of graceful red-throated divers. The loch nestles in a partially sheltered hollow on the west shoulder of Cnoc Beul na Faire (565ft).

The water by the west shore is deep, although I have waded, very carefully, along some of the bank. Ann never waded. Instead she kept about four or five feet back from the edge, crouched down, and cast a short line and invariably caught fish whilst I remained blank. The east shoreline is more accommodating to wade, although, in truth, the best approach when fishing any-where on the loch is to remain on terra firma. Skyline has a small, satellite lochan, Lochan nam Breac, down the hill to the west and that contained large stocks of tiny three-to-the-pound trout. It is now largely enveloped by forestry.

The largest trout that I have ever encountered in Caithness was when fishing Lochan Airigh Leathaid, 'the pools of the summer shieling', another Flow Country water. The three pools lie about a mile to the north of the track out from Loch More to Glutt Lodge and are again fished from the Ulbster Arms Hotel in Halkirk. They are a delight to fish, regardless of numbers of trout caught, which may generally, given their guile and cunning, be counted on the fingers of one hand.

Fishing is from the bank but, with care, wading is possible over a large area. Carrying the waders up the hill is another matter, for, in spite of being fairly close to an estate road, on a hot day the hike over the heather can be soggy and strenuous. One of the lochs is weed-fringed, barely half an acre in extent, and it is pos-sible to cover much of it from the shore. The water is dark, the banks soft and squelchy. Indeed, unless otherwise informed, one would pass by without even considering a cast. Which I almost did, and, in retrospect, perhaps should have done; for the memory of my first cast into that peaty darkness still haunts me, as does the sight of the 'one for the glass case' disappearing back into the depths.

Ann and I had set off early that morning, as much intent on a day's walking as on the removal of trout from their natural hab-itat. As far as we are concerned, catching fish is of secondary importance, which, given my ability as an angler, is probably just as well. Proud stags nervously marked our progress. A black-throated diver greeted us, gazing curiously from the middle of the loch as we settled in the heather by a promontory on the north-east shore. Meadow pipits complained crossly at our intrusion. Ann drank coffee as I put up the rods, standard Sandison practice prior to fishing.

After an hour or so of carefully inching round the shores of the main lochs, I decided to walk over and have a look at a little pool to the north. I reasoned that I couldn't do much worse. Two more fish at that stage and I would have caught a brace. I hadn't even seen a trout rise, let alone had an offer. On my way over the moor, I stumbled into a bog and dropped my rod. The 'killer cast', constructed with consummate skill, was hopelessly tangled. I decided to repair the damage as I stood at the water's edge, my feet slowly sinking into the marshy ground. Unhooking the tail fly, a size 14 Silver Butcher, I reeled off some line in order to give myself more space. The tail fly landed in the water by a clump of weeds and snagged; flies are designed so to do.

Cursing mildly, I tentatively tugged. A huge head appeared from the weeds and lazily grabbed the middle fly, a Soldier Palmer. I stood, speechless, wondering if I was imagining things. Had that really been a trout? Cautiously, I reeled in, tightening. A sail-like tail appeared above the surface, quickly followed by a monstrous, mile-long back. Good grief, it was the most enormous trout that I had ever seen.

My heart raced as I applied pressure. The big trout, lamb-like, followed the strain and wallowed towards me. Landing net, quick, before the trout knows what is happening. I twisted sideways and struggled to free the net. It was stuck fast, cramped between bag and body. Please Lord, I prayed, let the net come free. I slung the bag viciously round my neck, almost strangling myself, and attacked the net with maniacal fury. By this time my feet were rooted, irreversibly parallel, eighteen inches beneath the bog. The trout waited patiently, tantalisingly close, just out of reach: deep-bodied, gold-spotted, the fish of my dreams.

The net came free and I rocked back and forth, spluttering, lashing it upwards and trying to flick it into the locked position.

One arm of the net was caught in the mesh. What had I done to deserve such a fate? I was a good father, a loving husband, helped with the dishes, cut the lawn regularly. Why me? The fish shook its head, vigorously. I froze in terror. Now or never, I vowed. Reaching forward as far as my trapped position would allow, still cursing the half-open net, I reasoned that if I could manage to get part of the wretched net under the trout, then at least I would have a chance of landing him. Almost there. Another inch.

At that moment, the trapped arm sprang free and connected with the trout's tail. I staggered back, sinking into wet slime. The water exploded as the trout decided that enough was enough. Spray sparkled and the weeds parted. Back and tail clear of the surface, he turned and ran for the middle. My snagged Silver Butcher pulled free. The rod was almost wrenched from my hands as the reel screamed in anger. I hung on, watching helplessly.

Leaving a wake like the *Queen Mary*, the huge fish steamed across the loch. It gave one mighty, spectacular leap, and my cast broke. Waves rippled through the reeds by my feet. A lark sang, derisively. I slumped on the moor – wet, muddy, stunned and utterly dejected. Collecting together what remained of my broken tackle and spirits, I trudged miserably over the heather to Ann. I was greeted with a cheery wave and the sight of a brace of beautiful trout. 'There,' she said, 'I told you. Perseverance, that's all it takes. How did you get on?'

Through mist-filled eyes, I managed to gasp, 'Not bad. Had an offer, a huge trout, but it got away.' I poured out my tale of woe.

Ann smiled knowingly. 'Yes, dear, I've heard it all before. Stop brooding, time for home. Come back another day. He'll still be there.'

As we trailed down the hill in the evening sunlight I knew that I would never go back. It wouldn't be right.

One of our happiest outings in the Flow Country was to Loch Tulachan and Sand in 1975; three-and-a-half miles south from the road end at Loch More. Park at Loch More, cross the gate and follow the track along the east shore of the loch. Within the first half-mile, hang a left and follow a narrower track up the hill over Druim nam Muc (453ft). This leads south-east, past a ruined cottage at Balavreed that was surprisingly still semi-furnished when we passed. The track rounds the east shore of Loch Tulachan and ends at a derelict lodge used now as a bothy by shepherds, shooters and stalkers.

There were six of us – Ann and me, and our four children, Blair, Lewis-Ann, Charles and little Jean. We intended to camp out at Tulachan for a few days and had received permission to do so, and to fish the lochs, from the Ulbster Arms Hotel in Halkirk. Because of the distance involved, and the provisions and equipment to be transported out to the lodge, we decided to do it in two trips. Well, to be completely truthful, Ann and Lewis-Ann did. They nobly offered to make the first trip out with some of the gear, whilst Blair, Jean and I fished nearby Loch Meadie. No point in wasting good fishing time, Blair and I had argued. The following day, we all walked out and, once away from the side of Loch More, the track degenerated into a soggy stumble. However, with Jean perched proudly on Blair's shoulders and Charles asking why I couldn't provide the same service for him, we eventually made it.

The lodge stood about 100 yards from the water's edge and was in a less than pristine state, but with a little effort we made the main room habitable. The most difficult part was persuading the sheep that it was time for them to go. Any door the slightest bit open instantly resulted in half-a-dozen lazy-eyed ewes glaring unblinkingly at what they obviously considered to be intruders. But apart from a few semi-wild ponies, our companions were red deer, peregrine, Arctic skua, whooper swan, redthroated diver and a curious otter. Tulachan gave us super sport with brightly marked little brown trout, providing a meal fit for a king.

The day we visited neighbouring Loch Sand, three-quarters of a mile to the west of Tulachan, the skies opened and it poured. And to keep the rain company the wind howled at gale force. Undaunted, we struggled across the wet moor and huddled in the shelter of an overhanging bank at the south end of the loch, close to the inlet burn; Tulachan drains into Sand and the flow exits down the Backless Burn to Loch More. I was determined to show willing and reached for my rod, intent upon a few casts; I had been more than particular in selecting the flies and they were my prize selection, all guaranteed to catch fish. The rod had gone. At the far end of the loch, Lewis-Ann was using it, busy catching fish, regardless of the weather.

Eventually the rain stopped and we fished on until suppertime, fighting our way back over the heather against the unrelenting force of the wind. Poor Charles was suffering and I had to help him along over the last few hundred yards, with frequent rest stops and endless encouragement. Sitting in the comparative shelter of the lodge, he quickly regained his composure and claimed that he hadn't really needed any help. At that time he was in his 'Bionic Man' stage. 'I'm all right,' he exclaimed. 'A little bit of wind can't hurt me. Look!' He stepped out of the lea of the building and was almost instantly blown to the ground. I dragged him back to safety. Charles is always the optimist. He doesn't understand the need for fear.

Another memorable Flow Country long walk was to Loch Breac, to the south of Ben Alisky (1,142ft), a lesser peak of the mountains that mark the southern boundary between Caithness and Sutherland. The loch is on the Dunbeath Estate and permission to fish may sometimes be available. Unlike the lairds who owned the Caithness Flows, the Dunbeath Estate, happily, resisted the blandishments of the factory tree-farmers, so walking here is a constant pleasure, amidst a landscape that has remained substantially unchanged for generations.

Loch Breac drains south-east through the Raflin Burn to

Dunbeath Water, but, for us, the easiest approach was from the north, at Dalnawhillan Lodge. On the first occasion we fished Loch Breac, Lewis-Ann, in a sudden, rebellious teenage fit, declined to join us, so our company comprised Ann, Blair, Charles, Jean and me. At that time, there was a bridge across the Thurso River that gave access to a stalker's track on the other side.

The bridge was our first challenge: there was no walkway, the boards having long since been swept away by winter storms. The supporting wires and ropes were, however, still in place. Think in terms of an Asian mountain rope bridge over a raging torrent. There was no torrent when we crossed the Thurso River, but it required a degree of confidence and patience to do so, particularly with little Jean. However, we all made it and set off in good heart along the track. The track skirts the north shoulder of Ben Alisky and after three miles it crosses over the Backless Burn. At this point we bid farewell to the track and followed the line of the burn upstream for half a mile before striking south-east to find Loch Breac.

Loch Breac is about a quarter of a mile north/south in length, and slightly less than that in width. I can't remember now why we chose to fish it, but the most probable reason was because it looked so isolated: a small circle of blue surrounded by magnificent hills and moorland. We fished from the bank, taking turnabout to keep Jean happy and amused. In all my years fishing I have had no finer day's sport. We all caught fish, all day, the most successful patterns of flies being these old friends of mine: Black Pennell, March Brown, Soldier Palmer and Mr Silver Butcher. They were not large, averaging about 8oz to 10oz, with a few approaching the 1lb mark. But they were beautiful.

Our lunch was enjoyed amidst the heather, loud with the call of golden plover, piping from sphagnum tussocks. Ann spent an hour or so plant-hunting, which is her special pleasure. It was hard, very hard, to leave and we did so reluctantly, Jean, again, perched on her big brother's strong shoulders. We trekked north line astern playing 'I Spy With My Little Eye' to keep our spirits high and safely crossed the rope bridge over the Thurso River to reach our car. We drove home with memories that have remained with us ever since, which is the real treasure of our well-loved art.

A few miles to the south of Wick are a number of useful trout lochs. The first, Loch Hempriggs, is immediately adjacent to the main road; featureless, often wild and windy, and containing small wild brown trout. Bank fishing only and I always found it uncomfortable to do so, along with the noise of traffic thundering along the A99. However, you will find more peace and quiet if you turn left in Thrumster Village and follow the minor road east towards the sea and Loch Sarclet. Well, to be exact, peaceful for most of the year apart from the days when the local model yacht sailing club are holding an event. Sarclet is fished from the bank and has a well-deserved reputation for holding trout of exceptional quality and of exceptional size, although it has to be said that they are not easily tempted, no matter how hard you might try. Nevertheless, Sarclet is a lovely little loch, close to the sea and always a pleasure to fish.

Less taxing sport may be found nearby on Loch of Yarrows. The loch supplies water to the Royal Burgh of Wick and a somewhat ugly pier structure struts out into the loch from the northeast shore. Yarrows is one of the lochs we first fished when Ann and I came to Caithness in 1975. It was a mild mid-June evening and we were fishing from a boat. The trout are small but numerous and not fussy eaters, taking virtually any fly presented to them, and we were enjoying constant sport. It was a wonderful evening and we had decided that we should do one last drift. However, when I looked at my watch it was nearly 11 p.m. and hardly really dark; we learned later that Caithness was famous for its midsummer fishing competitions. Close to Yarrows is the little Marl Loch, relatively new, or more accurately re-born: there was a loch there until the early years of the twentieth century, when it was drained so that lime-rich marl could be extracted and used as fertiliser. In the late 1970s the loch was recreated and stocked with trout from Yarrows and they have thrived, mightily, and now average close to 1lb in weight.

If you prefer a bit of a walk with your fishing, then head for tiny Loch of Warehouse on the eastern skirts of Hill of Yarrows (656ft): about a mile south-west from Loch of Yarrows, less than 400 yards long and so narrow that it is possible to cast from one side to the other. The water is dark and peat-stained, but, surprisingly, there are trout of some considerable size; one of Blair's friends had a fish of 2lb from the loch. The view from Hill of Yarrows is disfigured by forestry, but raise your eyes to the horizon and a splendid vista of moorland and water entraps the soul: to the north, a distant prospect across the Pentland Firth to the Orkney Islands; east, a sparkling blue sea pegged with the black outline of oil-drilling platforms; and west, the shapes of Ben Loyal and Ben Hope in Sutherland.

The other remarkable aspect of fishing here is that you are surrounded by almost 100 sites of archaeological significance, built here more than 4,000 years ago and now being meticulously excavated by the Yarrows Heritage Trust; the Trust has its headquarters in Thrumster, in the old railway station buildings, where you will find information on the sites, the people who built them and the volunteers who are working to commemorate their passing, and for the angler, fishing permits for the lochs mentioned above.

But for me the real gem here is Loch Watenan, approached from the village of Whaligeo, six miles south from Wick on the A99. The loch is barely half a mile from north to south, narrow and almost impossible to fish because of the extensive growth of plant life – quillwort, water lobelia, awlwort, reeds and water lilies. But there a few areas where you can cast a fly without becoming entangled; one is close to where you park the car, at the south-west corner of the loch, by a small bay; and on the east bank, from the ruined cottage halfway up the loch, where there is a strip of clear, fishable water. Further north it becomes impossible, and wading is not recommended. Having said all of that, I should also point out that the loch is dour – ultra-dour. However, I have had a few trout and they have been worth the effort involved in catching them: beautiful fish, deep-bodied, small heads, perfect in shape and golden in colour. These fish were between 1lb and 2lb in weight, but I have seen a trout of 4lb 8oz taken. Walking the south shore during late autumn, I have watched trout on their spawning beds, close to the bank, and many were of considerable size.

I kept going back to Watenan because, fish or no fish, it is, quite simply, utterly lovely. An overwhelming sense of peace seems to envelope the loch. In spring, birdsong is louder than you could ever imagine. Myriad wildflowers crowd the banks – golden saxifrage, wild hyacinth, wood sorrel, red campion, marsh marigold, forget-me-not and violets. And on the high crag guarding the east shore and built 3,000 years ago, the ruins of Garrywhin Fort, more than 200 feet wide by 590 feet in length, with walls that were eight feet thick. The track up to the fort is on the line of an old drove road and Garrywhin is considered to be one of the finest examples of these structures in the north of Scotland. Perhaps it is this sense of history, of continuous occupation by people for almost 8,000 years, that lends the spot its peace. Perhaps a sense of their presence is still there. Whatever it might be, Watenan is one of my very special places.

Two further lochs, at opposite ends of the country, always warmed my heart: in the south, on the Welbeck Estate near Berridale, little Loch Borgue, which flows into Berridale Water, and in the north, Loch Scye, sixty-odd acres of angling delight and one of the most remote lochs in Caithness. Borgue is tiny and, if I remember correctly, man-made: there is a plug-like affair in the middle, which I think could be operated to drain the loch.

Whatever, for many years the estate stocked it with a few brown trout and these fish gave a splendid account of themselves and could grow to a considerable size. The loch is accessed by a rough mile-long track leading west directly off the A9 Inverness/Wick road. Park the car at the end of the track and a short walk brings you to Borgue.

When we fished Borgue, we obtained permission from Robert Howden, then factor on the Welbeck Estate. His office was in Berridale and we always enjoyed meeting Robert, a courteous, kindly man with a wonderful sense of humour. The estate was one of the premier stalking estates in the north, famous largely because the sixth Duke of Portland, who owned the Berridale Estate, was a keen stalker, recording his passion for the sport in his book *50 Years and More of Sport in Scotland*. When one of his grandsons was told that his grandfather had died, the boy asked, 'Who shot him?'

I was also indebted to Robert for giving me a copy of a hilarious report published in a French newspaper on 20 July 1917, giving a description of King George V as an angler. It must be one of the best angling stories ever written and it is certainly worth repeating here. A classic.

THE KING AS A FISHERMAN

He is an angler of the first force, this King of Britain. Behold him there, as he sits motionless under his umbrella, patiently regarding his many coloured floats. How obstinately he contends with the elements. It is a summer day of Britain. That is to say, it is a day of sleet, and fog and tempest. But what would you? It is as they love it, those who follow the sport.

Presently the King's float begins to descend. The King strikes. My God, how he strikes! The hook is implanted in the very bowels of the salmon. The King rises. He spurns aside his footstool. He strides strongly and swiftly towards the rear. In due time the salmon comes to approach himself to the bank.

Aha! The King has cast aside his rod. He hurls himself flat on the ground on his victim. They splash and struggle in the icy water. Name of a dog! But it is a braw laddie! The gillie, a kind of outdoor domestic, administers the *coup de grâce* with a pistol. 'The King! Hip-hurrah!' On these red-letter days His Majesty George dines on a haggis and a whisky grog. Like a true Scotsman, he wears only the kilt.

I recounted the story one day in September when Ann and I, along with a friend, Stan Tuer, a famous Scourie Hotel boardmaster, fished Loch Borgue. Bank fishing only and Ann, as always, kept well back from the bank and fished a short line into the shallows. I was on the other side of the loch and saw her rod suddenly bend furiously as a fish took. I sprinted – well, walked quickly – round, landing net poised. I could see the dorsal fin of the trout above the water and it was clearly a fish 'worth the huddin''. Ann played the fish carefully and I successfully landed it. It was lovely and nearer to 4lb in weight than 3lb, the heaviest trout Ann had ever caught. Thinking of supper, I despatched it and, to keep it fresh, placed it in a plastic bag, and looped the bag over a stubby post in the water near the boathouse.

As we were having lunch, Stan casually remarked that it looked as though the bag floating in the water didn't have a fish in it; he waded over to examine the bag.

'I was right, Bruce, it is empty.'

'Very funny, Stan, very funny,' I replied. But when I looked, the bag was indeed empty. I must have only stunned the trout, and, by placing it in what was, in reality, an oxygen tent, the fish had recovered and headed back into the depths of the loch. I headed immediately into the depths of despair, having lost Ann's best ever brown trout. She has never reproached me, but I will never forgive myself for being so careless.

I spent another memorable day on Borgue with Peter Fluck, one of the creators of that outrageously hilarious and satirical television puppet show *Spitting Image*. Peter had called at our house one day to ask me to sign a copy of my first book, *Trout Lochs of Scotland*, and we have remained friends ever since. *Spitting Image* ran from 1984 until 1996. The show was a must-watch for our family, and for up to fifteen million viewers nation-wide. The series featured puppets of well-known people during the 1980s and '90s, including Prime Minister Margaret Thatcher. Perhaps one of the most memorable incidents in the show was when Thatcher took her cabinet ministers out for lunch and ordered a steak, rare. The waitress asked, 'What about the veget-ables, madam?' To which Mrs Thatcher famously replied, 'They'll have the same as me.'

Peter ties most of his own flies, many of which have a distinctly 'political' feel: the Edwina – large body with huge eyes – and the Geoffrey – bushy with a yellow stripe down its back. I don't tie flies, so one evening when Peter was staying with us I asked him if he would introduce me to that aspect of our gentle art. Peter readily agreed. James Paterson, a long-time family friend and expert fly-tier, was staying with us at the time and also volun-teered to help. After an hour of intensive coaching and extensive advice, I managed to produce a size 10 Silver Butcher that in my mind was every bit as weird and frightening as the wildest of Peter's *Spitting Image* puppets.

Peter was meticulous in everything. On a fishing expedition, his fly-tying cabinet lived on the back seat of his car. It had five drawers, all neatly arranged with materials and flies various. One morning, when Ann had to dash to the village, Peter sugges-ted she take his car to save time moving vehicles about to get her car out. Unaccustomed to Peter's car, Ann, on the road from Watten Village round the loch, applied the brakes too fiercely on a corner, thus emptying the shelves from Peter's fly cabinet and several hundred flies onto the back seat and floor of the vehicle.

Peter, ever the gentleman, simply smiled and said, 'Don't worry, Ann, I'll soon have them in order.' The cabinet now wears a seat-belt.

Although some of Peter's flies were weird, the Borgue trout approved of them mightily and we had a splendid day, fishing and talking amongst 'the large religion of the hills'.

Loch Scye also lies amidst 'the large religion of the hills', deep in the heartland of the Flow Country. Two small hills guard it, Beinn nam Bad Mor (688ft) to the west, and to the east Beinn nam Ban Beag (490ft). The loch drains out through a tortuous route, north and east, to eventually flow into the Forss River, a wonderful little salmon stream. Scye is accessed by a stalker's track, a track that begins by Shurrery Lodge and ends five miles later at Loch Truim Ghlais. Scye is three miles along this track, a step to the north. On the occasions Ann and I fished the loch, the estate kindly loaned us a Land Rover so we would have a lot more time to enjoy the loch than if we had been using 'shank's ponies' to reach it. Scye is a little bit of paradise. The boat is by a golden beach; the water clear, yet with a hint of peat. There was invariably a red-throated diver on the loch when we arrived. Greenshank and golden plover called plaintively. Buzzard circled gracefully. And the trout, though not large, were all that an honest heart could wish for.

The little River Forss is another of my special places, not so much for its fishing but more so because it is a small piece of sanity amidst the hustle and bustle of nearby Dounreay Atomic Power Station and a US naval base. It lies a few miles west from Thurso, along the most northerly road on mainland Britain, the A836. Forss House, an old, grey building built in 1810, nods sleepily over the river amidst twenty acres of natural woodlands and an arboretum that is carpeted in springtime with celandine, snowdrop and bluebell; tree-creepers carefully scrutinise the bark of insect-rich pines; woodcock whirr stiff-winged through the dark forest.

41

A pair of buzzards rule the glen from the throne of a new plantation above the banks of the river, close to where brown and white peat-stained waters dash over the shining black rocks of Forss Falls, where magnificent wild Atlantic salmon hurl themselves in silver bars at the cascading torrent, urgent to reach their ancestral upstream spawning grounds.

Forss House is now a comfortable hotel (www.forsscountryhouse.co.uk) and to the left of the house a path leads to a promontory overlooking the falls. A thoughtful seat provides comfort for you as you wait and watch for the sudden splendour of the king of fish rising majestically to challenge the stream. The largest salmon taken from the river was a huge fish weighing 42lb, caught in August 1954 by local angler David Couper.

Early one morning, whilst I was sitting there, I watched an otter sidle cautiously into the pool below the falls. His eyes sparkled and whiskers twitched as he sniffed the air for scent of danger, but the wind was right for me. I watched him slide below the waves and pursue, capture and land a salmon of about 9lb, rushing the doomed fish into the undergrowth, anxious for breakfast. Wish I could catch them so easily.

A track leads from the back of the house, through an iron gate, along the side of pine-wooded hills above the river. Forss slides gently seawards through green meadowlands, decked with purple and spotted orchid, tormentil, bugle, milkwort and primrose. Grey and pied wagtails dip and bob by the stream as it hurries under a footbridge to greet the cold Atlantic in Crosskirk Bay.

On the cliffs above the west shore and within the confines of a walled burial ground cluster the ruins of one of Scotland's oldest places of worship, the twelfth-century St Mary's Chapel, built in about AD 1100 and the oldest church building in Caithness. To the south of the chapel is St Mary's Well, from which the church derives its name, and nearby are a Pictish symbol stone and signs of eighth-century occupation.

Long, wave-washed rocky ledges wed the river to the sea in an

ever-changing pattern of crests and tiny storms. Oystercatchers
pipe by the shore; seals black-bob the bay; brisk eider duck drakes
roller-coast the tide; in warm corners *Primula scotica*, that rarest of
Scottish plants, blushes purple-pink in early summer sunlight. A
special place.

I find it impossible to say which my favourite Caithness loch is;
there are so many. But Toftingall, yet another Flow Country loch,
comes pretty high up the list. Perhaps this is because Ann and I
had the rental of the loch for a few years and came to know it
intimately, not just the fishing but also the wonderful wildlife
that surrounds it. Well, that was the case up until the late 1970s.
Then the factory tree-farmers moved in and ploughed and
planted the moorlands with regimented rows of Sitka spruce and
lodge-pole pine.

Toftingall was one of the first lochs we fished when we came to
live in Caithness. It lies between Watten Village to the east and
the main Latheron/Thurso road to the west – the Causiemire (*the
way across the mire*). Before the building of modern roads, crossing
this vast peat bog was a hazardous affair. Often travellers spread
tree-branches ahead of their steps to make the passage secure for
themselves and their animals. Toftingall is accessed from the
minor road between Watten Village and the Causiemire. The loch
lies at the very heart of this bog, which is part of the famous Flow
Country, one of the last remaining areas of blanket peat moorlands in the world.

Toftingall covers some 140 acres, has an average depth of four
feet and drains out at its south-east corner into the Burn of
Acharole, which, after a few miles, joins the Wick River just to the
south of Watten Lodge. The afternoon we chose to fish Toftingall
was dull, cold and wet, and there was barely a track down to the
loch. Nevertheless, we set off cheerfully and, because of the wind
direction, decided to make for the south end, a hike of about two
miles from our start point. Why is it that no matter which way
you approach a loch, when you arrive, the wind is always

blowing directly in your face? Is this another of angling's great insoluble mysteries, or just my luck?

We did not anticipate much activity from the trout, so we hunched in the shelter of a high peat bank and warmed ourselves with coffee. We fished from the bank, wading cautiously in water that was new to us, and allowed the wind to assist our casting efforts. To our great surprise, and in spite of the weather, we were soon raising and catching trout. We both use a three-fly cast and each of our six flies excited interest from below the peat-stained water; lovely trout, about 10oz in weight, beautifully marked and fighting fit. We kept the best two, both around 1lb 8oz, and marched triumphantly home, promising ourselves a return visit in better weather.

The forestry was in progress by the time we became fishing tenants of Toftingall, but it did not yet completely surround the loch. A boathouse had been built and a picnic table and benches erected. The loch became a much treasured place to all the family – aunts, uncles, nephews, nieces and friends; I suppose I should also include animals: Heathcliff, Ann's bad-tempered thug of a Yorkshire terrier, and my golden retriever, Breac, the Gaelic name for trout. Heathcliff had many unfortunate traits, one of which used to drive me particularly mad. The moment we decided to head home, Heathcliff would disappear. I still blush when I think of the hours I have spent squelching amongst the flows, shouting, 'Heathcliff, Heathcliff!' like some latter-day Cathy from Emily Brontë's *Wuthering Heights*. Eventually, Heathcliff would return, his face twisted into a hairy, white-toothed grin.

Secretly, I admired the little dog. He would walk miles, uncomplaining, over terrain that I found difficult, behind Ann and in front of me; we climbed a lot of Munros, Corbetts, Grahams and Donalds together. However, he couldn't, or more probably wouldn't, swim. This may stem from the time, as a puppy, when a mallard duck led him away from her chicks and into a Sutherland hill loch. The wind caught him and he was drifting away. I struggled to get my boots off so that I could rescue the dog, but my son, Blair, beat me to it. I see him now, half-naked in the freezing loch, grabbing Heathcliff. Unceremoniously, he hurled the dripping dog ashore.

I did, however, rescue Heathcliff from another disaster when Ann and I were fishing Toftingall. Heathcliff went everywhere with his mistress and he was perched behind her as she cast. A trout rose in front of Ann and she quickly cast to cover it. In doing so, her elbow caught Heathcliff's rump and propelled him into the loch. Ann didn't notice at first, till I shouted, grabbed the oars and pulled the boat round so that I could reach him with the landing net. He had sunk under the surface. Desperate, I lunged with the net and caught a glimpse of the white of his eyes. I got the net under him and hauled him aboard. Thanks? As I freed him from the net, he bit me.

I think, on balance, I preferred fishing from the bank, rather than from the boat; you really begin to understand a loch when bank fishing. That, of course, depends on the size and character of the loch. Toftingall was perfect for bank fishing and, given the depth of the loch, it was easy to cover a very wide area. I waded from one side of the loch to the other on a number of occasions. Apart from that first visit, when we did well at the south end, there always seemed to be less action there in later years, perhaps because of the advance of the forestry planting; sometimes, the run-off from forestry ploughing would so discolour the water that the loch was unfishable for several days. Also, in high winds the bottom was stirred mightily, again making fishing impossible.

I always avoided the north end as well; the bottom was soft and wading uncomfortable. But for the rest, trout could be taken everywhere. I suppose the average weight was 8oz–10oz, although there were much larger fish: a nephew had one of over 3lb. It was always a joy taking young ones up to Toftingall, there was always something to see: if not trout, then exciting birdlife.

The moorlands were home to greenshank, golden plover and dunlin. In the early evening, a hunting long-eared owl would float by silently on ghostly wings.

An osprey was a regular visitor and many times we all watched, spellbound, as it fished. As with anglers, however, some fish got away. I remember one afternoon seeing the bird take a good trout, only to drop the fish as he tried to regain height. Other regular visitors were black-throated divers, gliding down, stiff-winged to the surface. They often swam close to the boat, inspecting us curiously. Otters were also frequent callers. Fish would suddenly stop rising and, sure enough, an otter would break the surface, whiskers bristling, intelligent bright eyes smiling at us.

We also visited the loch during the winter months when Icelandic whooper swans and greylag geese graced the loch. These birds arrive in October and generally remain in Caithness until March or early April. One spring, we were delighted to find that a pair of swans had remained on Toftingall and hoped that they might breed there. As such, we kept quiet about their presence and just crossed our fingers. I saw them, frequently, in April and May, then, towards the end of the month, they had gone. But not quite: I found the female, dead, on the shore of the loch. She had been shot. It was impossible to establish who had shot the bird, but I cursed whoever it was.

Charles, our second son, who was by then a competent angler, loved visiting the loch. He was ten years old at the time and had a group of good friends, including Peter Sinclair, Duncan Robertson and Stewart Macdonald, who regularly shared in his adventures; one memorable occasion being when he persuaded me, against my better judgement, to let the four of them camp out overnight in the boathouse at Toftingall. I was surprised the boys' parents had agreed, given the results of previous outings organised by Charles; they invariably ended in one or other of the gang arriving home soaked to the skin ('It was Charles, Mum, honest, he asked me to wade in to land a trout he had caught').

I took them up to the loch and made sure that they had everything they needed, banned them from using the boat, gave a briefing about hazards and left them to it. About 2 a.m. I was wakened by the phone ringing. Expecting the worst, I grabbed the handset.

'Hi Dad,' said Charles.

'Where are you?' I asked.

'In Watten,' he answered. That meant Charles must have walked about four miles to reach the phone box in the village.

'What's wrong, Charles? Is everybody all right?'

'Yes, Dad, everything's fine, it's just Peter, he wants to go home. Can you come and get us, please?'

'Stay where you are, Charles, and I will come and get you.'

I picked up Charles, who was suspiciously silent, in the village, collected the rest of the gang at the loch and got them home.

It was not until some months later that I discovered what had really happened. I had been worried that they had gone out in the boat. No, Charles had been telling them ghost stories and, I suppose, to add dramatic effect to his tales, he had been creeping round the outside of the hut, banging on the walls, scaring them all, and in particular Peter.

I made the mistake of buying the boat without trying it out first. The farmer selling it took me round to his back yard to inspect the vessel, which was perched on a trailer, in pristine condition and newly painted. It seemed perfect: clinker-built, broad beamed, deep keeled, sharp at both ends and very Shetland-looking. We agreed a price, including delivery to the loch, and, although I offered to help with the removal, he assured me that there was no need: 'No, no, Bruce, just leave it to me. I'll put it in the water for you. Don't worry.'

I should have been suspicious, but foolishly said nothing. All was revealed the next time I went fishing. Yes, the boat was sound and water-tight, but it rocked from side to side, alarmingly, the moment you twitched a muscle. Furthermore, the keel was so deep that it required Herculean effort to get the wretched thing afloat. The children would wait at the mooring-bay whilst I dragged the boat out into the loch, returning for each embryonic angler, carrying them on my back, one at a time, out to the malicious tilting craft.

In the slightest wind, the boat rocked dangerously. That season, we invented a new Olympic sport: synchronised fishing. Casting by numbers. It was essential that we moved at the same time, and changing places was a death-defying nightmare. My worst moment with the boat came when we had friends staying, Mavis and Peter Greaves. Peter was an experienced angler but had never managed to persuade his wife to join him in the delights of fly-fishing.

I decided to set about changing her mind. One of my missions in life is to persuade people at least to try fly-fishing because I am convinced that it will greatly enrich their existence; introducing them not only to a wonderful pastime but also engendering in them a fuller appreciation of our countryside and environment. Eventually, with some trepidation, and I suspect much against her better judgement, Mavis agreed to join me for an evening expedition to Toftingall. I got Mavis into the boat at the mooring bay, smothered in wet-weather gear. Then, pretending that everything was quite normal, heaved her and the boat over the shallows into deeper water.

'Do you always have to do this when you go fishing, Bruce?' Mavis enquired.

'All part of the adventure, Mavis,' I replied, emptying out a soaking wader. 'I'll row up to the top, out of the wind. We'll soon have you casting and catching trout with the best of them.'

I am convinced that the moment beginners catch their first fish they are hooked for life, and our loch was absolutely full of free-rising trout. I thought warmly of Peter's delight when I returned with Mavis, an enthusiastic angler and convert to the gentle art. I noticed Mavis gripping the sides of the boat tightly as we lurched and pitched through the ever-strengthening wind, and I chattered away reassuringly about the pleasures of angling.

It started to rain. Lightly at first. Then heavily. An unremitting Highland downpour. The skies darkened ominously, but I was determined that Mavis should at least have the opportunity of seeing a fish caught, if not actually catching one herself. What had begun as a moderate breeze quickly grew into a full-scale gale and, as luck would have it, half a mile up the loch the elongated keel of the boat got stuck between two rocks. I tried to keep up a brave face, in spite of the imminent danger of capsizing. 'Soon have it free, Mavis. Just you sit still,' I said calmly, instantly followed by a sharp bark of alarm as Mavis tried to stand up and help: 'Sit down, Mavis! Don't move!'

As I poled the boat round out of the rock-trap, it turned sideways on to the wind. Water began lapping over the sides. 'Nothing to worry about, Mavis, just keep still.' I could see by the look on her face that she was not convinced and had decided she was in the hands of a complete lunatic. Eventually, I forced the boat free and the wind instantly grabbed us like a giant hand and hurled us down the loch, back towards the boathouse. Mavis was white as a sheet. So was I. 'I think we'll finish now,' I said, trying to sound noncommittal, in control, at ease. 'Too windy, really. We'll make for the shore. Please, keep still.'

With all thought of fishing or casting lessons abandoned, I concentrated upon keeping the boat afloat and directly in line with the wind. Even so, water splashed in by the bucketful over the sides. As we approached the mooring-bay I realised that I would have to make one final, dangerous dash, across the wind, to get to safety. There was no way in which I could ask Mavis to step out and wade ashore. It was all-or-nothing time.

I judged my moment, and then turned suddenly shore-wards. Using all my strength, mightily assisted by the wind, I virtually levered the boat over the bottom and into the mooring-bay, breaking one oar in the process. Without waiting for a second invitation, Mavis leapt out. Showing remarkable restraint, she collected herself bravely and smiled down at me: 'Bruce, did I happen to see you with a hip-flask?'

She had, and it was, for some unknown reason, filled with Green Chartreuse. I handed it to her and she disappeared behind the boathouse. A moment or two later, Mavis reappeared and gave me back the flask. It was considerably lighter.

'Now,' she announced brightly, 'I think that I would like a cigarette.' Mavis hadn't smoked for three years. 'Thank you, Bruce,' she said. 'That was one of the most interesting evenings of my life. An evening I will never forget.' The very next morning I placed an ad in the local paper: 'Loch-style boat with trailer for sale. View at the above address.' But I am sure in retrospect Mavis laughs and dines out on the story of her introduction to fishing on a Highland loch.

As the factory tree-farmers continued to plant around the loch, we visited Toftingall less frequently. Our two older children had flown the family nest, off to university and new adventures of their own, so we gave up the rental of the loch; it had given us, our family and friends, hours and hours of pleasure and happy memories too deep for words. It is years since I have fished the Toftingall, although by all accounts it still provides excellent sport. But I miss the wild moorlands that once surrounded this lovely little loch in the heart of the Flows.

This section of the book is dedicated to Hugo Ross, affection- ately known as 'Mr Caithness Angling', a good friend to the members of Clan Sandison for many years. Thank you, Hugo.

SHETLAND

Hail sheetin doon wi a Nort wind ahint it
Blottin oot laand an sea frae da scene,
An iron coortin closin ower aa thing
Winter has come ta da islands ageen.

— Jack Renwick (1924–2010)

Many people have only the vaguest idea of where Shetland really is, apart from it being in that little box at the top right-hand corner of UK maps. These northern lands, a wild scattering of more than 100 islands, cover some 550 square miles of the Atlantic Ocean and lie on the same latitude as Norway's capital city, Bergen, and the southern tip of Greenland. They are 200 miles north of Aberdeen and 230 miles west of Bergen. Indeed, Shetland is closer, both physically and emotionally, to Norway than it is to either Edinburgh or London.

The largest island is Mainland; the other principal islands being Yell, Unst, Fetlar, Whalsay and Bressay. They are a never-ending delight of sound and sunlight guarded by seabird-clad crags. There are near-deserted shining white sandy beaches, and moorlands abound with Arctic and great skua, whimbrel, piping golden plover and the plaintive call of red-throated divers. Springtime is a riot of wild flowers, thrift-covered headlands, the tiny blue flowers of squill, red campion, and thyme and loveage. During summer months, beneath the magnificent silence of the midnight sun, the 'simmer dim', it never becomes really dark.

Shetland has been home to the world's travellers for 4,000 years. At Jarlshof, near to Sumburgh Airport at the southern tip of Mainland, lie the ruins of Bronze Age dwellings intermingled with the remains of succeeding settlements right down to Viking times. The sequence of occupation begins with houses of the type excavated in Orkney at Skara Brae and which were in use until well into the Late Bronze Age. Iron Age dwellings next, followed by the enigmatic builders of the brochs, and a round house and a wheel house, then the Viking era; Shetland belonged to Norway from AD 875 until 1468, when the islands were ceded to Scotland as surety for the dowry of Margaret, daughter of King Christian I, who married James III of Scotland. The money was not forthcoming so Shetland (and Orkney) became part of Scotland.

In pre-Christian times, writers referred to Shetland as Ultima Thule and in 325 BC explorer and geographer Pytheas of Marssalia (the name given to the settlement the Greeks founded at the site of present-day Marseilles) sailed 'six days from North Britain' to reach Ultima Thule.

The old capital of Shetland was Scalloway on the west coast, but this distinction now belongs to Lerwick in the east. Lerwick is a bustling town and its harbour plays host to most of Europe's fishing fleets; boats from Russia, Poland, Denmark, Norway, Germany and France ride at anchor off Commercial Street and a dozen different dialects may be heard in shops and bars. Visitors admire and buy the world-famous hand-made Shetland knitwear, which uses the natural colours of the wool from the island's hardy sheep; Shetland sheep are not shorn in the traditional manner, the wool is teased from the sheep by hand. Shetland is also famous for its delicately spun lace from the island of Unst, so fine that a square can easily be passed through a wedding ring. There are also sheepskin rugs and coats, and a wide range of locally designed silverware and jewellery.

Due to the warming influence of the Gulf Stream, extremes of temperature in Shetland are unusual; it is neither too hot nor too cold. However, rather less can be said for local variations in weather, it being fickle and devious, bright sun one minute and pouring rain the next. The wind is ever-present and what a Shetlander refers to as a gentle breeze, BBC weathermen might report as a gale.

Shetland has some of the best game fishing in Scotland. Ask a Shetland angler how often he changes his flies during the course of a day's fishing and he is most likely to reply, 'Oh no, we don't bother changing our flies up here. If the fish aren't rising, we just change the loch.' This is easy to do when there are more than 300 to choose from. Most of these contain wild brown trout, which vary in size from bright half-pounders to fish of up to and over 6lb in weight. Salmon run the larger burns, although they are rarely caught, whilst sea-trout, for which Shetland was once world famous, are now largely absent due to fish-farm pollution and disease.

As a visiting angler, your first and most important call should be to the Shetland Anglers Association. With so many fishing possibilities available, it is essential to seek advice on the best place to start. Otherwise, precious days could be lost thrashing away fruitlessly on one water whilst the fish are rising on another, a step over the hill.

The Shetland Anglers Association was formed in 1920 and, including ladies and juniors, the club now has more than 500 members. The association has a comfortable clubhouse in Lerwick and owns fishing rights on some of the best Mainland lochs, with permission to fish on many others. The members do a vast amount of work managing and maintaining their fishing, and are usually in the midst of some ambitious new scheme for improving the quality of their island's sport. But, above all, the members are a most friendly and welcoming group, always ready to tell you which flies to use, which fingers to cross and how to get to the lochs that are producing best results at that time.

The Shetlanders are enormously proud of their boats and they maintain them meticulously. They are also very lovely to look at – the boats, that is – although, to be sure, Shetland has more than its fair share of pretty girls. But the boats are marvellous: sleek, narrow-bowed, finely crafted works of art and owe as much to Viking traditions as to the skill of modern-day boat builders. On the islands, it is said that you may do as you please with another man's girlfriend but you must never lay a finger on another man's boat.

MAINLAND

One of the most popular Shetland waters, and one of my favourites, is Loch of Tingwall, a few minutes drive from Lerwick. The name 'Tingwall' derives from Old Norse, meaning *'field of the Ting assembly'*, or parliament; a small promontory at the north end of the loch was the site of the earliest Shetland parliament, once an island accessed by a stone causeway but now part of the mainland since the water level in the loch was lowered in the 1850s. Nearby is Tingwall Kirk, built in 1788 on the site of an earlier church, dating back to the twelfth century. The Shetland parliament moved from Tingwall to Scalloway when the latter became the capital of Shetland in the 1570s.

There is a good mooring-bay, jetty and fishing hut at the loch and access is easy. My friend and angling association member Rae Phillips showed me round the loch and pointed out the most productive drifts. Tingwall is over one mile long by some 200 yards wide and, to the south of the boathouse, divides itself into two sections. The association stock the loch and the average weight of trout is in the order of 12oz. These fish are of exceptional quality, rise to the fly like rockets and fight hard; during

my first visit to the loch, with Rae's guidance, I had ample opportunity to find this out for myself.

The north end of Tingwall is shallow and the water becomes
cloudy and coloured after high winds, with weed growth an
increasing problem as the season advances. Boat fishing is best
and, whilst fish may be caught all over this north section, a
favoured drift is from the north-east corner down the shore for
some 300 yards to an old dyke. Another good drift is from the
same starting point but over towards the boathouse. The southern part of Tingwall is much deeper and the water is very clear.
Drift down either shore, fairly close in, and look out for action.
Take care if wading, however, since there are deep holes close to
the bank on the east shore ready to catch you unawares.

South from Tingwall and joined to it by a little feeder stream is
Loch of Asta, sheltered by the Hill of Steinswall to the east, with
Asta golf course laid out along its west bank. The first tee is close
to a Neolithic two-metre-high standing stone, which is also
known as 'Murder Stone'. It was here, in the last decade of the
fourteenth century, that Earl Henry of Orkney killed his cousin,
Malise Sperra, and seven of his unsuspecting companions, in a
dispute over the lordship of Shetland.

There is no dispute over the quality of Asta trout. The loch
offers good sport and is easily accessible from the B9074.
However, the best bank fishing on Asta is down the east shoreline.
Cross the feeder burn from Tingwall to reach it. Asta trout are of
the same quality as Tingwall, but it can produce larger fish. Both
Tingwall and Asta are limestone lochs with a high pH and excellent feeding. My enduring memory of these lochs is of haughty
mute swans and the marvellous banks of yellow flag adorning
their shores.

To the west of Tingwall, beyond Gallow Hill, are a series of
smaller waters where, apart from the splash of rising fish, you
may wander undisturbed all day without meeting another soul.
Park the car to the north of Tingwall and follow a track out to fish

Loch of Griesta, then on to Broo Loch and south to Loch of Ustaness. South again brings you to four smaller waters: Jamie Cheyne's Loch, Maggie Black's Loch, Loch of Garth and Loch of Houlland.

In the larger lochs, Griesta and Ustaness, expect trout in the order of 10–12oz, with heavier fish in Griesta, whilst Jamie Cheyne's and Maggie Black's, although being singularly dour, might surprise you with something much larger.

I fished these lochs during a hot summer day. Not the best weather for fishing, but nevertheless a wonderful and unforgettable journey. For me, the highlight was having lunch on the promontory at the south-west end of Ustaness. It was obviously also much used by otters for grooming, as was evidenced by the bright green grass. Shetland probably has the highest population of otters in the UK. They are my kind of animals: a love of wild places, a sense of humour, great swimmers and highly competent fishers.

As with so many of the Shetland lochs I have fished, my guide and mentor on Loch of Spiggie was Rae Phillips. I fished it a number of times, with Rae guiding my inexpert efforts, and have always enjoyed every moment afloat. Spiggie is a large, clear water loch one-and-a-half-miles long, north to south, by up to half-a-mile at its widest point. It lies close to the sea in South Mainland, to the west of Skelberry, and is owned by the Royal Society for the Protection of Birds (RSPB) and leased to the Shetland Anglers Association. The RSPB restrict access to some areas of the loch to prevent disturbing nesting species. The loch is an important winter site for migrating Icelandic whooper swan. These most graceful birds arrive in October and stay until late April; although, recently, and for the first time in nearly 100 years, whooper swans have remained at Loch of Spiggie to rear cygnets.

Spiggie fish are very beautiful and average in the order of 10–12oz, with good numbers of larger fish as well. Bank fishing is generally comfortable over much of the loch, although boat fishing seems to be more productive. No one place is better than another, so fish with confidence wherever you go, bank fishing or from the boat. One of my most favoured parts of the loch is off the west shoreline, particularly in the vicinity of Halleluiah Bay, so named because the Baptist community, before they had a church building, used to baptise their adherents in that part of Spiggie.

Nevertheless, no matter what fishing fortunes bring, Spiggie is a most magical place to spend a day: amazing birdlife – widgeon and teal in winter, long-tailed duck, mallard, lapwing and redshank during spring and summer – and the dunes between the loch and the sea and the surrounding croft lands abound with wildflowers, including yellow rattle, meadow buttercup, devil's-bit scabious, and red and white clover. To visit Shetland and not spend at least a day on Loch of Spiggie would be a sad mistake.

Perhaps the best Mainland Shetland water is Loch of Benston, complete with a scenic island and surrounded by well-cultivated fields. As I write, above my desk is a front-cover page from the magazine *Trout & Salmon* dated January 1984. It shows a much younger Rae Phillips and a much younger Bruce Sandison on the island in Benston, consulting a fly-box. That was my first visit to the loch, again with Rae, and it is one of the most attractive and exciting lochs that I have ever fished. A couple of years back, Rae landed a splendid trout that was nearer 5lb in weight than 4lb. Loch of Benston is dressed overall with fishy corners, points and skerries, and holds trout which average 1lb as well as fish over 41b. The last time I fished Benston, within minutes of starting I had a lovely fish. Then, for no apparent reason, the loch went dead. Nothing daunted, Rae decided it was time to change lochs.

The boat was hauled ashore, loaded onto its trailer and off we went to Loch of Girlsta, to the north of Lerwick. Girlsta is named after Geirhild, a Norwegian princess who drowned on the loch whilst trying to escape to her lover. Girlsta is a mile long by about 300 yards wide and it deepens very quickly from the margins to more than seventy feet. Consequently, the best fishing areas are at the shallow north and south ends, or close to the shore down either side. Wading is dangerous. Halfway down the west shoreline is a small cairn that marks the spot where an incautious angler lost his life in the mid-1900s. Searchers found the fisherman's dog guarding his master's basket and tackle, but the unfortunate angler was never seen again. Stay on terra firma. Leave bank fishing and wading to the locals, who know their way around. When fishing from a boat, you really must have someone on the oars all the time to keep the boat in the best fishing position, and on this exposed water an outboard motor is essential.

On its day Girlsta can produce spectacular sport. We had a long drift down the east shore and my fishing partner was rewarded with two fish, each weighing 1lb 8oz. The trout were in perfect condition, fought like demons and were virtually unseen until brought to the net. My introduction to Girlsta trout came later, during our lunch break. As we sat by the shore I saw a fish rise within a couple of yards of the bank. Over the years I have noticed that, before doing so, they wait until you have taken a large bite from a soggy tomato sandwich whilst balancing a cup of scalding coffee on one knee and a large dram on the other.

Abandoning coffee and dram, and spluttering sandwich-muffled curses, I grabbed my rod and sprinted – well, lumbered – loch-side. One cast, out over the still-widening rings, and my Black Pennell was grabbed with the utmost fury and the rod almost wrenched from my hand. A huge trout set off for the depths, sending the reel screaming in protest. As always happens in these circumstances, the fly came free and I staggered back, fishless and fuming.

'More coffee, Bruce?' was the only comment made by my companions.

Girlsta has a reputation for serious trout: the largest caught in Shetland came from Girlsta and weighed 12lb 8oz. It is also the only Shetland loch known to contain Arctic char.

For anglers who enjoy a good walk with their fishing, I heartily recommend a visit to the lochs around North Mid Field (482ft) in Weisdale: little Whitelaw Loch, Truggles Water, Maa Water and Lamba Water. My wife Ann and I walked that way when we were staying in a cottage overlooking the Voe of Browland at Bridge of Walls. When we arrived at our cottage and were unloading the car, we were welcomed by a pair of otters splashing amongst the green and brown fronds of seaweed and rocks that bordered the shore. They seemed quite unconcerned by our presence and carried on with their affairs, giving us a unique opportunity to watch them at work. Moments to treasure.

Our walk the following day was also treasured but took considerably longer than a few moments, involving a tramp there and back of about eight miles. We parked the car at Houlland and headed up the hill to fish Truggles Water first, then on to Maa and Lamba, leaving Whitelaw Loch for the way home. It was a bright, sunny day and the hill was dry, almost parched, as we skirted round and over peat banks. We knew that the lochs we were going to fish held only modest-sized trout but were more than happy just to be there. I'll say it again: there is more to fishing than catching fish.

Our day was spent amongst whimbrel, Arctic skua and golden plover. We enjoyed lunch by Maa Water, more comfortably and at ease than if we had been dining in the best restaurant in the world. And, yes, we did manage to catch a number of beautifully marked 8oz trout. Ann's faithful hound, the irascible, bad-tempered Yorkshire terrier Heathcliff, was with us and he was responsible for creating for me an angling 'first'. I was caught by a trout. I had two fish on the cast and was removing the top one, preparatory to putting it back, when Heathcliff jumped up and grabbed the lower trout. In doing so, the fly that I had removed from the top fish dug itself deeply into the back of my hand.

The fly was removed by Ann, using the traditional method – a bit of line round the hook, press down hard on the eye of the hook and jerk the line, firmly, back and upwards. I wouldn't say that I didn't feel a thing, but it certainly did not hurt, and not nearly as much as the hurt I proposed to lay on Heathcliff the moment the deed was done. Needless to say, he very sensibly avoided my company all the way back to the car. By the time we reached home and I was ensconced behind a glass of red wine, watching the otters again, my anger had gone.

However, of all the wonderful fishing Mainland Shetland has to offer, for me none is finer than the series of lochs lying at the north of Mainland in the vicinity of Ronas Hill (1,486ft), the highest point on these northern isles. It is the end of the road as far as the A970 is concerned. Park your car near Skelberry. There is a gate to your left, go through it, walk down the grass field, over a fence, then follow the burn up the valley in front of you.

When you arrive at the top and climb onto the moor, a wonderful vista opens: a scattering of granite boulders, glistening in sunlight; silver and blue lochs and lochans beckon; golden plovers flit over rough peat hags and Scootie Allan, the Shetland name for Arctic skua, turn and twist overhead. The song of the wind, tugging persistently at your clothes, urges you on.

Ahead lie more than thirty waters, varying in size from the ragged straggle of Many Crooks to the half-mile-long windswept Roer Water. All have good stocks of trout that average 8oz in weight but some have much larger fish. Finding out which of the waters contain the larger trout is the real pleasure of fishing on Ronas Hill.

You really need Ordnance Survey Map 1 Shetland – Yell & Unst, Second Series Scale 1:50,000 to find your way round. Make sure that you have a cast or three at the Loch of the Grey Ewe; this water is noted for sometimes producing brilliant sport with seriously large trout. However, at other times – in fact, most times – you would swear that it was fishless. The secret of success is, as ever with our well-loved pastime, being in the right place at the right time.

Swabie Water (grid ref: 310854), fed by a burn flowing down from Black Button Hill (984ft), is another small, shallow clear water loch that can make strong men weep. The majority of the residents are bright little 8oz trout, but the loch is also known to contain fish over 4lb in weight. All you have to do is tempt them to rise to your fly.

Whatever, a journey into the wilderness lands of Ronas Hill is right any time, but Shetland weather is notoriously fickle, one moment bright and smiling, the next grim and unforgiving. As such, if you venture this way, and particularly if you decide to camp for a few days, you must be prepared for whatever the elements decide to chuck your way. A compass and map, and knowing how to use them, are essential. Even then, if a sudden mist descends you might have problems finding your way home.

When I last tramped Ronas Hill, I fished Birka Water, a classic Scottish trout loch. The sudden shock of its sheer beauty is almost impossible to describe: 700 yards long by 300 yards wide and crystal clear water with a glorious sandy beach at the north end. The most dramatic aspect of Birka, however, is the magnificent waterfall that drops from high crags along the south shore. I saw the falls after heavy rain on a warm, sunny afternoon; full, silver and thunderous, they tumbled into the loch, sending urgent wavelets rippling over the calm surface.

Birka collects together all the waters from the lochs on the north slopes of Ronas Hill: Many Crooks, Loch of Hadd, Swabbie Water and Sandy Water. Sadly, in my view, they are now part of a public water supply system that has partially robbed poor Birka of its magnificent falls. From Birka Water, I climbed up the side of the falls to explore the Moshella Lochs. As I reached the top, there, at eye level and only a few yards in front of me, swam a proud pair of red-throated divers. They soared skywards, as I breasted the crest of the falls, and swung away over the moors. The Moshella Lochs are a modest, narrow affair, but I did manage to take a 2lb trout from their dark waters.

After a wonderful day I walked slowly homewards, stopping once or twice to cast into small lochans along the way, thinking of Shetland past and present and of the marvellous wonder of the moors. Before descending to the road I stopped and looked back, trying to fix the scene firmly in my mind. Of all the places I have wandered, throughout Scotland, few have made such a deep and lasting impression on me as the wide sweep of blue, loch-specked moorlands on Ronas Hill.

Before leaving Mainland, it should be said that sea-trout fishing from the shore, in the sea and voes around Shetland, was once considered to be amongst the finest in the world. Indeed, as a boy I thrilled at stories from anglers such as Moray McLaren, who wrote about his experiences fishing for sea-trout in Shetland. Sadly, these days seem to have gone and it is hard to resist the conclusion that the huge expansion in fish-farming that has taken place in Shetland in recent years is linked to this decline in sea-trout numbers.

Shetland now produces some 50,000 tonnes of farm salmon each year and the sea lice that breed in their billions amongst these captive fish attack and kill wild sea-trout as they pass by their cages. The fact that these fish farms are almost exclusively Norwegian-owned is, to me, infuriating: wild fish that have survived in our waters since the end of the last Ice Age are being driven to extinction by, as I see it, sheer greed and materialism. Here is what Moray McLaren, author and broadcaster and one of my favourite angling writers, had to say about Shetland sea-trout in 1959:

> The Shetlanders are unanimous in telling you that, pound for pound, their sea trout are stronger and more sporting than any other. They may or may not be right; but I who have felt their sea trout in the full blood of their vigour am not going to deny this patriotic island belief. On a day when the freshwaters are welcoming them in, and when

the tide is beginning to flow, the sea trout come rushing up the voes and can be caught in salt water on sand-eels, lures of blue and silver, or indeed almost any gleaming object cast into their midst like a wet fly and then treated like a lure. I have enjoyed many other forms of autumn angling and with larger fish. But for sheer, intense, exciting joy, give me a Shetland sea trout of 2 to 3lb, coming up with the flood of the tide during the autumn season. There is no fish quite like him.

Thanks to the ungentle administrations of the fish-farmers, I never had the opportunity of experiencing that joy, nor will succeeding generations, as long as the dirty business of fish-farming persists. I have listed here, with the OS Map number first, followed by a six-figure grid reference, for the record, a number of traditional sea-trout fishing locations, for 'auld lang syne':

Bixter Voe (3/331520); Seli Voe (3/337480); Olas Voe (3/287470); Voe of Snarraness (3/239560); The Vadills (3/291546); Club of Mulla (3/393648); Olna Firth (3/402638); Gunnister Voe (3/319742); Hamar Voe (3/314765); Ura Firth (3/310787); Orr Wick (3/333813); Gluss Voe (3/358775); The Vadill (3/401756); Dales Voe (3/412689); Colla Firth (3/430690); Boatsruom Voe (3/497707); Ayre of Duty (3/462604); Quoys of Catfirth (3/443540); Olas Voc (4/288468); Stead of Culswick (4/271444); Wester Wick (41284426); Sil Wick (4/295419); Skelda Voe (4/313441); Bur Wick (4/395408); East Voe of Scalloway (4/404395); West Voe of Quarff (4/404350); Voe of North Ho (4/378315); Banna Minn (4/365304); May Wick (4/376247); Bay of Scousburgh (4/373181); Muckle Sound Bay (4/367178).

If you should decide to have a throw for sea-trout, take great care. Danger is never far distant from sudden tide surges, waves, slippery rocks and unstable bottoms, and it is always advisable to go with a partner. Also, always tell someone where you are going and when you expect to return. Better safe than sorry.

Sea-trout have soft mouths and are hard to hook, but when hooked look out for spectacular sport.

UNST

Just saying the name 'Muckle Flugga' brings pleasure. Being close to Muckle Flugga is even nicer; this seabird-whitewashed outcrop lies just off the north coast of the Hermaness National Nature Reserve in Unst in Shetland. Muckle Flugga is crowned by the most northerly lighthouse in the UK: 200 feet above sea level, sixty-four feet high, with three-and-a-half-foot-thick walls, designed and built at a cost of £32,378 15s 5d between the years 1854 and 1858 by the famous lighthouse-building brothers David and Thomas Stevenson. Scottish writer Robert Louis Stevenson came north to see how his father and uncle were getting on with the job and is said to have used the shape of the island in his adventure story *Treasure Island*.

I must declare an interest here because my ancestors came from this lovely island and, to me, returning to Unst is like returning home. Unst is the most northerly of the Shetland archipelago islands and covers an area some twelve miles by five miles. It is hardly densely populated, being home to fewer than 700 souls, but Unst has some of the most dramatic scenery on Planet Earth. The island lies like a multicoloured garnet stone – red, orange, violet, green and yellow – embraced by endless ultramarine waves and near deserted beaches of white sand. The moorlands are carpeted with wild flowers and guarded by dramatic cliffs that rise to a height of nearly 700 feet, and always the constant music of the sea.

One bright August morning Ann and I set off from the Ness by Burra Firth in the north of the island to explore the Hermaness peninsula. An old Unst tale tells of two giants, one called Herma, who lived on Hermaness, and the other, Saxa, who lived across Burra Firth on the hill of Saxa Vord, the Shetland name for 'hill'. The giants fell in love with a mermaid who sang mournfully from

Flugga Rock at the mouth of the Firth and they began to quarrel over the mermaid, hurling huge rocks at each other over Burra Firth. Tired of the racket the giants made, a local witch turned Herma into a mist, and Saxa into turf to form the Vord.

Keeping a weather-eye open for giants, Ann and I climbed west over Mouselee Hill to reach the sheer cliffs at Bluescudda Kame. The walk is not taxing, though we were seriously dive-bombed along the way by bonxies, the Shetland name for great skua; 800 pairs of these aggressive birds nest on Hermaness. In windy or misty conditions keep well back from the cliff edge – it's a long way down. We hoped to catch a glimpse of Muckle Flugga and of Albert Ross, a black-browed albatross that had strayed from its principal stronghold in the Falkland Islands. The bird was first sighted in Scotland in 1967 in the Firth of Forth, courting gannets on the Bass Rock. Unrequited in love, Albert then settled at Hermaness to see if any of the Unst gannets were more game. During the course of that unforgettable day, we didn't see Albert, but we did see Muckle Flugga.

Stevenson was an angler, although there is no record of him fishing when he was in Unst, which is a pity because the island has a number of excellent trout lochs. The most popular is Loch of Cliff, over two miles from north to south, with a narrow, crooked arm extending east at the north end for a distance of about half a mile. This arm hosts one of Shetland's oldest salmon farms and in recent years Loch of Cliff has suffered from serious algal bloom outbreaks, perhaps associated with untreated waste from the farm. Whatever, the local angling club has boats on the loch and, although Loch of Cliff is perhaps not for me, it does produce some handsome baskets of fish.

A few years ago I was invited by Unst Angling Club to open their annual midsummer fishing event. Kick-off was 8 p.m., the weigh-in at 8 a.m. the following morning. Eyebrows were raised when I appeared with a built-cane trout rod on the roof of my car; I have always fished with a cane rod and probably always will.

'My grandfather had one like that,' one of the young lads said. 'Can you cast far enough with it?' he asked.

'Yes,' I replied. 'As far as I need to.'

Most of the competitors headed for Loch of Cliff, but Ann and I decided to fish Loch of Watlee.

The loch drains northwards into Loch of Cliff via the Burn of Caldback and we mounted our assault from Heilia Brune, just off the A968 road. The loch enjoys a degree of shelter from the wind by the hills that enfold it on the east and west sides. Bank fishing is comfortable and we soon had sport with lovely trout of about 8oz in weight. Speaking to club members at breakfast, some mentioned a tiny loch, the Black Loch, which lies just to the north of Watlee. 'Wading is not advised,' I was told. 'It is dangerous but, believe me, there are some huge trout in that little loch, if you can catch them.'

As I have mentioned before, Shetland has long been famous for the quality of sea-trout fishing. However, in the early 1990s, and exacerbated by the massive expansion of fish-farming throughout Scotland's West Highland and Island areas, sea-trout numbers collapsed. In the autumn of 1992 Unst Angling Club members and supporters decided to do something about it. Since then, club members have worked hard, clearing up the burns and streams through which sea-trout reach their traditional spawning grounds. The club developed a hatchery and began a unique sea-trout restocking programme, rearing native fish that are then released into their natal streams. Two small waters in the south of the island, near Uyeasound, used to be prime sea-trout fisheries, Easter Loch and Dam Loch, and both are still worth a cast or three today.

The best of the Unst fishing, relatively speaking, is to be found in the south-west corner of the island, near the pier at Belmont. There are five waters deserving of your close attention: Loch of Belmont, Loch of Snarravoe, Loch of Stourhoull, Loch of Snabrough and Loch of Vigga. Stourhoull and Snabrough will tax your legs a bit, particularly Snabrough, but the other three are easily accessible. Belmont extends to about twenty acres and is comfortably fished from the bank. The water is clear and the trout generally accommodating, averaging in the order of 10oz–1lb, but there are also fish of up to and over 2lb in weight. These fish are of exceptional quality and fight hard. In windy conditions, not unknown it these airts, Belmont is ideal because you can simply adjust your position on the bank according to wind direction.

Snarravoe lies a short distance north from Belmont Pier along the A968, the only main road on the island. It is reputed to be the best loch in Unst, and here again, like Loch of Belmont, it is principally fished from the bank. It was stocked many years ago with progeny from Loch Leven, which perhaps accounts for the almost golden colour of its trout. Hope for great sport with lovely fish and, possibly, trout of over 4lb in weight. The loch drains westwards into the sea at Snarra Voe, so from July onwards there is also the chance of sea-trout. Stourhoull and Snabrough are also said to have been stocked with Loch Leven trout and have a well-earned and deserved reputation for being dour. They are both small waters, a few acres in extent and fished from the bank. The trout they contain are very beautiful and average 12oz. However, many local anglers insist that these lochs also hold fish in the teens of pounds.

The last water, Loch of Vigga on the hill to the south of Lunda Wick, always reminds me of my Unst ancestral connections; particularly the remains of St Olaf's Church, built in the twelfth century on the foundations of an even earlier place of worship, where there is a cemetery where numerous Sandisons lie at rest; Sandison has always been a pre-eminent name in the island and it is my belief that my people came from Unst, initially to Caithness, where my grandfather was born, and thence to Edinburgh, where I was born. However, on the ferry over Bluemull Sound from Yell to Unst the ticket collector noticed my name and remarked, 'Well, be careful who you tell, that's all I'm saying.'

I am sure Vigga, like the other waters mentioned above, must also, in the past, have been stocked with Loch Leven trout. It has a reputation for being excessively dour, as well as being home to some seriously large residents. If so, I have never managed to persuade any of them to take my flies, no matter how carefully I present them. But for me, the setting of this little loch is just about perfect: the sparkling waters of the bay; the calm sea, shaded silver and green and blue, where foam-tipped wavelets gently caressing the black rocks by the old church; snow-white gulls wheeling and crying plaintively. I can think of few other places in the world where I could be so happy and be so utterly and completely fishless.

YELL

Crossing from Toft in Mainland Shetland to Ulsta on Yell can be a pain in the 'buttocks' – the name given to that part of the journey between the uninhabited island of Bigga and the pier at Ulsta, where the sea rides over an underwater shelf, causing unsettling turbulence. Peter Guy, in his guide to Yell, notes:

> At certain tides, when a strong wind is blowing, it is possible to watch the waves crashing over the broken rocks of the Holm of Copister (130ft). The current can be so strong that the waves stand out like teeth as they career on the outside of the Holm and resemble 'da bittel grice', Shetland dialect for 'the biting pig'.

Nevertheless, for the angler at least, this is a small price to pay for the pleasures that lie ahead.

Although Yell is the second largest of the Shetland isles, it is sparsely populated – some 1,000 souls – with most of the communities being located on the east coast, rather than the west, which receives the full brunt of seasonal storms. There is little agricultural land – peat, to a depth of ten feet, is the dominant feature and it makes up more than two-thirds of the landscape. The island narrowly escapes from being cut in two in Mid Yell, where Whale Firth in the east is separated from Mid Yell Voe in the west by not much more than half a mile. The only main road is the A968 from Ulsta to Gutcher, where the ferry departs for Unst.

Most of the trout lochs lie in the north of the island and to the east of the main road. Some are more accessible than others, but, as is ever the case, the best of the fishing will adequately exercise legs and lungs. The North Yell lochs offer a great variety of fishing, with three of the waters being particularly noted for producing specimen trout: Loch of Brough, to the west of Cullivoe; Loch of Papil, immediately to the east of Greenbank; and the third loch, a step north from Papil and approached from Brough, is enigmatic Kirk Loch, reputed to hold fish of up to 5lb in weight and very dour with it. However, this fertile corner of Yell is dramatic, particularly in the stormy months of winter. During spring, wildflowers abound, and in summer, if you have non-fishing companions with you, then they will find here one of the UK's most lovely beaches and safe, albeit bracing, swimming in shallow, sheltered waters.

Another group of lochs, in Mid Yell, on the peninsula between Whale Firth in the east and Yell Sound in the west, are the Cro Waters and Virdi Water on The Herra. They involve a decent walk out from the village of Grimister and offer excellent sport, with bright little fish averaging 8–12oz. They also have the reputation of holding some much larger trout as well, and it is bank fishing all the way. Do not wade: it is unnecessary to do so and only scares the fish out into deeper water. Regardless of the size of the inhabitants of these lochs, this is a very special place – wonderful scenery, and wonderful wildflowers, and wonderful birdlife.

However, one of the most memorable days that Ann and I have enjoyed in Mid Yell was spent on Loch of Vollister, a little loch on the hill above a deserted village on the east shore of Whale Firth. But before walking out to fish, we explored one of Yell's most infamous properties, the ruins of the haunted house at Windhouse; ragged ceilings seeping dampness, broken roof beams spear-pointing the sky; empty window frames gaping like missing teeth; the remains of the staircase hanging crookedly from the wall, most of its steps missing. My spine tingled. I turned to Ann to ask if she felt uncomfortable. She was nowhere to be seen. Then I heard her call: 'Come on, Bruce, time to get on with our walk.'

I learned later that the house was haunted not by one ghost but by a whole family of spirits; the 'Lady in Silk', the ghost of a woman whose skeleton with a broken neck was found under floorboards at the foot of the main staircase; the 'Man in Black', a tall spectre in a black cloak seen outside the kitchen window; the ghost of a child whose remains were discovered built into the kitchen wall; and, to keep them all company, the ghost of a black dog.

But the most infamous ghost that haunted the house was a trow, the Shetland equivalent of a Scandinavian goblin or giant. Andrew Mathewson, writing in about 1863, recounts that the only survivor of a ship that had been wrecked in Whale Firth on 24 December was the vessel's Master. He sought refuge at Windhouse. To his surprise, he found everyone preparing for departure. He asked his host, a Mr Neven, why they were going. Mathewson relates:

> He received for answer that for this night of the year, namely Yule E'en or the 24th of every December, that he would have to seek lodgings for himself as no mortal who had ever attempted to sleep in the house that night was found alive in the morning, but was destroyed and slain by some evil spirit from the sea called Trows.

70

The ship's captain persuaded Neven to let him remain at Windhouse so that he could confront the demon.

> At one o'clock a sound arose as of rolling thunder and the whole fabric of the house shook and trembled as if going to ruins ... to sit still and die so ignominiously was not his desire. In the name and strength of the Blessed he made ready, felt his dagger and grasped his axe, tore down the barricades from the door and threw back the bar.

A dark shape fled from him and he pursued it towards Mid Yell Voe. Just before the creature reached the sea, the Captain hurled his axe, striking it in the head. When he examined the body, all that he could make out was a shapeless mass. He disposed of the creature 'in a large hole, covered it with earth and then formed the fence around it which still remains'. The Windhouse, a listed building, remains unoccupied today, the roof now entirely gone. I noticed recently (February 2015) that yet again the Windhouse is looking for another occupant. It is up for sale, again, open to offers of over £25,000.

I turned from the sombre ruin and joined Ann on the hill. Together, we tramped the golden moor – harried all the way by the angry great skuas who build their nests there – for two easy miles to reach the deserted village of Vollister. But unlike Windhouse, the tumbled ruins of Vollister greeted us happily and, borne on the soft wind, I thought that I heard the sound of dogs barking and children's laughter echoing amidst the tumbled grey stones.

Vollister is a small loch and was allegedly stocked in the early years of the twentieth century by the Windhouse Estate. The feeding in the loch must be excellent because over the years it has produced some specimen trout of considerable proportions. The current average weight of the residents is said to be in the region of 2lb. The loch drains into Whale Firth and is fed from north and east by two feeder streams. The water is crystal clear and deepens from the east side, where wading is comfortable and easy; this is true around most of Vollister apart from areas of the west shore and near the mouth of the outlet burn, where wading is virtually impossible. The loch is a few acres in extent and generally circular in shape, which is ideal in windy conditions: there will always be a suitable casting position, regardless of wind direction.

As we arrived, a large dog otter gave us a haughty stare before lolloping off seawards. It was not the best of fishing days – bright sun, calm and little chance of disguising evil intent, made more difficult by the presence of Ann's constant companion, the hyperactive Heathcliff. Nevertheless, I fished as carefully as I could. I had one sudden and huge tug at my flies, almost pulling the rod from out of my hand, but, after a few seconds, the fish was gone. That was the sum total of piscatorial action, so we eventually retired to the village ruins for rest, coffee and recuperation.

It is hard to describe the sense of peace that surrounded us, intangible and yet somehow almost physical. We left reluctantly and walked north for a mile or so between Muckle Swart Houll and Little Swart Houll to explore Loch of Windhouse, a bleak, long, dark and peaty puddle on Hesta Mires, where we found dark little trout. We also found a decent track by the Burn of Windhouse, and in the gathering dusk followed it back to our car, being careful to keep a keen lookout for marauding trolls and well clear of the grim ruins of the old house.

FETLAR

We caught the early morning ferry at Belmont on Unst for the thirty-minute crossing to the island of Fetlar. It was a glorious, sun-bright July morning. The sea was calm and sparkling, specked yellow and white with diving gannets. A 'good to be alive' day. It was our first visit to Fetlar, and Ann and I watched with increasing excitement as we approached that magical isle.

The ferry docked at Hamars Ness, and we bumped ashore and drove south to Brough to join the B9088, Fetlar's principal road, which serves the needs of the island resident population of some sixty people. The island school, near Houbie, the main village of the island, recently counted a role of seven primary pupils and two nursery pupils.

Fetlar is the fourth largest of the Shetland Isles and covers an area of some 15 square miles. It is a fertile island, known as the 'the Garden of Shetland'. It is also renowned for its wildlife. There are upwards of 200 species of wildflowers and Fetlar is an outstanding sanctuary for birds, with Arctic and great skuas, whimbrel, golden plover and large colonies of storm petrel. During the 1960s and early 1970s a pair of magnificent snowy owls famously nested on Fetlar. However, the most notable bird is the delicate and lovely little summer visitor, the red-necked phalarope, which nests at the Loch of Funzie – pronounced 'Finnie' – in the west of the island at one of the most important UK breeding sites for this species.

In 2013, many national newspapers reported on the vast distances some of these small birds make on their migratory journeys. One article revealed:

> The Royal Society for the Protection of Birds (RSPB) working alongside the Swiss Ornithological Institute and Dave Okill of the Shetland Ringing Group, fitted individual geolocators to ten red-necked phalaropes nesting on Fetlar. After recapturing one of the tagged birds when it returned to Fetlar last spring, experts discovered that it had made an epic 16,000-mile round trip during its annual migration. It had flown from Shetland across the Atlantic via Iceland and Greenland, south down the eastern seaboard of the US, across the Caribbean and Mexico, ending up off the coast of Ecuador and Peru. After wintering in the Pacific, it returned to Fetlar following a similar route.

73

However, there was one other species that we were anxious to see during our visit: wild brown trout. The island does not have many lochs, but they have a considerable reputation for the quality and size of the fish that they contain. The principal lochs are, from west to east, Papil Water, near Tresta; Skutes Water, to the north of Houbie; Loch of Winyadepla, an invigorating two-mile hike north from Houbie to the Hill of Morgisdale; and Loch of Funzie, at the end of the B9088 road. Winyadepla is noted as being exceptionally dour but also as holding exceptionally large trout. Sea-trout are most noticeable by their absence. Feltar has no rivers and the dramatic cliffs that surround the island do not provide many opportunities for fishing from the shore.

We decided to have a look at Papil Water, reputed to be the best of the Fetlar lochs. It is certainly one of the most beautiful, with banks of yellow flag in full bloom. Access is easy and the loch lies close to the sea, where machair flats were carpeted with wildflowers. Sadly, however, and marring the beauty of the loch, there were smolt rearing cages at the south end. A man fishing from a boat later told me that all he had caught were escapee salmon smolts. I suffered likewise and soon tired of doing so. The water was also so discoloured that it was impossible when wading to see your feet a few yards out from the shore. Nevertheless, on checking recently with friends on the island I was delighted to learn that the smolt cages had been empty for several years and that Papil Water had returned to its former excellence, producing seriously sized trout of up to and over 4lb in weight.

Our next call was to Loch of Funzie, easily accessible and crystal clear. I didn't see any phalaropes, or, indeed, any trout, but I did see a lot of binocular-clad ornithological visitors at the RSPB hide. There are areas round the loch were access is restricted because of nesting birds and I was told later that the island's rain geese, red-throated divers, had probably eaten most of the trout in Funzie. With that in mind, and feeling uncomfortably exposed, we decamped and headed back to Houbie.

After calling at the Fetlar Interpretive Centre, where everything you want to know about Fetlar past and present is on display, we decided to investigate Skutes Water. It is easily accessed from bleak Fetlar Aerodrome, a brisk thirty-minute walk across the moor. Skutes Water instantly captivated me. It lies in a wonderfully remote setting with not a dwelling in sight, loud with the call of whimbrel and golden plover. The loch is shallow and safe to wade, and although the trout may not qualify for a glass case they are beautifully marked and fight well. A very special place.

WHALSAY

Whalsay lies two miles off the east coast of Mainland Shetland and is known as 'the Bonnie Isles'. It has a population of about 1,000 and its lifeblood is fishing; when the fleet is in, the harbour at Symbister is crowded with boats both large and small. Regular ferries run from the pier at Flugarth on Mainland across Dury Voe to Symbister and it is easy to spend a day fishing the island's trout lochs and be back on Mainland in time for tea. The name of the island derives from the Old Norse 'Hvals Oy', which, translated, means 'whale island'; Vikings sailing to Whalsay would have seen the massive cliffs of Clett Head (390ft) at the south of the island which, to them, resembled the hump on a whale's back.

One of Whalsay's most notable residents was the Scottish poet Hugh MacDiarmid, the pseudonym of Christopher Grieve. Grieve lived in a croft house on Whalsay in the 1930s until he was called up for service in 1942 during the Second World War. He did not really 'fit in' to the community and remained, essentially, an outsider, but he wrote his poem 'On a Raised Beach' there; to this day, a challenging work, uneasy to read and just as uneasy to understand. There is no record of Grieve ever having picked

75

up a trout rod, which is, in my view, a pity because had he done so his work may have become more accessible and, certainly, less sad.

There are ten lochs on Whalsay and all are easily accessible from the road that circles the main body of the island, with a spur that continues from Brough to Skaw at the north tip of Whalsay. Trout average in the order of 10–12oz in weight, but with the possibility in some of the lochs of much larger fish. The little Loch of Sandwick is unnamed on the OS Map but lies on the hill to the west of the community of the same name. It can produce trout of up to 2lb, but it becomes very weedy as the season advances; Loch of Isbister, East Loch of Skaw and Loch of Houll fall into the same category. Nuckro Water, a small loch immediately adjacent to the road on the west side of Whalsay, is an exception and is said to hold very large trout. However, they are rarely caught and Nuckro is the loch to fish if you are keen to break your heart. Like Loch of Sandwick, it becomes weedy from June onwards.

The largest Whalsay trout, weighing 9lb 8oz, came from Loch of Huxter and fell to the well-presented fly of George Irvine, a notable Whalsay angler who, rumour had it, used to get up at midnight if he was going fishing the next day. I fished Huxter with George and another expert Shetland angler, David Pottinger, both great companions and full of tales about the ones that got away – and the ones that didn't. Boat fishing brings best results on the loch and although we worked hard the trout remained singularly uncooperative. But it is a lovely loch to fish, surrounded by wildflower-covered banks and vibrant birdlife. It is also remarkable in that a small island at the west end of the loch contains the ruins of an Iron Age fort. The island is connected to the mainland by a now-submerged causeway and the fort was probably constructed around 3000 BC. No doubt its inhabitants then took trout from the loch, although I guess that they would have used rather more direct methods to do so than rod, line and delicately feathered fly.

BRESSAY

Bressay is the most accessible of the principal Shetland islands, a few minutes' ferry sail (a bridge is being suggested) from the hustle and bustle of busy Lerwick. The population of the island is in the region of 400 and the Isle of Noss, 200 yards off the east side of Bressay, is famous for its seabird-crowded cliffs that are close to 600 feet in height. Isle of Noss is a National Nature Reserve managed by Scottish Natural Heritage (SNH) and in the breeding season the sound that tens of thousands of anxious parent birds and their chicks make is like that of a huge orchestra tuning up: 40,000 guillemots, 20,000 gannets, 5,000 kittiwakes, puffins, shags, razorbills and fulmars. For information about Isle of Noss Nature Reserve, have a look at the Scottish National Heritage website.

One year when Ann and I were in Shetland, Rae Phillips and his wife, Loreen, and their son, Robert, took us to see the Isle of Noss cliffs and their raucous residents. We spent an unforgettable day on Rae's yacht, sailing from Lerwick to see and hear the amazing sight and sound of the birds on the one-mile-long guano-whitened Noss cliffs. The noise was almost deafening, yet at the same time entirely enchanting.

After leaving Isle of Noss, we sailed south for a few miles across a millpond-flat sea, rounding the east side island of Mousa before turning north again into Mousa Sound to see its famous broch, the finest example in the world, being nearly forty-three feet in height with sixteen-foot-thick walls. The brochs were built, generally, during the period 100 BC to AD 200, and the remains of many are scattered throughout the Highlands and Islands of Scotland, but Mousa Broch, probably because of its situation on an island, is the best preserved of these structures. The mystery of the brochs, however, is why they were built: they are clearly massive defensive buildings, with only one easily guarded entrance; the puzzle is, who were they defending themselves against? No one knows. Mousa Broch is also famous for a less war-like reason: it is the nesting home for some 6,800 pairs of our smallest seabird, the storm petrel, which is 8 per cent of the UK population and about 2.5 per cent of the world population of these beautiful little creatures.

When you arrive on Bressay, you will be greeted by the Bressay Heritage Centre, opened in 1996, and owned and operated by the Bressay History Group. This will give you an overview of the island's history and geology, and point you in the direction of the site of one of the most beautiful Pictish symbol stones in Scotland: the ninth-century Bressay Stone in the graveyard of St Mary's Church at Cullingsbrough in the north-east of the island. The stone was found in 1852 and later removed to the National Museum of Antiquities in Edinburgh. A replica of the stone was erected in 2000 by the Shetland Council of Churches to commemorate the millennium.

For the angler, Bressay offers sport on about a dozen lochs scattered throughout the eleven square miles of the island. They all offer decent sport, perhaps the best of it being amongst the Lochs of Beosetter, easily accessible from the ferry terminal after a short walk over the moor. There are four lochs here: Beosetter itself, Mill Loch, Loch of Cruester and Gunnesta Loch. Mill Loch becomes weedy as the season advances and, as it is with most of the Bressay waters, it is best to avoid wading. Stay safe on terra firma. The Shetland Anglers Association has stocked these lochs and the average weight of fish is in the order of 12oz, although fish of up to 4lb have been taken.

There are four further lochs, frequently unforgiving, on the west side of Bressay, approached from the road to Isle of Noss: in the north, Loch of Aith; then Loch of Setter, where a large trout would weigh 1lb – clear water and do not wade, and again very weedy as the season advances; in the middle, dour Loch of Brough, the island's water supply and with a reputation for holding some specimen trout; and, to the south again, Loch of Grimsetter, which is thought to be virtually fishless. As to flies, perhaps the old standard-pattern Scottish loch flies will suffice. They have done so for me for more years than I am prepared to confess: Ke-He, Black Pennell, Soldier Palmer, March Brown, Greenwell's Glory, Woodcock and Hare-lug, Invicta, Dunkeld, Silver Butcher and Silver Invicta, all good friends of mine.

However, for a real Bressay adventure, walk two miles south round the east shoulder of Ward of Bressay Hill (712ft) to explore distant Loch Sand Vatn. Wading is possible, with care, and although somewhat dour, the fish fight well and average in the order of 8–10oz. Sand Vatn is rarely fished, but is a very special place.

This section is dedicated to my Shetland friends, Rae, Loreen and Robert Phillips, with affection and thanks for the many acts of kindness that they have shown to Ann and me over the years.

ORKNEY

Beyond the red-scarred cliffs of Hoy
My being mingles with times past.
Amidst the sentinel grey stones of
Stenness and Brodgar I hear dogs
Barking and the laughter of children.

Over the sea to the magical islands of Orkney, and I hope that you are a good sailor because the vagaries of the Pentland Firth can test the strongest sea-legs. I remember with fond horror a passage in 1967 before the advent of roll-on roll-off ferries. Our car was lifted onboard by sling and dumped none too ceremoniously on deck, but that was as nothing compared to the dumping we received when the boat left the comparative calm of Scrabster Harbour near Thurso in Caithness.

House-high waves, mad walls of tormented, flying spray roared in from all quarters as the vessel cork-screwed and bobbed crazily northwards until we eventually pitched drunkenly into the lee of the island of Hoy and, slowly, calmer waters settled our pounding hearts. We were not, as I had previously expected, every minute, doomed to a watery grave. Ashore, surrounded by the solid stones and cobbles of the old grey town of Stromness, I felt like Mr Fletcher Christian waving farewell to Captain Bligh from the *Bounty*. Then, from a great height, they dropped my car onto the pier: a final gesture of disgust from proper seamen to fair-weather sailors and landlubbers like me.

In spite of that violent introduction to the Orcades, this very special place has held us enthralled ever since and the journey from mainland Scotland is not always so stormy. We have sailed, millpond calm amidst myriad seabirds, chased and chivvied by porpoise and gannets, lazing past sunburnt sentinel stacks, barely aware of time passing. What finer way to go fishing, and few islands offer such a warm welcome to anglers.

Most people think of the Orkney islands in terms of the mainland view from Caithness; across the firth to the russet-red crags of Santoo Head, Sneuk Head and Robie Geo on Hoy. But beyond the hills of Hoy lies a vista of gentle fields and soft moorlands; of farmlands, filled with safely grazing sheep, handsome cattle and fine crops. Mainland Orkney is famous for the vitality of its agricultural land, which produces outstanding crops of oats and barley, and fine crops of seed potatoes. These farmlands are surrounded by wonderful, heather-covered moorland and one is never far from the eternal sound of the sea.

This is the scene that unfolds as you drive east from Stromness towards Kirkwall, Orkney's administrative centre: at the crest of the Brae of Howe, before you glints Loch of Stenness, incredibly blue, with Loch Harray beyond, stretching into the hazy distance; and between these two waters, the ancient standing stones of Stenness, forming a 100-foot circle, and nearby the majestic Ring of Brodgar, built before the construction of the great Pyramids of Egypt. Now, adjacent to Brodgar, the remains of a Neolithic settlement is being excavated and it is vast, almost certainly the principal population centre in Orkney in Neolithic times.

There are more than 1,000 known sites of prehistoric man scattered throughout the islands. In 1958, Ronnie Simison, a farmer in South Ronaldsay, discovered and over a number of years excavated a 5,000-year-old burial chamber, now known as the 'Tomb of the Eagles' because it contained the talons of an estimated fourteen white-tailed sea eagles; it is thought that before bodies were taken into the tomb, they were exposed outside for the pleasure of the eagles, the remains then being collected and ceremoniously interred in the tomb. It is thought that the Tomb of the Eagles contained the bones of more than 340 people, interred there over a period of some 800 years.

This dramatic tomb lies close to a cliff-top edge near Isbister on the south-east shore of South Ronaldsay, and Ann and I visited the site on a windy day when white waves were shattering on the base of black broken rocks and flinging themselves madly up the face of the cliff. We were alone amongst this stark landscape and entered the tomb by lying face down on a wheeled trolley, using a rope to pull ourselves into the centre. Light entered the tomb through a small roof-light, casting dark shadows into the confined space, illuminating an area where lay the skulls of the dead. And yet it was not disturbing. A sense of peace pervades this burial place, a level of calmness that one can almost touch; the same sense I always experience at every prehistoric site I visit in these magical isles.

Further afield and close to the Loch of Harray and Loch of Stenness in Mainland is Maeshowe chambered cairn, considered to be the most magnificent European example of such a burial place, sealed by its priests more than 5,000 years ago, and reopened and looted by the Vikings in AD 1150. (Norsemen conquered Orkney in the ninth century when the islands became dependencies of Norway and Denmark.) It was during the time of that Viking domination that Rognvald Kolsson began to build his magnificent red-sandstone cathedral in Kirkwall, named after martyred St Magnus, killed on the island of Egilsay in AD 1116. It is said that before he died Magnus asked his executioner to kill him by an axe stroke to the head, rather than suffer decapitation: 'For it is not seemly to behead chiefs like thieves.' When the remains of the saint were found in 1919, in a pillar in St Magnus Cathedral, the skull was deeply marked, by an axe blow.

The Stone Age village of Skara Brae in Sandwick – built during the same period as the building of the other Neolithic structures mentioned – is perhaps one of Orkney's most dramatic monuments. In the winter of 1850 a huge storm uncovered the remains of ten houses buried in the sand dunes. They have been carefully excavated and nestle on a bluff overlooking the Bay of Skaill, half a mile of golden sand washed by green Atlantic waves, warmed by the Gulf Stream.

We often swam from the beach at Skaill; indeed, I taught my first dog, a shy golden retriever named Jean, to swim there. She showed a distinctively un-retriever-like fear of water so eventually I carried her out and set her afloat. She swam happily ever after. Visit Skara Brae on a midsummer evening amidst the cry of seagull and twittering late larks. Then, it is as though small axe-carrying, sheepskin-clad men will come to greet you, with their prehistoric dogs yapping loudly around their calloused feet.

Orkney is also an ornithologist's delight. I remember, as a boy, lying on the cliffs to the east of Birsay, watching fulmar petrels sweeping along the cliffs, and my first glimpse of a hen harrier, floating ghost-like over the moors. There are many rare species to be seen, including great northern diver, black-throated and red-throated divers, purple sandpiper, golden plover, great skua, Arctic tern and puffins. Orkney wildflowers are also splendid: that uniquely Scottish jewel, *Primula scotica*, and grass of parnassus and Scottish lovage; Alpine bearberry, mountain everlasting, spring squill, oysterplant and bog pimpernel. Everywhere you turn on these lovely islands some new pleasure greets you.

I first visited Orkney in 1952, on a family holiday, and I suspect that experience had a lot to do with stimulating my love of islands. We lived in Edinburgh then, and sailed from Edinburgh's port of Leith via Aberdeen on the RMS *St Ninian* to Kirkwall; my first real adventure into the unknown. The overnight passage to

Aberdeen was wild and stormy, and my brother Ian and I were amongst the few passengers onboard capable of doing proper justice to the excellent dinner provided. Afterwards, we clung to the rail, listening to the wind howling, watching vast angry waves crowding in on every side.

Mother and Father had retired, along with my younger brother, Fergus, and they spent an unhappy night wrestling with the toils of seasickness. Stirred, still green and shaken, they emerged the following morning to greet the new day. My parents had rented a cottage on a farm at Backakeldy, ten miles south from Kirkwall overlooking the sea on the eastern shores of Scapa Flow. The farm was owned by three bachelor brothers and three spinster sisters. Senior brother, John Isbister, smiling brightly, met us on the pier at Kirkwall and I instinctively knew that I was going to like him. Our cottage lay on stubby cliffs close to the sea. There was no road to it, or track, merely a worn path, two fields distance from the farm, but to us, big-city born-and-bred, it was paradise, the stuff of which dreams are made, and for two weeks we lived a life of unadulterated bliss.

Outside the cottage door was a huge, ominous-looking shell which we were told had been fired from a battleship during the First World War, and John pointed out to us exactly where the HMS *Royal Oak* had been torpedoed in 1939; sunk there by the German submarine *U-47*, commanded by Captain Gunther Prien, who had managed to penetrate the defences to Scapa Flow. John told us that oil slicks from the stricken leviathan still sometimes marred the bay.

One of our greatest pleasures was collecting early morning provisions from the farm. We always found an excuse to linger round the milking parlour, warmed by the steaming animals, watching in admiration as one of the ladies coaxed milk from pink teats into a foaming bucket. An invitation to tea in the farmhouse kitchen was an almost unbearable delight; bright cinders glowed in the polished black stove; hot, freshly baked scones, butter, cheese, ten-minute fresh eggs and milk from the sombre-eyed cows round the door; the scent of peat smoke, soothing all cares.

Like all Orcadians, the Isbisters were supremely gentle, kindly people, always with enough time to stop and talk to two excited small boys and my lifelong interest in birds was greatly encouraged by their patience and kindness. One evening, as we stood talking by the shore, I saw a strange, beautifully shaped bird flying fast over the sea, rising in a long, slow arch, calling hauntingly as it flew. John told me that it was a red-throated diver, and those lovely creatures have remained favourites of mine ever since.

We were allowed to help with the work of the farm, although more often than not I suspect we hindered the wheels of labour. In those days, horses were still used on many farms for ploughing and I soon found myself staggering red-faced up a furrow, furiously gripping the wooden handles, astonished at the power of the mighty beasts plodding sombrely ahead. Ian, being older, was even luckier. He was allowed to drive the old red Ferguson tractor. One day we all crowded, laughing, aboard the trailer, to help the Isbisters bring home peat for winter fuel. That day we nearly lost young Fergus.

One minute he was there, the next gone, vanished from the face of the earth. I saw him disappear but, before I could say anything, Fergus started yelling. He had stumbled into a deep peat hole, hidden by heather, and worse, the heather had closed above his head, hiding where he had fallen. John Isbister shouted, 'Keep yelling, son, I'm coming.' He bounded across the moor, guided by Fergie's howls, and eventually discovered the spot. Parting the heather, he reached down and grabbed Fergus by the hand. With difficulty, John hauled my terrified little brother to safety. Just in time. Fergus had been waist deep and sinking fast.

We had another narrow escape, and for years afterwards Father would go red with embarrassment when the subject was mentioned: 'I must have been off my head,' he would mutter ashamedly. The incident happened on the Churchill Barriers, the great concrete causeways Winston Churchill ordered to be built to protect the fleet in Scapa Flow from further submarine attacks after the sinking of the *Royal Oak*. Four causeways were built, mainly by Italian prisoners of war: from Mainland to Lamb Holm, Lamb Holm joining Glims Holm, Glims Holm to Burray, and Burray to South Ronaldsay. The Isbisters had lent Father their car and we spent the day exploring, visiting the Italian Chapel on Lamb Holm, built by Italian POWs, now guarded by a statue of St George, before driving south to the little hamlet of St Margaret's Hope.

Ian and I were particularly impressed with the half-submerged hulks the block ships sunk there during both world wars, prior to the building of the Churchill Barriers, to protect the fleet at anchor in Scapa Flow. We were both young enough and old enough to have vivid wartime memories of the Second World War, and were fascinated by the ominous array of masts and dark shapes in the bay. The peace treaty ending the First World War remained unsigned by Germany six months after the eleventh hour of the eleventh day in the eleventh month of 1918. Rear-Admiral von Reuter, anticipating renewed conflict, on 21 June 1919 commanded his fleet of seventy-four ships to be either scuttled or beached. As SMS *Hindenburg* went down, the German Ensign was lowered and this flag may still be seen in the German Fleet Exhibition in the excellent Stromness Museum, founded in 1837 and portraying Orkney's maritime and natural history.

But after a glorious day's exploring, by the time we turned for home the weather had become very wild. As we approached the first barrier, waves were breaking fiercely over the road. Nothing daunted, Father continued, in spite of protests from Mother. Matters grew worse by the minute as Father pressed on, windscreen wipers working furiously. Waves flew over the car. How we survived remains a mystery, but when we eventually arrived at Backakeldy we were told that the coastguard had been alerted and that our mad passage across the barriers had been watched in amazement by worried would-be rescuers.

By the time I returned to Orkney I had been stricken by the incurable disease of angling and, for anglers, Orkney boasts some of the most exciting wild brown trout fishing in Britain, and the bays and seaweed-fringed shores round the islands can also offer excellent sport with sea-trout. However, as is the case with Shetland and the West Highlands and Islands, the impact of disease and pollution from factory fish farms has greatly reduced the numbers of sea-trout returning to these shores.

Nevertheless, good sport might still be had with sea-trout and here is a note, with OS map number and six-figure grid reference, of the places to try: Marwick Bay (6/227242); Bridge of Waithe (6/282110): Swanbister Bay (6/352050); Skaith (6/377063); Scapa Bay (6/434088); Graemshall (6/491017); Sandside Bay (6/590068); Bay of Suckquoy (6/522044); Grimsetter (6/476087); Bay of Isbister (6/391182); Wood Wick (6/395240); and Sands of Evie (6/376263).

On Hoy, visit Bay of Creekland (7/236047); Bay of Quoys (7/242033); Lyrawa Bay (7/291988); Pegal Bay (7/297978); Mill Bay (7/300955); Ore Bay (7/305939); Heldale (7/284912); Saltness (7/278899); and Myre Bay (7/328910).

In the spring of 2006 a sea-trout of 11lb 3oz was taken from Bay of Cleekland.

In recent years, fish-farm activity has declined in Orkney and – surprise, surprise – sea-trout have begun again to populate their traditional spawning grounds. Sadly, however, in 2014, a Canadian fish-farm company, Cooke Aquaculture, acquired a considerable interest in Orkney (and Shetland) fish farms. This looks as though it might bring about a new expansion in fish-farm activity in Orkney, which will almost certainly result in a drop in the numbers of wild sea-trout returning to spawn. The Orkney Trout Fishing Association (OTFA), which recently celebrated its 100th anniversary, actively and regularly opposes new fish-farm planning applications and is to be congratulated for doing so.

The majority of Orcadian sea-trout are caught in the sea, fishing from the shore, although they may also be encountered in Loch of Stenness, Loch of Harray and Loch of Kirbister. But few angling experiences match the thrill of hooking and playing a wild sea-trout from the shore and the vast majority of the fish so caught are returned to fight another day. The season runs from 25 February to the end of October, with the best times being March and April. Take great care wading, and check tide times and seek local advice before setting out, and remember to wash your tackle in fresh water when you return.

MAINLAND

There are five principal trout lochs – Harray, Stenness, Swannay, Boardhouse and Hundland – on Mainland, and other smaller waters, both on Mainland and in the outer islands. However, of all Orkney lochs, Swannay is my favourite. Not only because of the quality of fish but also because of the serenity of the surroundings. My wife and I know Swannay in its every mood, from millpond calm to raging turmoil. And yet, even in the worst of weather, Swannay has rarely sent us home supper-less.

I once fished the loch in a snow storm, from the bank near Dale, and was rewarded with two of the most beautiful trout I have ever seen, each weighing just about 1lb 8oz. Given my angling ability, my success was probably due more to luck than any skill on my part; at least that's what the rest of the family said and, being outnumbered six to one, not including Ann's Yorkshire terrier Heathcliff, I was in no position to argue.

Boat fishing brings the best results. I discovered this fact many years ago, fishing from the shore at the north end. The bottom was uneven and rocks slippery. A good place for a ducking. The most productive areas of the loch seem to be at the south end.

Begin in the bay where the burn of Etheriegeo enters. Fish from the burn-mouth westwards, then explore the drifts between the island of Muckle Holm and Loudenhill Farm. The east shore should be given careful attention, from the OTFA site down to past Southend and Dale.

Swannay trout do not give themselves up easily and you will probably count your catch on the fingers of one hand rather than two. However, they make a meal fit for a king. Our last visit ended more modestly, with four fish in the boat, but I shall remember that day for many years to come due to the astonishing weather. One moment we were bathed in brilliant sunlight, the next shivering, hunched in torrential rain. At times the sun was so hot that perspiration flowed down our faces; the next minute, ice-cold rain was dripping from jackets and sleeves whilst distant thunder rumbled and roared.

At the end of the day we retired, stunned but happy, marvelling at the perversity of nature and the perfidy of trout. Nevertheless, a local angler, fishing throughout the same conditions, had a lovely basket of twelve fish, the heaviest being a splendid specimen weighing 3lb 8oz. I had been watching him during the afternoon and he told me that he had taken most of his fish on a small Blue Zulu fished very rapidly across the surface, hardly allowing the flies time to settle before beginning the retrieve. I made rapid mental notes for my next visit. The most productive flies on the loch seem to be Black Pennell, Black or Blue Zulu, Ke-He, Loch Ordie and Silver Butcher.

One Easter we rented a cottage in Sandwick and, in spite of fierce, cold weather, we decided to assault Loch of Swannay. Fighting our way through a raging snowstorm, we arrived at the north end by Costa Hill and huddled in the car astonished by the force of the blizzard. Ann, made of sterner stuff than the rest of her tribe, leapt from the car, determined to fish. Within moments of setting off she was lost from view, swallowed up in the white mist. We waited, wondering whether or not to follow. After twenty minutes I glimpsed her figure, red hat and green coat, shoulders bent, struggling back, snow-woman-like, with a lovely brown trout that weighed almost 2lb.

We nearly got stuck in a snowdrift at Setter on the way back to our cottage, but dinner that night was wonderful. Then, with wind howling round the windows and rattling the doors, we sat in front of a peat fire and played games. That was really our last family holiday, our four children – Blair, Lewis-Ann, Charles and Jean – Ann and me. The following year, Blair and Lewis-Ann were off chasing their own adult fortunes. But the memory of that last holiday together in Orkney lingers forever.

On our first family holiday in Orkney, Ann booked a caravan from a lady in Finstown. She asked the woman taking the booking exactly where the caravan was located and the reply was: 'Where do you want it located?' The selected location was a few yards from the shore of Loch of Boardhouse, on the west side of the loch, close by Castlehill and Nicol Point. And there was a boat ready and waiting for our use. The loch lies in the parish of Birsay in north-west Mainland, near to the Viking island of Brough of Birsay and the dramatic ruins of the Earls Palace, built in the sixteenth century by Robert Stewart, the illegitimate son of James V of Scotland and a despotic ruler of the islands.

Boardhouse is approximately two miles long, lying north-west/south-east and pinched in the middle by narrows. The south bay is three-quarters of a mile wide, between Nicol Point and Midhouse; the north bay is just under half a mile across from the standing stone at Stanger, north-east to Newhouse. It is accessible from the A967 road, which parallels the west shore, and by a minor road along the east shore. The loch drains north via a narrow stream and enters the sea at Point of Snusan. It is possible that Boardhouse once had a run of sea-trout and, perhaps, could have one again, were the outlet stream improved, but as far as I am aware there are no plans to do so.

I remember one evening, out with my son, Blair, who was five at the time. It was calm and fish were rising almost constantly. However, I couldn't persuade them to take my fly – which is when I noticed a large daddy-long-legs floating by. I netted it. 'This will do the trick, Blair,' I said, confidently. 'I will bind it carefully to a hook.' I did so and cast, gently, so as not to dislodge the insect. When I brought the rod forward, it was obvious that I hadn't been gentle enough; the daddy was sitting on the water behind the boat. As we watched, an enormous trout rose and took the daddy.

'That was exciting,' Blair said. 'Can we do it again and maybe you might catch the fish?'

Unlike other Orkney waters, Boardhouse is almost entirely free of skerries, underwater outcrops of jagged rock, and the loch has an average depth of eight feet to twelve feet. The bottom is soft and an ideal habitat for insect life. Consequently, trout thrive mightily and, frequently, so do anglers. Fish average 12oz, although each season much larger specimens are landed and trout of 41b are by no means uncommon. One of the principal pleasures of fishing Boardhouse is the sure and certain knowledge that trout may be caught throughout the whole loch, from margins to middle. Some areas are perhaps better than others; for example, during August, when weed grows strongly in the middle of the south bay, good baskets may be taken by carefully inching round their edges. There is also weed growth in the north bay during the back end and good sport may be had there as well.

Bank fishing on Boardhouse is bad news and uncomfortable, due to the depth of water close to the shore and the muddy nature of the bottom. Nevertheless, I remember catching fish, in a howling gale, near the stone surround by the waterworks, so if all else fails go thou and do likewise. When trout are in the mood, sport is fast and furious, so it is important to be selective about which fish you keep. Offer them Ke-He, Black Pennell or Sedge-hog on the 'bob'; Kate McLaren, March Brown or Greenwell's

Glory in the middle; Silver Butcher, Silver Invicta or Dunkeld on the tail.

East of Boardhouse, and joined to it by a little stream, is Loch of Hundland, a small water which, as the season progresses, has substantial weed growth. When we visited the loch some years ago, it had all but disappeared due to a long dry spell. Things have much improved since then and Hundland is noted for the size and quality of its fish: heavier than Boardhouse trout, with occasional monsters sometimes encountered in amongst the weeds. Because the loch is shallow, fish rise and may be caught all over, from middle to margins. So cast with confidence every-where. Another plus-point with Hundland is that it produces good results in bright conditions, when other Orkney waters tend to be dour.

The Loch of Harray is Orkney's largest and most popular loch and is considered by many to be the most productive wild brown trout water in Europe; some years it can produce upwards of 20,000 trout. The fish are of very high quality, silver bodied and pink fleshed, marvellous to catch and marvellous to eat. Their average weight is in the order of 12oz, but some huge fish have been taken over the years: in 1964 a magnificent trout of 17lb 8oz was landed, and fish of over 5lb are not uncommon. During a recent National Angling Competition on the loch, nearly 400 trout were recorded during the day.

I am not a fan of angling competitions, national or otherwise. To me, the only acceptable form of competition in fishing is between the angler and his quarry, with the odds very much weighted against the angler. But in the late 1970s, along with three friends, I formed a private fishing group known as the MacSob Log. We were Donnie Mackay, me (Sandison), Harry Officer and Adam Black – thus 'MacSob'. The idea was that once a year we would have a fishing outing when each member would fish with his son. The most successful pair would have the priv-ilege of writing a note, generally scurrilous, of the day's activities in a book-cum-photograph album, thus the 'Log'. Donnie was of a religious turn of mind, so we often described ourselves as: father and son, father and son, father and son, and Holy Ghost – the ghost being Donnie Mackay.

One of our most memorable and happy outings was to fish Loch of Harray. We stayed at the excellent Merkister Hotel and, because it was a special occasion, we were accompanied by wives and other friends, in total a party of twelve. Heather and Arthur Howard owned the Merkister then and could not have been more welcoming. As, indeed, was Harray, with a brisk wind and enough of a wave to disguise evil intent, and comfortable for fishing. There was good sport all day, with trout rising freely and readily to well-presented flies – bushy bob-flies, Greenwells and March Browns in the middle and attractors on the tail. Landing nets got wet and, in the evening, so did those who had used them. I am the last surviving member of the founders of the MacSob Log, but the memories of our many outings remain ever fresh. Such is the joy of fishing.

Harray is six miles long by up to one-and-a-half-miles wide, encompassing an area of some 2,500 acres. The loch is shallow, and consequently warms up quickly, and spring fishing can be spectacular. It all depends upon the weather. Fish may be caught throughout the whole system and most anglers launch their attack from boats. However, bank fishing can be just as productive and, in high winds, one of the most delightful aspects of fishing Harray is that it is always possible to find a sheltered corner somewhere along its fourteen-mile margins from which to cast. One of the most popular bank-fishing areas is at the south end of the loch, close to the standing stones and Maeshowe. Fish round to the mouth of the burn that feeds Harray from the moorlands of Nisthouse and Heddle.

In a strong west wind, make for Mill of Rango, close to the A967, and fish down past Whilliastane to Pontooth on Ness of Tenston. When the storm howls in from the east, head for Bigging and ply the shoreline southwards past Nistaben to Ballarat House. There are endless numbers of points, headlands and fishy corners where trout await your well-presented fly. You do not need to cast far to be amongst them, so wade sparingly.

Afloat is a different matter. The loch is full of skerries and around them is where most fish are caught, just as the water begins to deepen. Finding these feeding areas is not easy and my best advice is to seek local knowledge. The way to do this is to join the Orkney Trout Fishing Association. The high quality of Orkney sport is maintained and supported by the association, a group of unpaid, keen local anglers who expend much time, energy and effort in looking after the island's fisheries. Membership of the association allows visitors access to all the association sites and fellow members are always willing to guide the newcomer to the most productive drifts.

Merkister Bay, at the north-east end of the loch, is a popular fishing area; very shallow and downright dangerous in low-water conditions. Buoys mark the safe channel out from the jetty. Halfway down the loch, between Ballarat House on the east shore and Ness of Tenston on the west shore, can be a highly product-ive drift, as are the skerried bays of Ling Holms on the west and Long Holm by Grimeston on the east. As a general rule, when fishing Harray, if you can't see the bottom you are probably fish-ing too far out; keep to the margins and shallows.

Talking about skerries, I remember having an unwelcome closer look at one. I was covering an international competition for *Trout & Salmon* magazine and because there was a shortage of gillies I agreed to look after two members of the Welsh team. Although I did not have an extensive knowledge of Harray, I most certainly knew more about the loch than my companions, one of whom insisted on taking over on the outboard motor. When he ran aground on a skerrie, he looked at me expectantly. I carefully exited the boat and heaved it free. To my horror, for a moment, I thought that they intended to leave me there in the middle of the loch, so I was mightily relieved when they eventually edged back and allowed me to clamber aboard. Ever since, I have always been cautious in the company of men from the valleys.

If Loch of Harray is a lady, her neighbour, Loch of Stenness, can be an infuriating, maddening, perverse teenager. It probably has the finest quality trout of all Orkney waters, but they are also the most difficult to catch. Blank days, even for local anglers, are frequent. However, this dramatic loch still produces superb trout of unequalled quality and sometimes sea-trout, fresh from the tide that races through the outlet at Bridge of Waithie into Bay of Ireland and Hoy Sound. But when Stenness decides to behave, then rewards can be outstanding. It is all a matter of being in the right place at the right time.

The famous standing stones at the south end of the loch dominate the view, and when our family first visited Orkney in 1967 the centrepiece of the circle was two upright slabs, topped by a flat stone. We discovered that the horizontal stone had been placed there by a well-intentioned Victorian historian in the mistaken belief that a similar stone had been removed from the site centuries previously. Not so. There never was such a 'table' and the offending slab was removed.

Loch of Stenness water is brackish, providing an excellent environment for the production of food beloved by fish, including shrimp, midges, snails, seaweed fly and daddy-long-legs – even eels and shore crabs. The largest trout ever caught on Orkney came from Stenness and was reputed to have weighed over 29lb. Fish of up to 7lb are still taken, and most seasons produce trout weighing 4lb or more.

Sadly, with such an abundance of natural food available under their noses, your artificial flies, no matter how lightly danced overhead, are often studiously ignored; I have had more despairing blank days on Stenness than on almost any other loch in Scotland. However, to help you on your way, I suggest that you concentrate your murderous efforts round the margins. Fish lie in very shallow water, so, whether fishing from bank or boat, stay close to the shore and pay attention.

Stenness fish tend to follow the fly, waiting until the last moment before grabbing, or not, as is more often the case. So remember to pause before casting again. Otherwise you might spend the whole day pulling the fly from the fish's mouth – annoying for expectant trout but infuriating for expectant anglers. Wading is uncomfortable, particularly at the south end, where seaweed makes one stumble about a bit, much to the amusement of the mute swans that invariably grace the loch. But persevere: creep up on them because bank fishing here often produces better results than fishing from a boat.

Stenness can also produce good sport with sea-trout and they are most likely to be encountered towards the end of the season, from August onwards. They tend to gather in the vicinity of the outlet burn and the south-east bay, close to the Standing Stones Hotel, where Stenness is linked to Loch of Harray, and around the Ness, a peninsula near Voy at the north end of the loch.

Don't expect large baskets of fish, although, like everywhere else, on its day Stenness can produce great results. Do expect trout of matchless quality, finely marked and fighting fit. If the fates are unkind, take comfort in the knowledge that perhaps even the early inhabitants of Orkney experienced similar problems in removing fish from Stenness. In fact, I have a theory that the standing stones have nothing whatsoever to do with ancient rites or mathematical calculations. They are really a memorial to Neolithic anglers driven daft after returning fishless from Loch of Stenness. Prove me wrong, if you can.

North of the standing stones is the majestic Ring of Brogar, a collection of more than thirty upright stones laid out in a perfect mathematical circle; and on a small promontory, jutting out into the loch near Bridge of Waith, are the remains of a chambered cairn. Round the margins of Stenness, other relics of times past crowd the shoreline: burnt mounds, tumili and cairns. And, most recently, and noted earlier in this piece, at Ness of Brodgar the excavations that have exposed what appears to have been a small 'town' – one of the most exciting and extensive Neolithic habitations ever discovered.

When things get tough on Stenness, take comfort in the fact that little Loch of Kirbister will always welcome and restore your angling self-confidence. This delightful water lies to the south of Stenness close to the A964 road midway between Stromness and Kirkwall. Kirbister is the ideal place to introduce newcomers to the gentle art; the fish, though not large, give a good account of themselves. There is even the odd chance of a sea-trout, but they seem loath to use the fish ladder from Waulkmill Bay and few are taken. The loch is, however, a very pleasant place to spend a few hours and on most days breakfast will be assured.

Mainland Orkney has a series of other small waters all of which have their own particular attractions: Clumly, north of Stromness, has a reputation for holding some excellent trout, whilst Peerie Water and Loch of Wasdale have good stocks of small brown trout. But the best and, I think, the dourest of the smaller waters is undoubtedly Loch of Skaill, where fish of under 2lb must be returned to fight another day.

OUTER ISLANDS

For many years, the Orkney Trout Fishing Association (OTFA) has followed a policy of stocking trout lochs on the islands of Sandy, Stronsay and Westray. This work has been very successful and, consequently, Meikle Water in Stronsay, Burness and Saintear Water in Westray, and North, Roos and Bea in Sanday offer both OTFA members and visitors the opportunity of some outstanding sport. I have seen wonderful trout of over 6lb in weight – caught and returned – in Loch Bea. As ever, it all comes at a price, that price being patience, determination and, above all, skill.

These lochs can be unforgivingly dour and, because they are generally shallow, are often discoloured due to high winds, a not entirely unknown occurrence in these airts. They are primarily fished from the bank and you should wade carefully since there are unexpected holes and soft places waiting to catch you unawares. It is always best, to be safe, to fish these waters with a friend. But, oh, the joy when the residents are in the right mood.

The island of Rousay has three good lochs, all containing stocks of wild brown trout. The largest is Muckle Water, close to its little brother, Peerie Water, and they are approached by a track that leaves the island's circular road at Westness, a few miles west of the ferry landing stage. Trouble is, though, the bus goes anti-clockwise round the island, so you will have to be patient. Or stop off at Loch of Wasbister, in the north, and have a few casts there on the way.

For me, the most dramatic of the outlying lochs are those on the island of Hoy, south from Stromness past the little island of Graemsay. The most accessible loch in the north of the island is Sandy Loch, to the south of the road out to the remote village of Rackwick. The loch lies between Cuilags (1,421ft) to the north and Ward Hill (1,631ft), the highest Hoy hill, to the south; it is dark and dour but reputed to hold some large fish.

In the south of Hoy are Heldale Water, Hoglinns Water and Sands Water, on the cliffs above Sweinn Geo and Little Rack Wick. Heldale used to be the main water supply for Lyness, the most populous community on Hoy. Follow the road south from Lyness for about six miles to find Heldale. A good track invites you out onto the hill from Heldale, following the Burn of Heldale westwards up Cairn Hill (538ft), and both waters can be easily fished during the course of one day, although Holginns has not been stocked by the association. Sands Water is a considerable step further north from Haldale, round Bakingstone Hill (1,553ft) and is rarely fished.

Heldale Water is the 'star' here and unique in Orkney in as

much as in some areas it is more than 15m deep. This is a large loch, one mile from east to west in length, and a few hundred yards wide. Forget wading. It is dangerous and, because of the steep sides, bank fishing is uncomfortable. But the OTFA has stocked the loch with brown trout and, in 2002, a well-meaning fish-farmer put in some Arctic char. Therefore, for those prepared to accept the challenge, the potential rewards could more than repay the effort involved in tackling Heldale.

The only problem, apart from persuading trout to rise to your well-presented fly, will be leaving. The setting is magnificent and it is unlikely that you will meet another soul. Meeting the fish will also be a problem, for they are few and far between. However, if you should be fortunate enough to tempt one, then, as we say in Scotland, it will be 'well worth the huddin" – as was discovered by a friend of mine, Mark Bowler, publishing editor of the magazine *Fly Fishing and Fly Tying*, a couple of years back. He landed a 7lb trout from Holginns Water. Go there and try to do likewise.

My friend Colin Kirkpatrick gave me more information about the Heldale Arctic char:

Historically Heldale was reputed to hold an indigenous population of Arctic char. They are mentioned in early twentieth-century Melsetter estate records and a few books.

In the mid-'90s Sandy Kerr, Neil Firth and myself founded the Orkney Arctic Char Group to look for them. Along with Dr Johan Hammar, Eva Hammar and Ron Greer of the International Society of Arctic Char Fanatics, we surveyed the loch with char nets but found nothing but trout.

The theory was that when the loch became a water supply in the '70s, the raising of the water level removed the littoral zone where the char would have spawned, thus creating an extinction scenario. A local Arctic char farmer

SECRET LOCHS AND SPECIAL PLACES

then took it upon himself, against all scientific advice, to put some alien Arctic char in the loch. Few, if any, of these char have been caught since. The last original char we heard of being caught was in the 1950s by very experienced fly-fisher Alan Bullen. Just recently, the Orkney Arctic Char Group tracked down a jar of Heldale char in the depths of the British Natural History Museum in London, collected in the 1850s.

Many years ago I visited Orkney along with Roy Eaton, who was then editor of *Trout & Salmon*. At the end of our stay, as I waited for the ferry to leave, I wondered where my companion was. Then I saw him, striding purposefully away from the ferry and heading into the heart of Stromness. 'Roy,' I yelled. 'For goodness sake, you'll miss the boat!'

Later, safely Scrabster-bound, he explained, 'Bruce, if you hadn't shouted at me I think that I would have stayed in Orkney for the rest of my life. I don't know whether to thank you or curse you.'

So, be warned: it's not just the fishing that is special in Orkney. There is magic there, too.

This section is dedicated to the Orkney Trout Fishing Association, with thanks for all the work they have done, and do, to protect and preserve the wonderful quality of wild fishing on their islands, with a special thank you to Colin ('Puk') Kirkpatrick, angler, conservationist and artist, for the friendship and kindness has shown me over so many years.

100

INTERLUDE

Be not afeard; the isle is full of noises,
and sweet airs that give delight and hurt not.
               – Shakespeare, *The Tempest*, Act 3, Scene 2

ISLA MONITA

Between 1990 and 1992, I spent two periods, each of six months between October and March, looking after a fishing lodge in Chile; a friend had contacted me to ask if I knew anybody who would be able to undertake the position, but I couldn't come up with a name. 'Why don't you do it?' Ann said, and the matter was settled. Ann joined me for the second expedition, taking over the running of the kitchen and staff that looked after guests, and we both enjoyed the experience.

Thus in October 1990 I found myself flying from Edinburgh to Amsterdam, thence to Sao Paulo in Brazil and on to Santiago in Chile. I wore my kilt for the journey and it was relatively unremarkable in Amsterdam. However, the sight of a Scotsman in his national dress in Sao Paulo at 4.30 a.m. raised a few eyebrows. I was met in Santiago by Chris Brown, one of the syndicate who owned the island, and he diplomatically suggested that I change before meeting the other owners.

The island, Isla Monita, lies about 800 miles south from

Santiago at the southern end of Lago Yelcho in the Los Lagos region of Chilean Patagonia. Yelcho is vast water, twenty-seven miles long by up to three miles wide and 2,000 feet deep, surrounded by jagged peaks rising to over 6,000 feet in height. It is fed by the Rio Futalefu, which has its source in Argentina as the Rio Grande and becomes the Rio Yelcho when it flows into Chile, through a landscape described by local people as *un paisaje pintado por Dios* – a landscape painted by God. I flew from Santiago to Puerto Montt and then south again in a tiny plane to the town of Chaiten at the mouth of the Rio Blanco. An oil-sand and potholed road wound its way south-east to Puerto Cárdenas, where Lago Yelcho tumbles from the lake into a fast-flowing river. This road is part of the Carretera Austrial, a 700-mile route built in 1976 through the wild, largely unpopulated lands that lie between Puerto Montt in the north and Villa O'Higgins in the south.

The lodge was the only building on the island, close to an orchard splendid with cherry, plum and apple trees, regularly visited by brightly coloured hummingbirds. On the lake, giant grebes called and courted. Above the broken Andes Mountains, majestic condor soared. Patricio Suazo, the head boatman, had a workshop by the shore of the lake where he built the boats used on the lake and other waters we fished, small lagunas into which the river overflowed when it rose during winter months, thus naturally re-stocking them with trout each season. Flat-bottomed boats, fourteen-feet long, were used in the lagunas, whilst on Lago Yelcho, itself seventeen foot, we used long, sturdy traditional boats powered by 25hp outboard engines; in bad weather, the lake could be as wild as the sea, with the wind funnelled between the surrounding peaks to howl madly down the lake, building huge waves in the process.

Everything required for keeping the lodge and the boats running had to be brought in from Chaiten: food, drink, fruit and vegetables, domestic household supplies, fuel for the engines and generator. It was all transported from the mainland across the lake to the island and carried to the lodge. Shopping was therefore a regular part of my duties, as was greeting arriving guests at Chaiten Airport – little more than a shed on the outskirts of the town. Consequently, I soon began to know most of the local traders and businessmen, and to speak a little Spanish. The café on the front street became my 'office', where I could recover from shopping angst with a sandwich and a cup of coffee. Next door was the post office, where I would phone home and keep in touch with the owners in Santiago. I often wore my kilt and the island became known as 'the Scotsman's island'.

The landing stage, where the boats were moored, was formed out of a huge fallen tree and guests generally fished from after breakfast until early evening, with the statutory siesta after a picnic lunch; often consisting of a fish caught during the morning and cooked over an open fire. The fishing was – more often than not, quite spectacular – for brown trout, rainbow trout and brook trout. There were two distinct brown trout populations: those imported from German forest streams and trout descended from Loch Leven in Scotland. Initially, these fish were introduced into the Rio Grande in Argentina and had migrated via the Rio Futaleufu into Lago Yelcho and the surrounding lagunas. The brook trout and rainbow trout were of Canadian origin, and there were also Atlantic salmon, escapees from a smolt-rearing farm at the north end of the lake, owned and run by the Norwegian company Marine Harvest. Given my understanding of the way farm fish were reared, what they were fed and the chemicals used to try and keep them disease-free, I made sure that they never reached the dining table in the lodge.

The brown trout averaged around 4–5lb in weight, with many double-figure fish as well. Whilst the brook trout were smaller, they were amongst the loveliest fish I had ever seen. The stocking of trout had taken place towards the end of the nineteenth century and the early years of the twentieth century, so the fish we caught were close enough to being 'wild' as makes no difference. Certainly, the rainbow trout in particular were spectacularly beautiful; firm, muscular, classically shaped bodies and so brightly coloured that they dazzled the eye. I took Ann once to what we called 'the Secret Laguna', where specimen rainbow lived. She hooked a wonderful fish that leapt into the air, sending a rainbow of crystal and diamond droplets sparkling through the sunlight. When I netted and returned the fish, I saw that Ann had tears in her eyes. 'It was so beautiful,' she said. After that incident Ann never again fished in Chile.

Most of our guests were American, although there were occasional parties from the UK. During phone calls to Santiago, I was given details of the people arriving, their names and other relevant information, which is how I once found myself in a most embarrassing situation. I had been told that one of the members of a UK party was 'Richard, who is deaf'. As such I made a point of facing him when I was speaking. He appeared to have an amazing ability to lip-read and although I did, from time to time, get the odd quizzical look from Richard, I always tried to speak clearly. We were tackling up one morning prior to going down to the boats when I heard one of the party speak to Richard, who had his back to the person. Richard responded to the question quite normally. Later I had a quiet word with the leader of the group and asked just how deaf Richard was.

'Deaf? What do you mean, Bruce? Richard is not deaf,' he said.

I explained that I had been told that he was.

'Ah, I think I can guess what has happened. His name is Hughes D'Aeth.'

Like every water in the world, no matter how high its reputation, I did have blank days – not many, but yes, a few. There was one laguna that held a lot of trout, and a lot of them were over 6lb in weight. Previously, I had seen the water boiling with rising trout. Before we set out to fish the laguna, I explained all of this to one of our guests, 'Mad Dog Malchon', a retired medic and

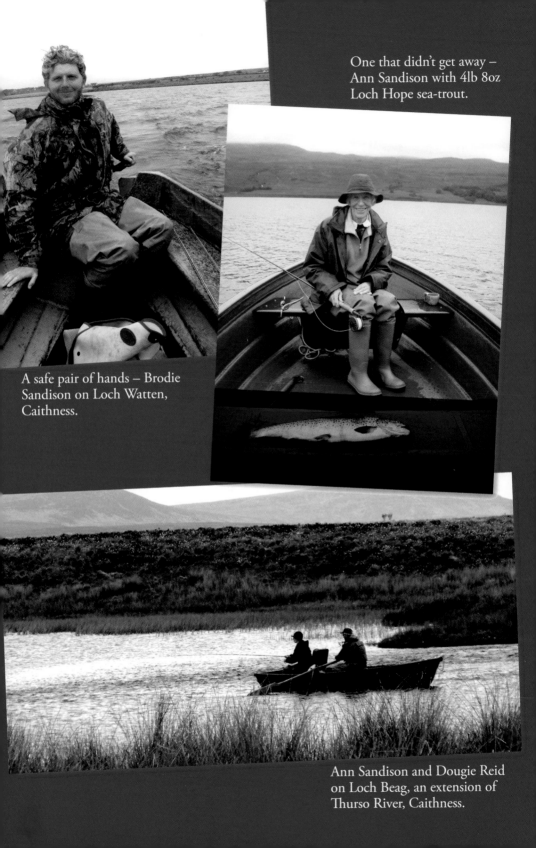

One that didn't get away –
Ann Sandison with 4lb 8oz
Loch Hope sea-trout.

A safe pair of hands – Brodie
Sandison on Loch Watten,
Caithness.

Ann Sandison and Dougie Reid
on Loch Beag, an extension of
Thurso River, Caithness.

Happy angler. Grandson Sem August Sandison with first pike, Finland.

Lunchtime at Loch Sletail, Sutherland. Blair, Charles and Jean.

Family picnic at Loch Hope, 2013. Ann, Barbara, Bruce, Brodie and Ann's hound Daisy.

Bruce Sandison and Father
Nicholas Court fishing at Loch
Achall, Wester Ross.

Rain stopped play. Pollaidh
and Jake at Plantation
Loch, Sutherland.

Granddaughters Fearn and Mey having lunch at South End, Loch Hope.

Patricio Suazo with 11lb rainbow trout, returned to Laguna Chava, Chilean Patagonia.

Ian and Jean Smart fishing at Loch Meadie, Sutherland.

Artists Nanna and Charles
Sandison, the Finnish
branch of Clan Sandison.

Jessica Sandison at
Loch Loyal.

Cousins Jean, Vicky
and Becca on Loch
Toftingall, Caithness.

Lewis-Ann Sandison fishing at
Loch Haluim on the south skirts
of Ben Loyal, Sutherland.

Lago Yelcho, Chilean
Patagonia.

Blair Sandison selecting flies for
afternoon session on Durness
limestone loch, Caladail.

The ruins of the church at
Howmore, South Uist.

The descent from Canisp,
Sutherland, and a very special
little loch.

Clan Sandison, August 2008
– celebrating Bruce and Ann's
70th birthday.

Vietnam veteran with a wonderful sense of humour. Over a period of four hours we thrashed the water fruitlessly to foam and never saw single a fish rise. 'Say, Bruce,' Mad Dog eventually remarked, 'are you the guy who called the Witchdoctor a son-of-a-bitch?' He was a memorable fishing companion and we still correspond.

Most of the fishing followed a similar fashion. All of the lakes and lagunas were deep and because of the nature of the undergrowth around the margins it was impossible to bank fish. There were also, generally, extensive reed-beds that extended out into the lake. Thus, the boatman positioned the boat in such a way that the anglers could cast in towards the reeds. It was enormously exciting to see a large trout suddenly emerge from the cover of the reeds to grab a carefully presented dry fly. This was difficult for some of the women to do, who were mostly far less experienced than their partners, so when I went out to Chile on my second visit I took with me a traditional dapping rod – light and telescopic, extending to seventeen feet in length. This delighted the girls, who immediately re-christened the technique as 'dappling'. It worked famously and hook-ups in the reeds were few. The only problem was getting them to let the fly settle on the surface, which seemed to be beyond many of them. Nevertheless, I have seen trout in the teens of founds leaping three to four feet into the air, attempting to take the 'dappling' fly, and sometimes succeed in doing so.

One of the lagunas, shaped like a butterfly and lying at the foothills of a mountain, had a swift stream flowing into it, bringing in ice-cold meltwater from glaciers that coloured the lake green and white. The water was particularly clear and it was in a corner of this laguna that a rainbow trout of 12lb was taken. It was a stunningly beautiful fish and carefully returned to fight another day. Just as exciting was to see a dark shape rising from the depths and parallel the course of a fly as it was worked towards the boat, then, at the last moment, turn suddenly and take the fly. We also fished the river, from a drifting boat. It was also possible, in some areas, to beach the boat and fish from the bank. Enormously rewarding and satisfying work.

If there were guest-free days, when the staff went home to their wife and family, Ann and I would have the island to ourselves. These were special times when we relaxed, explored the island and enjoyed a break from caring for our guests. There was a track round the island and, just by the lodge, another track that led up the hill to the high point of Isla Monita. Forty species of birds called the island home and more than 100 species of flower, shrub and tree. Along the way it passed through wildflower-clad meadows, ideal for post-lunch siestas. In the blackness of night, we would sometimes lie flat on the ground in a meadow, immersed in the hum of insects and the enormous, unending canopy of twinkling stars, crowned by the magical Southern Cross.

The climate was that of a temperate rainforest, but, apart from one large, black biting insect which was easily despatched, there were no untoward environmental surprises. There were mountain lions in the area, and we saw their footprints in the soft sand, but never the animals themselves. Landing anywhere along the shore of Lago Yelcho was difficult because of its steep banks, but there was one area, about twenty minutes' sail up the lake, that was perfect for a picnic and where bank fishing was possible. A twenty-foot-high waterfall plunged from a cliff at the foot of which was a deep, clear pool. From a ledge above the pool you could quite clearly see trout, tree-long shadows, moving in the depths. They were impossible to catch, and I know, because I tried and tried and tried again to tempt one to take my fly, but to no avail.

I passed through Chaiten once again in 2007, when environmentalist Douglas Tompkins invited an international group to Pumalin Park, to the north of Chaiten, an 800,000-acre conservation project, to discuss the implications of the disastrous impact that salmon farming was having on the Chilean environment. I stopped at my 'office', the café, and the post office, for old time's sake. A few months later, in May 2008, disaster struck Chaiten: the Chaiten volcano erupted for the first time in 9,000 years and destroyed the town. A plume of ash and sulphurous steam rose nineteen miles above the volcano and the Rio Blanco burst its banks, flooding Chaiten. One thousand five hundred people were evacuated. None of the Isla Monita staff lived in Chaiten, but it was the focal point of their community, and Ann and I were greatly saddened by what these people must have suffered, their homes, businesses and community devastated. Initially, the intention was to rebuild the town, to the north, but in 2011 it was agreed that the town should be rebuilt on its original site. Work that is still in progress.

Perhaps my most enduring memory of the time I spent on the Isla Monita was of the kindness of Patricio Suazo, who was one of the most remarkable men that it has been my privilege to meet. Patricio did not speak a word of English, and my Spanish was elementary, but I think we became friends. I know that there were times on the lake in a storm when I was terrified and he probably saved my life. He was always utterly courteous and patient and seemed to read my mind. I watched him building boats in his workshop, confident and assured in all his actions. We fished together sometimes, and he was a skilled angler who tied perfect flies. Ann and I also got to know his wife and family; his sister was the district nurse and his brother, Manuel, also worked with us as a boatman. Patricio helped and advised Ann in the kitchen, where his standards of hygiene were exacting and demanding. I don't think that there was anything that Patricio could not do; indeed, I believe that the word 'can't' was absent from his vocabulary. I guess that Patricio has retired now, but Ann and I always think of him with the greatest of affection.

SUTHERLAND

A wind from Suilven sweeps
Across the blue loch, chasing
A rain-goose from its stippled
Surface. The splash of a rising
Trout throws crystal to the air.

By the time I was sixteen years old, I had successfully convinced my father that standing up to the waist in the middle of a stream trying to catch trout was far more rewarding than bashing an entirely innocent small white ball around a golf course. The result of doing so was that Father decided, in 1954, that he would forgo his golf in favour of a fishing holiday in the far north. Thus it was that I was introduced to 'Suderland', the south land of the Vikings.

Back then, it was a long, wearisome drive from our home in Edinburgh: crossing the Firth of Forth at Queensferry, then north along traffic-packed roads, in and out of every town along the way, and not an inch of dual carriageway to be seen. Our destination was Strathnaver and we followed the A9 road through Inverness then up the east coast to Helmsdale, where we turned left up the strath to Kinbrace, then left again to across over the moor to Syre in Strathnaver.

By the time we were heading towards Syre, night had fallen, accompanied by heavy rain, and the windscreen wipers were hard at work. Which is when the car gasped, stalled and stuttered to an ignominious halt. We were all tired and Father, not the most even-tempered of men at the best of times, got out, torch poised, opened the bonnet and tried to see what had gone wrong. My younger brother, Fergus, and I remained diplomatically silent in the back, just hoping that Father would be able to find and fix the fault.

Fergus saw him first and nudged me: 'Look,' he said. Through the rain, coming towards us, was a strangely dressed old man cycling a rusty old bike with a ragged black-and-white sheepdog by his side. He stopped and talked to Father. Father handed him the torch and the old man disappeared under the bonnet. He reappeared and we heard him say to Father, 'Now, just you get back into the vehicle and when I make the signal, give the engine a turn.' I could see by the look on Father's face that he had little confidence in the proposal, but he did as he was told.

When the old man waved an arm, Father turned the key in the ignition and, yes, the car started. Overjoyed, Father got out to thank our saviour, insisting that he accept payment for his help, but in spite of all Father's urging and pleading the old man refused.

'You must be a mechanic,' Father enquired.

'Oh no, dear me no, I'm a Mackay from Strathnaver.' With which he remounted his bike, gave us a cheery wave and cycled off down the road with his sheepdog trotting obediently behind.

Mackay is the foremost name in these northern airts. Indeed, this part of Scotland is known as 'the Land of Clan Mackay' and we stayed with a Mrs Mackay at Skail, a few miles downstream from Syre. One of the most famous regiments in the British Army, the 93rd Sutherland Highlanders, was raised in Strathnaver in 1799 by Major General Will Wemyss on behalf of his cousin, the sixteen-year-old Elizabeth, Countess of Sutherland. A total of 419 men were enlisted, with more than half of them having the same surname, Mackay, and half again sharing the same first name, John.

The regiment fought with distinction during the war to recapture the Cape of Good Hope from the Dutch in 1808 and with steadfast bravery during the bloody and unsuccessful attempt to capture New Orleans in 1814. But perhaps their greatest moment came in the Crimean War in 1854 at the Battle of Balaclava when the 93rd withstood and broke a massed Russian cavalry charge: 'There is no retreat from here, men,' their leader, General Colin Campbell told them. 'You must die where you stand.' And the reply of John Scott, the right-hand man, was taken up by them all: 'Aye, Sir Colin, an needs be, we'll do that.' William Russell of *The Times* immortalised the action in his title, 'The Thin Red Line'.

Father had some idea of fishing the River Naver, but very little knowledge of how to go about getting permission to do so and nobody locally seemed particularly willing to help. Thinking back, I am quite sure that this was the moment when the thought of writing a book to redress that situation first came into my mind; a task that had to wait thirty years before being tackled in my volume, *Trout Lochs of Scotland*; followed thereafter by the first edition of *River and Lochs of Scotland*, which was published in 1997 and is still going strong eighteen years later.

However, our hostess at Skail, the said Mrs Mackay, didn't seem to be heavily burdened with problems about when and where to fish the river that ran by a few yards from her back door. She strictly observed the Sabbath Day, but come the first stroke of midnight I saw her setting off for the river carrying a bundle that to me looked very like a net. Fergus also fished the river one day, for trout, and astonishingly returned with a fish that weighed over 2lb. I congratulated him through gritted teeth but had no desire whatsoever to put a foot anywhere near the forbidden stream. Instead, Father and I set off to look at some of the little lochans near the road between Syre and Kinbrace, beginning with Palm Loch, sweetly edged by water lilies. It was also full of brightly red-speckled little trout. However, the greatest excitement Father experienced when fishing was when he put his landing net down on a slumbering adder. Later, Father dropped me off on my own at the bridge over the Allt Lon a'Chuil burn, which drains into Loch Rimsdale, and I set off upstream to explore.

I think that the hours I spent by that burn were key moments in my life, when, really, for the first time, I felt as though I was a part of the landscape; a part of the wind whispering across the moor; part of the heather and the red-tipped sphagnum moss; at one with the scent and sound of the flowing stream; singing the same song as meadow pipit and greenshank; I experienced an overwhelming sense of content; not happiness, content. I didn't understand then, but I felt it, deep in my soul. I knew that I had discovered something very special. As I write, it is still with me.

And the burn was very special as well; narrow, but surprisingly deep, with dark pots joined by runs and little tumbles. I found myself crouching down, well back from the river, and casting a short line upstream, gathering in line as the flies came towards me and then letting line out as they flowed past and downstream. Maybe I was just lucky – after all, the primary essential for success in angling is, in all honesty, being in the right place at the right time. I had half a dozen lovely trout, the largest of which weighed almost 2lb, all taken on a three-fly cast of traditional Scottish patterns: Messrs Black Pennell, March Brown and Silver Butcher.

It was seventeen years before I returned to Sutherland, during which time I had found and married Ann, my partner for life, and we had two children, Blair, eleven years old and Lewis-Ann, nine years; both, by then, briskly brainwashed into a love of fly-fishing. We were living in Northumberland at the time in an old house overlooking the river South Tyne, where we all fished. But that year, 1974, Ann and I determined that we should head north and, having researched the possibilities, decided to centre ourselves at the Scourie Hotel in north-west Sutherland.

Ian and Mary Hay owned and ran the hotel then and we instantly felt at home. The hotel had access to almost 300 wild brown trout lochs and lochans, and could also arrange splendid fishing for sea-trout and salmon on Loch Stack and Loch More and, occasionally, further north, on Loch Dionard. The hotel also had a unique method of allocating the fishing to make sure that all their guests had an equal opportunity of fishing the best beats. New arrivals had their name entered at the bottom of a list on a blackboard containing the names of all the guests fishing. In the evening, after dinner, a senior guest, known as the Board Master, invited the guest whose name was at the top of the list to choose where he or she would like to fish the following day.

Thereafter, the Board Master worked his way down the list, as each of the names on the board selected where they wanted to fish, excluding, of course, the beats already selected by guests higher up the list. The next morning, the name at the top of the list was returned to the bottom and in this way guests' names steadily climbed the board to have their moment of glory at the top. If a guest should suddenly leave, however, his name was still held on the list as a 'ghost', otherwise you might be suddenly propelled to top place, missing the equally attractive third- and second-top options in the process.

The Board Master was invariably a guest who had been fishing the Scourie waters for many years and who undertook his duties voluntarily, sometimes having to mediate during occasional disputes, which he did with courteous skill. He was formerly known as the Chief Fork and it was his right to be served first at meal times. He was also expected to sit alone during meals to ensure that no 'undue' influence was brought to bear upon any decisions he might have to make; in the days when the hotel had only one bathroom, the Chief Fork also had first use of the facilities in the morning, before breakfast, and at the end of the day, before supper.

Few of the lochs are close to a road and most days involve a not inconsiderable hike to reach the fishing; it is perhaps a truism to say that the best sport generally lies in the least accessible places and it is, but, believe me, Scourie had more than its fair share of these locations. What a fishing paradise awaits those who are prepared to search for it; bronze and purple moorlands; majestic hills and mountains; sudden, steel-grey waters; secret, dark pools; clear, stone-specked shallows with gold sand beaches; and, in some lochs, the wild brown trout of your wildest dreams.

The first morning we took the children to a roadside loch, Loch na Claise Ferna, that was full of small brown trout, but too near the road for our liking. The weather was being unkind as well, so, to warm ourselves and search for shelter, we tramped south up the hill to a small loch, unnamed on the OS Map (Sheet 9, Scourie, Scale 1:50,000) but known locally as Mrs Little's Loch. We found the required shelter, but it had started to rain and our spirits were low. Well, not all of them. Lewis-Ann marched purposefully down to a promontory and began casting furiously in all available directions, lashing the water to foam. We smiled benignly, until her rod bent double and she unceremoniously hauled a good fish onto the bank. Not a big trout, but one that pleased her, and us, mightily.

A more taxing walk for little and large legs out of training began at a shepherd's hut at the south-west corner of Loch Stack on the A838 Scourie to Lairg road. A stalker's track begins here and climbs the east shoulder of Ben Stack (2,366ft), with a glimpse of Loch na Seilge to the north along the way. Our destination was a mile further south, Loch Eileanach: a straggle of four small, island-dotted interlinked lochans that, eventually, after a convoluted journey of a dozen miles south and west, drain into the sea at Badcoll Bay. The stalker's path at this point is about 100 feet above the loch and we happily stumbled down to see what we could see.

I stopped to have a look at a small lochan on the way. It lay north-east/south-west in a depression and looked interesting. It was. Fishing from the bank, which was sandy, I had instant, great sport, with trout averaging 8–10oz in weight, with one fish of about a pound. Satisfied, I walked over to the first of the main lochs, which I had been told contained some specimen trout. I arrived, clumsily, at the loch's edge just in time to see the wake of one such specimen as it rapidly headed for the depths. The water was so clear I could see every mark on its body and I knew that it would have been 'well worth the haudin''. In the afternoon, tramping back down the hill, we sang happily, tired but content after a memorable well-spent day.

We had other memorable days on that, our first visit to Scourie. A comfortable walk out to fish Loch Calbha, a group of six lochans, unnamed on the OS Map and lying about a mile to the west of the A894 road between Scourie and Kylestrome, and to the north of Duartmore. We parked the car near Loch a'Mhinidh and set off with the spark of battle in our eyes. We all caught trout and I remember how excited Blair and Lewis-Ann were. There was a tangible sense of utter calm about the location, a stillness that one could almost touch. And a blessing: one of the largest trout that I have ever encountered. It was a quiet day with just enough wind to disguise evil intent. The others scattered to the other lochans whilst I contemplated the wonders of life by a stunted rowan tree – more a large bush, really, given the harshness of its habitat.

I thought that I saw a disturbance in the water to my left, about half a dozen yards from the shore, so I watched more carefully and, sure enough, it looked like a 'cruising' trout. Leaping to my feet, sort of, I began false casting over the land to get enough line out to cover the trout, which was definitely heading my way. At what I judged to be the appropriate moment, I cast towards it.

Almost the moment my 'bob' fly, a Black Pennell, landed on the surface, it was grabbed with such force that the rod was nearly jerked from my hand. I staggered back, wrestling with rod and reel, but there was little I could do to halt the trout's express-train-like run. It leapt once, gloriously scattering crystal droplets from its body, and as it landed back in the water my fly came loose. We have all experienced that moment of loss, the utter finality and despair. But for me that time it was different. I simply felt enormously privileged to have had such a moment of supreme joy.

There was less supreme joy when we all tramped off to fish the Black Lochs below Creag Dhubh (803ft). There is no track and the going was rough to downright wicked. We parked by an old hut on the roadside at Geisgeill on the A894 Kystrome road, by Loch Bad nam Mult. A hundred yards or so to the south, we found the outlet burn that drained the lochs and followed it up the hill, eastwards for a mile towards the ominous face of Creag Dhubh. It was tough going, particularly for Blair and Lewis-Ann, but they persevered, and with frequent stops for coffee, biscuits, breath and encouragement, we achieved our goal.

Throughout my life I have always had difficulty trying to find appropriate words to describe the majesty of Scotland's scenery. Such words as there are seem unequal to the task, and this was most certainly true of the calm that greeted us when we arrived at the most northern of the lochans. Blair and I lay on our tummies, peering into the crystal-clear water. We could see trout, lots of them swimming, turning, twisting, rising to take some-thing from the surface, darting at objects, invisible to us in the water column. I don't think we spoke, we just watched, fascin-ated. I knew immediately that I didn't want to catch them. It seemed wrong to disturb them, to threaten them in their home. I didn't fish that day.

Working south, we found that the last lochs were on a lower level and fed by the silver ribbon of a waterfall. A lone red-throated diver rocketed skywards on our arrival and a pair of pitch-black ravens watched us curiously from the crags. We had lunch, listening to the song of the falls, and in the late afternoon headed down the hill to the car. Going down was a lot less arduous than going up, and Blair and Lewis-Ann were in good spirits as we drove north to the Scouire Hotel and supper. It was an unforgettable week and we all have happy memories of that time. Much has changed during the intervening years, however, not least the upgrading of the road system, now fast, wide and excellent. But for me, my enduring memory is one of majestic peace, broken only by the rusty-engine cough of amorous corncrakes, and having by me those that I love.

In 1975 we were living near Morpeth in Northumberland, where we had North Whitehouse Farm, and 40,000 hens. Because of circumstances, and probably my lack of business acumen, we had to pack up and move out. After much soul-searching, we decided to go to Caithness, where my grandfather had been born in the fishing village of Staxigoe, a few miles from the Royal Burgh of Wick. By that time Clan Sandison had expanded considerably: Blair, fourteen years, Lewis-Ann, twelve years, Charles, eight years and Jean, a few months old. Once settled, we began to fish the lochs of Strath Halladale, out beyond the Split Stane. This huge boulder is split in two as if it had been cleaved by a mighty sword; it stands on the north side of the A836 Thurso to Bettyhill road and used to mark the old boundary between Caithness and Sutherland – legend has it that the devil, in a bad mood one day, split the stone with his tail when he was travelling the road. It also marks the beginnings of the Land of Clan Mackay; thus, if you live in the wilds of Sutherland, to those who live in Caithness you bide *beyond the split stane*. The Split Stane also plays a more sombre part in the history of the region: during the dreadful nineteenth-century Sutherland Clearances, when families were evicted from the homes of their ancestors to make way for more profitable sheep, many fled to the east, where they were welcomed with comfort and kindness by Caithness people who gathered to receive them at the Split Stane.

However, for Clan Sandison, speeding past on our way to, hopefully, a close encounter with the wild brown trout of Strath Halladale, it was always a happy journey. The first lochs we fished were deep in the heartland of the Flow Country and factored then by the Forsinard Hotel. The lochs were to the east of the A897 Helmsdale road, beyond Sletill Hill (919ft): Sletill, Talaheel and Leir, and a step north from Sletill Hill, little Lochan nan Clach Geala, with its unnamed satellite. To the west of the road are the tangled, dark, enigmatic Cross Lochs and crystal-clear Jubilee Loch.

Loch Sletill became our favourite, a wonderful loch where we were invariably greeted on our arrival by a pair of black-throated divers. We would leave home early in the morning and park the car at Forsinain Farm, then hoof it east across the moor for about three miles to reach the Sletill. A track is marked on the map, but it was less obvious on the ground. At some stage in the distant past marker posts had been placed at intervals along the way, but when we walked there the remains of these grey, lichen-covered sentinel stubs were only just visible. It was a comfortable walk, although care had to be taken to avoid unexpected bogs. I remember on one of our early outings to the loch, when Ann and number two son, Charles, were way ahead of me, Ann suddenly disappearing up to her waist in a peat bog. Thankfully, Charles was a strong lad and soon pulled his mother free.

Sletill is a shallow loch, covering about 100 acres, and the north-west end, where the boat is moored, was dominated by a single, large shark-fin-shaped boulder; presumably deposited there when the ice retreated during the last Ice Age. The bay has a sand bottom and wading is easy, but, for some reason, it didn't fish well. Further along the north shore there is a perfect little strip of golden sand backed by the heather-clad moor. This was our lunchtime dining room and we had many happy times there with family and friends. Nearby, there is a headland and when the wind was blowing hard from the south-west I often had great fun casting across the wind and dancing my flies over the tops of the waves. Trout would suddenly launch themselves from the side of a wave to snatch a fly; vigorous casting work, but wonderfully rewarding.

Up until then Charles had never caught a decent trout in a loch, so, on one occasion, Ann and I took him out to see if we could get our son into a fish. It was a perfect day, but after half an hour I sensed that Charles was beginning to flag. It was a pity because he was casting and working his flies well. I was on the oars and quite certain that it was only a matter of time before a trout rose to his flies. When it did, it was as though Charles had been hit by an electric shock. The trout took immediate control of the situation and roared off to the horizon like an express train. Charles just held on, the reel screaming.

The fish jumped spectacularly and I yelled at Charles to drop the point of the rod. The trout then headed back towards the boat, with Charles furiously reeling in. Clearly the fish was well hooked because it then began running left, then right, passing close to the boat, but Charles was unable to bring it to the net. Eventually I took a deep breath and, just as the trout was passing, I plunged the landing net in front and it swam in and was safely landed; a fine Sletill trout, perfectly shaped and coloured, and weighing in at around 2lb 12oz. The incident sealed Charles's fate as an angler, an affliction that he has borne ever since with the greatest tenacity.

Ann and I also applied great tenacity in fishing one of the least well-known of the Forsinard waters, little Lochan nan Clach Geala, the *white loch*. We didn't fish it often because it was a couple of miles north from Sletill Hill and we invariably headed straight for Sletill. The loch was only a few acres in extent, but I heard that it contained excellent trout; this was confirmed for me when I read over past records in the hotel fishing logbook. One entry in particular aroused my interest: a basket of eight trout weighing 27lb 8oz caught in the early 1970s. The loch lies north/south, so an east or west wind, preferably west, helps with casting, which is from the bank. Maybe it was just luck, but every time we fished there, the water level was high, almost overflowing onto the moor, so we kept well back from the margin to disguise evil intent. Another curious aspect, the water was peat-tinged, bronze almost, but still relatively clear. In all the hours we spent there we never saw a fish rise, let alone take any of the flies on offer. But I was sure that they were there. Clach na Geala simply screamed out to the angler in me that this was the case.

The Cross Lochs, to the west of Forsinard, have always been most famous for two things: the size of their brown trout population and the difficulty of persuading the blighters to rise to a fly. I can personally vouch for the latter, and by hearsay to the former. There are six principal lochs, varying in size from a pond to a few acres. There used to be a boat on the main loch, but I have only bank-fished. The surrounding soggy peatland makes for really uncomfortable walking, and downright dangerous wading. Strangely, the adjacent Jubilee Loch is crystal clear, so presumably it must lie on a limestone base. I have been told that in the early years of the 1970s the then owner of the land, a retired military gentlemen from Cumberland, stocked the loch with Canadian brook trout, but by the time I arrived there was no sign of that species and all I encountered were modest, but nevertheless very pretty, brown trout.

In the last years of the 1970s change came to Strath Halladale, a change that brought havoc in its wake to the peat moorlands around Forsinard and Sletill Hill. Basil Baird and Sons, prominent pig farmers in West Lothian, purchased several thousand acres, which they determined should be drained and set to growing grass. The grass would be dried and bulked into cubes to be used for animal food. Soon, huge quadruple-wheeled tractors were busy digging and ploughing up the peatlands, supported by a government grant alleged to be in the region of £500,000; as ever, the key that unlocked the public piggy-bank was based upon the premise of job creation in remote rural areas where jobs were scarce. Eventually, the scheme ran out of steam, and cash, and the company involved retired hurt back to its West Lothian base. Its intentions had been entirely honourable, but it left behind its ghastly, giant grass-drying plant and hundreds of acres of terminally damaged peatland.

Shortly after the Bairds left, Fountain Forestry Ltd, the tax-avoidance factory tree-farmers, moved in and continued the carnage; once again, rapturously supported by the government, the Forestry Commission, Highland Regional Council and the district councils of both Caithness and Sutherland. During his valedictory address, I understand that Mr Maclennan was reported to have said that one of the things he most regretted about his time in office was that more of the Flow Country had not been planted. As the ploughs cut four-foot-deep furrows in peat that had taken thousands of years to form, Clan Sandison turned its attention to the lochs at the north end of Strath Halladale.

At that time I was looking for a loch with free-rising trout not too distant from home and not too far from a road, so that our younger children, nephews, nieces and their friends various would be almost certain to catch fish; also, it had to have shallow margins, safe for little waders, and minimal undergrowth where novice fly-fishers would not have to spend most of their time retrieving flies from the heather. Loch Toftingall in Caithness had all these attributes, but I wanted to introduce into the equation the excitement and challenge of an adventure-walk. Loch Akran, to the east of the Melvich to Helmsdale road, the A897, met these requirements in every respect, as did Loch na Caorach, its near neighbour. Caorach could be less accommodating, but it had larger trout. A step further east again and joined to Caorach by a burn lay Loch na Seilge, pronounced *Shallag*, at about 100 acres, the largest of the waters in this area.

David Flett of the Melvich Hotel factored the lochs on behalf of their owners and was always open and courteous with his advice in connection with the flies to use and how to access the waters. Akran was all bank fishing, but both Caorach and Seilge had a boat. Like so many of our northern waters, booking the loch invariably meant that you had the exclusive use of it for the day, which was just as well, given the character and exuberance of my bunch. It was during these outings that I developed superior skills in putting up rods and reels and the knack of making up a two-fly cast in about five minutes; including a full blood knot, figure of eight knot and a turle knot for attaching the tail fly. I also developed an almost uncanny knack in unravelling tangled casts; or, as it was known in our family, for sorting out a 'bugger's muddle'.

These skills were thrust upon me not by choice but by necessity. 'Help, Uncle Bruce, I can't get the reel on,' or, 'Dad, she stood on my rod!'; 'He's taken the flies I wanted to use, tell him, Uncle Bruce.' Once they were all set up, who was to fish where became the next problem:

'No, Jean, you are far too close to your cousin, move along a bit.'

'But I was here first, she should be the one to move, not me!'

'Uncle Bruce, help, I'm all tangled up.'

'I can't find my cast, it's somewhere in the heather, over there, what shall I do?'

'My rod won't cast properly, Dad, can I have another rod please?'

'Look, Becca has caught a fish, it's not fair, I want one.'

Meanwhile, the adults were relaxing on the bank, enjoying morning coffee and biscuits, chatting merrily about this and that. 'Bruce is so good with them, so patient,' said my sister-in-law, Liz. 'I'll wait until he has them sorted out then get him to fix me up a rod – can't wait to have a go.' Or 'Gosh it's so peaceful here after the madness of Newcastle/Edinburgh/Glasgow/London – you are so lucky to be able to live here.'

It was during one such family outing to Loch na Caorach that the umbrella incident occurred. Some well-meaning soul had given me one for Christmas. Just the very thing I wanted; nobody uses brollies in Caithness, well, not for long, given the ferocious nature of the winds we live with. This is why when the brolly arrived I stored it carefully in the back of the garage. But for some strange reason, prior to setting off that day, one of my brother Fergus's daughters had spotted it and decided that it should be carted along.

'Why, Becca?' I asked.

'What will we do if it rains, Uncle Bruce?' she replied sagely. 'We have to take it. I won't go otherwise.'

In situations like these, I have discovered that reason, logic and general bad temper never work. So I packed the umbrella. This particular brolly was as bright as Joseph's multicoloured dream coat and the last thing I wanted to be seen with on a Scottish hill loch. It did not rain, so I was spared that embarrassment, almost.

We were a party of eight: brother Fergus, Liz and their two girls, Vicky and Becca, my little daughter Jean, Charles, Ann and me. I rowed the boat across the loch to the east shore and we set up camp close to where the stream comes in from Loch na Seilge. In the morning we fished from the bank and after lunch, and some serious pleading on the part of the young ladies, I capitulated and took the boat out. I have found that the most productive area of the loch, when fishing from the boat, is towards the south end just before the loch narrows and, sure enough, the trout were accommodating; they are not too particular about the flies they take and most of the standard patterns of Scottish loch flies please them. In the interests of safety, I insisted that they fished with just a single fly on the cast and I took the girls afloat one at a time. By the close of play, everyone was smiling and assured of breakfast for the following morning.

However, towards the end of the day, it did begin to rain and the wind got up, strongly, so we decided to head for home. To save the girls from having to walk all the way round the loch, Charles, who is enormously strong and absolutely fearless, courageously agreed to ferry the ladies across the loch whilst Fergus and I tramped round the south shore – as much gear as possible being loaded into the boat, including the umbrella. Fergus and I, like Tibetan sherpas, lugged the rest through the heather. Halfway there we stopped for a rest, slumping to the ground, sweating profusely.

'Good grief, Bruce, why didn't you bring the kitchen sink as well?' complained my panting brother.

'Don't blame me,' I snapped crossly. 'It was your daughters who insisted on bringing the tape recorder, a library of books and that wretched brolly.'

Through wet eyes we glanced up the loch to see how Captain Bligh was faring with the girls and were amazed by what we saw. Ann was sitting in the stern with two young ladies and my sister-in-law whilst Jean perched in the bow. Charles bulked in the middle, heaving mightily on the oars. Ann had put up the umbrella, using it as a sail. The boat was screaming across the loch at a vast rate of knots, the children yelling with delight, a blaze of colour, with water cascading from the bow and barely six inches of free-board. Mr Plimsoll would be revolving in his grave. 'Quick, Fergus,' I called, leaping to my feet and sprinting off. The west shore was very rocky, with uncomfortable boulders just below the surface. Unless they slowed down they were facing disaster. Fortunately, fate took a hand: a dozen or so yards from the mooring-bay, the umbrella blew inside-out, tearing the fabric to ribbons in the process, and the boat lurched to a sudden wallow amongst the shallows. I waded out, grabbed the bow and guided the boat to the shore.

'It wasn't my fault, Dad, honestly,' complained Charles. 'It just seemed like a good idea at the time.'

I smiled benignly, fingering the shattered brolly. 'That's all right, Charles,' I replied. 'Accidents happen.' I reasoned, with everyone safe and the exit of one unwanted Christmas gift, it couldn't be all bad.

Looking back on these young, green years, I wouldn't change anything. The sheer enthusiasm and excitement engendered during a day out in the hills with the family was reward enough; bright, shining faces, the shout of joy when a fish took, the cry of despair when one was lost; statuesque red deer on the hill, otters running by the shore or swimming in the loch; golden eagles, hen harriers and buzzard; glorious wildflowers – orchids, yellow flag, tormentil, milkwort, marsh violet and sphagnum moss. Neither Ann nor I ever lectured our brood about these things. If they asked, we told them what we knew; if not, we left them to themselves. I may be wrong, I probably am wrong, but I think that these moments stayed with the children and have helped to shape the way they think and behave today.

Loch Seilge, to the east of Loch na Caorach, became our favourite Strath Halladale loch. Because it was a step further from Caorach, it was less frequently fished. There was only one boat and booking it meant that the loch was yours for the day; bank fishing was uncomfortable and not nearly as productive as fishing from the boat. Seilge was endlessly fascinating, a broken circle in shape, with shallow bays at the north and south ends, and a wonderful little island just off the south shore. The island was a wildflower paradise, protected by its position in the loch from predation from sheep. Ann, who adores wildflowers, found wild pansy (*Viola tricolour*); a little purple, yellow and white flower, also known as 'heartsease' or 'love in idleness'. The perfect place for lunch.

I remember one blistering day on Seilge, when by half-time we were still fishless and my arms aching from rowing about the loch, trying to cover areas where fish were showing. After lunch we were lying on the island, working on an over-all tan, when we heard an aeroplane approaching. Glancing up we saw what looked to be an RAF reconnaissance plane, flying low and slow over the loch. We could clearly see the crew in the cockpit, white shirts and ties. As the plane passed overhead it tipped its wings at us and the pilot gave us a cheery wave.

Hot days, however, are not very common in the far north and in less than friendly conditions we found ourselves again at Seilge on a day that is forever fixed in my mind. It was cold, very cold, and windy, and I sort of built my better half into the stern: cushion seat, hat-ridiculous, full wet-weather gear, gloves and additional blanket for her knees. I had tied a three-fly cast to her line, Ke-He on the 'bob', March Brown in the middle and Silver Butcher on the tail, and had prepared a similar cast for my own rod. The light of battle glinting, I pushed off with a degree of confidence that belied the storm.

Almost immediately Ann's flies touched the water a fish rose and took the Ke-He. Tucking the handles of the oars under my knees, I landed the fish, unhooked the fly and grabbed the oars just in time to avoid being driven onto the shore. As I rowed out, I noticed that Ann's cast was tangled. I went further out so that I would have time to sort it out before starting the next drift. Which I did, and handed the rod back to Ann, who, by this time, had managed to light a cigarette. As I gave her the rod, the newly repaired cast touched the tip of the cigarette and burnt through the nylon. I rowed out and re-repaired the cast.

The moment Ann's flies touched the water a fish rose and took the March Brown. This was followed almost immediately by a third trout, on the Silver Butcher. 'Come on, Bruce,' said the love of my life, 'You are missing all the fun, have a cast.' Rowing out again to set up another drift, I grabbed my rod and set the flies, light as a feather on the surface. Nothing. 'Oh,' called Ann, 'I have another!' I landed it and returned to my rod. Still nothing, whilst Ann had two more. All this action, at least it was for Ann, took place along the south shore of the loch and at lunchtime I retired, hurt and troutless, to lunch on the island with Ann.

After lunch, my humiliation continued unabated. Ann kept catching trout, whilst I, using exactly the same patterns of flies, did not. I decided to fish the north end of the loch, rationalising that, for me, it could, at best, be no worse than the south end. The wind was still aggressive, although Ann, in between hooking fish, still managed to get involved in a few tangles. In the process of sorting out one such tangle, I had left my line on the water and the wind rapidly blew my line into a long arc, which is how, unbeknown to me, it snagged an underwater obstruction. I passed the now pristine cast back to Ann. We were drifting, quickly onto the bank, so I rowed furiously offshore and then picked up my rod. The top section broke a few inches from the tip, neatly rounding off my disastrous day. I looked at my wife and smiled. 'Darling,' I said, 'it's getting late. I think you have caught all the fish in the loch, so should we head for home?' Thus was born in my mind the conviction that any one woman angler is guaranteed to be more consistently successful than any ten men.

On the west side of Strath Halladale and accessed from a peat track half a mile west from Melvich lie two small lochs that also became firm favourites with Clan Sandison: Eaglaise Mor and Eaglise Beag. At that time, permission to fish came from the Melvich Hotel, then owned by the excellent David Flett and each loch was blessed with a boat. Bank fishing was possible, but not very comfortable, and booking both boats gave us the use of the lochs for the day. The walk out was taxing, particularly for little legs. The car was left at the end of the peat track and we walked south from there round the east shoulder of Cnoc Eipteil (564ft) and then over a wet, soggy moor to reach the north end of Eaglaise Mor after about three miles.

Along the way we passed close to Loch Baligill, reputed to be dour and home to some excessively large trout; a cast of one such fish adorns the walls of the Melvich Hotel, a trout weighing over 8lb and caught in the 1980s by the local policeman. A step further south brought us to the east end of Loch Achridigill, which is full of small trout. We never investigated Baligill, but sometimes stopped for a cast or two in Achridigill. The youngest member of our family, Jean, was only five when she joined us on one such outing. Jean was nervous of boats and had never caught a trout, so Ann and I decided to take her out on Eaglaise Mor, where modest, free-rising fish abound, whilst the other members of the tribe tramped further south to tackle larger things in Eaglaise Beag.

Jean, with an anxious expression on her face, sat in the middle of the boat grimly gripping her seat. The slightest movement of the boat elicited shouts of fear: 'Mummy, stop him, he's bending the boat!' Since nothing was happening at the top end of the loch, I turned to Ann and said, 'Shall we go down to the bottom?'

Jean screamed and yelled, 'Stop him, mummy, I don't want to go down to the bottom!'

Ann calmed her daughter and explained that I didn't mean under the water, but to row the boat down to the other end of the loch. Once there, I hooked a trout and passed the rod to Jean. She took the rod and howled, 'I've caught a fish! Look, I've caught a fish!' Thus anglers are born. The trout was reeled in, landed and released, and Jean spent the rest of the afternoon grousing at me, 'When is it my turn, you have caught a fish, now it's my turn, tell him, mummy, it's my turn.'

At the end of the day, when we regrouped prior to walking back to the car, Jean was very tired, so big brother Blair hoisted her onto his shoulders and we set off homewards over the damp moor. I didn't envy Blair because Jean was no lightweight. In those days there were a few marker-posts, showing the way. They were, even then, simply weather-worn stubs of wood stuck into any available dry patch of ground. We always travelled line astern, with me bringing up the rear and Ann leading the way, the rest of the clan spaced out in between. After about a mile and a half, I saw Blair stop at one of the marker-posts. Wearily, he lifted Jean from his shoulders and placed her on the ground. As he stretched his arms, I saw his little sister, clearly annoyed at being unseated, aim a vicious kick at his left leg. Blair is patience personified, always was and always will be. He hoisted her aloft and tramped on.

Eaglaise Beag is a fifteen-minute tramp south from its name-sake, Eaglaise Mor. It is a small loch but seems to contain much larger trout. My estimate is that the average weight of its fish is between 1lb 8oz and 2lb. There are patches of weeds that in the later months of the season restrict the area available for fishing, but it was along the outer edge of weeds at the south-west corner of the loch that we had an unforgettable hour. There were three of us in the boat – Ann, Blair and myself. We adopted the habit of each spending half an hour guiding the boat, then changing, with a new angler holding the boat whilst his companions fish from bow and stern. The system is fair and works well because the boat is constantly held in the best fishing position.

It was about midday and Blair was on the oars. I was fishing from the bow, Ann at the stern. Afterwards, I remembered that there had been a sudden stillness, a moment of unusual calm; the wind dropped, the sun broke through the clouds, something happened. A trout rose like a rocket to Ann's flies and screamed off across the loch. She held on, dropping the point of the rod as it leapt at the end of its run, and eventually Blair netted the fish, which weighed 2lb 8oz. Encouraged, I cast towards the weed beds. Nothing. Another trout rose to Ann, which she missed, then another, which was hooked, played and landed and was the twin of the first. I had a rise and missed it and, as I was preparing to cast again, Blair said, 'My half-hour is up, Father, would you like to take the oars?'

With as good grace as I could manage, I smiled weakly and

shifted to the centre thwart and grabbed the oars. During the next half-hour the loch seemed to be alive with rising trout: lovely, wild fish, beautifully shaped and perfectly marked. I can't remember, before or since, such excellent sport in such a short space of time. If the secret of fishing success is being in the right place at the right time, then that day on Eaglaise Beag was one such moment. Well, at least it was for Ann and Blair. At close of play, in the boat there were seven splendid trout weighing 16lb. Ann caught four, Blair three and I caught the rest.

I haven't counted them, but between Strath Halladale and Strathnaver there are probably more than 100 lochs and lochans; small affairs, like the Eaglaises, to vast waters such as the three interlinked lochs, Badanloch, nan Clair and Rimsdale. They cover an area of six square miles and feed the Helmsdale River. Presiding over this anglers' paradise is the Garvault Hotel, noted in the *Guinness Book of Records* as being the most remote hotel on mainland Britain. The hotel sits above the B871, the narrow road from Kinbrace in Strath of Kildonan in the east to Syre in Strathnaver in the west, guarded to the north by Ben Griam Mor (1,936ft) and Ben Griam Beg (1,903ft). Griam Beg is renowned for having on its summit the remains of a Pictish hill fort, the highest fort in Scotland and built some 2,000 years ago. A six-foot stone wall encloses an area of 500 feet by 200 feet, and in recent years small round stones, with a hole in their middle, were found there, which suggests they might have been used as weights for fishing nets; probably employed in Loch Druim a'Chliabhain and Loch Coire nam Mang, two trout-filled waters that lie off the west skirts of the mountain.

The B871 was the road where my father's car broke down in 1954 when we first came to Sutherland and were 'rescued' by the man who was not a mechanic, but 'a Mackay from Strathnaver'. Ann and I have fished many of the lochs in the area, but most memorable was the day we walked north from the Garvault Hotel to fish two of the remotest waters, Caol-loch Beag and

Caol-loch Mor. These waters drain to the north, through Loch Strathy and into the Strathy River, and we were fortunate enough to discover them before blanket forestry invaded this part of the Flow Country. Now, as I write, in 2015, the spectre of a huge wind farm also threatens to further disfigure this amazing landscape.

We set off after breakfast well prepared for whatever the weather would throw at us, in spite of early morning sunlight. But it was a 'good to be alive' day and lines of an unknown poet came to mind:

Now turn I to that God of old
Who mocked not any of my ills
But gave my hungry hands to hold
The large religion of the hills.

We followed the Coire nam Mang track and then struck north across the trackless moor to reach Caol-loch Beag after three miles. A red-throated diver rose from the water as we arrived and arrowed off northwards, gaining height as it flew. We fished the west shore and attracted gold- and brown-speckled little trout that gave a good account of themselves; the outlet burn from the loch lead us easily to Caol-loch Mor, a long, narrow water. As I fished from the bank, Breac splashed in, paralleling my progress along the shore at about the perfect casting distance. Nevertheless, the trout didn't seem to mind and I constantly caught fish inches from his black nose.

After consulting the map, we decided to visit a third water on the way home; Loch Sgeireach, which lay a mile and a half southwest from Mor in a hollow between Creagan Dubha Reihde Bhig (1,106ft) and Cnoc Bothan Uisge-beathan (1,036ft). It also gave good sport with classic, small wild brown trout and we had a late lunch in the shelter of a high peat bank at the south end. Enjoying the warmth of a cup of coffee and a sandwich, we suddenly heard a shrill little voice close by, calling, 'Oh dear me, oh dear me.' We looked up and there on the peat bank above our heads was a greenshank, piping plaintively: 'Oh dear me,' it repeated. Greenshank are glorious summer visitors and they nest in the Flow Country, returning each year to the same site, generally by a large rock that seems to help them find their nesting place. Their call sounds exactly like 'Oh dear me' and invariably indicates that it is just about to rain.

We thanked the bird for its timely warning, packed up, heaved on waterproofs and pulled down hats. With the dogs at our heels, we set off on the three-mile walk back to the Garvault Hotel. And it rained, heavily, and a cold, biting north-east wind blew in our faces. Strangely, though, it was a walk that we will always remember. There was something special, invigorating, about it, in spite of the storm. We were enormously happy with our day and with the 'large religion of the hills'; with our fishing, the wildflowers we had found, birds seen and heard. The storm seemed an integral part of the whole. We arrived back at the hotel, drenched, stirred and thoroughly shaken, to a warm bath, an excellent supper, an even more excellent nightcap and a sweet night's sleep.

In 1981 we were still living in Caithness, in a house on a hill looking south across Loch Watten to the Caithness mountains. Most of our fishing then was centred on Caithness and the hill lochs in Strath Halladale, with expeditions to Orkney and Shetland. I was working on my first book, *Trout Lochs of Scotland*, in which I had included a number of the Scourie lochs that, as a family, we had visited in 1974. So I was delighted to receive a phone call one day from Ian Hay at the Scourie Hotel. Ian wondered if I would like to come over to Scourie to discuss running a hosted holiday at the hotel. I did, and we agreed upon a late April date in 1982 for our first venture.

Scourie is a small village by the sea in north-west Sutherland; a few houses, attractive caravan site, shop, post office and not much else. The hotel stands on the site of the home of General

Hugh Mackay (1640–92), who joined the English army in 1660, serving in France and Holland, eventually returning to England in 1688, along with his famous Clan Mackay Regiment when William of Orange landed at Torbay at the start of the Glorious Revolution. Mackay had no love for the Jacobite cause and, in spite of his ignominious defeat at the Battle of Killiecrankie, he was given the task of subduing the Highlands. He built the fort at the head of Loch Linnhe that became known as Fort William. Mackay died in 1692 whilst leading his regiment into the thickest of the fight at the Battle of Steenkirk in the Netherlands.

On that first hosted holiday, Stanley Tuer, a Board Master and regular guest at Scourie, was there to help me. He had been fishing at Scourie twenty years and at times I thought that he knew every trout in the area, by name. Stan was a wonderful man, small in stature but huge in personality. He was a bachelor and a teacher by profession. Stan was from the Midlands and had organised his teaching career via a progression of different schools, each move taking him further and further north until he was teaching in Carlisle. At the end of the summer term he would close up school and head for Scourie, where he spent the long holiday fishing. When he retired, Stan settled in the cathedral town of Dornoch in Easter Ross; close to excellent facilities, shopping and medical services, but, and of far greater importance to Stan, an easy hour's drive to Scourie. His knowledge of the fishing was enormous and he kindly shared much of that knowledge with me, often taking Ann and me on long hikes into the hills to explore his favourite waters. Stan always travelled light, carrying his rod, with his lunch tucked in his fishing jacket, along with a few flies, nylon and reel.

On one such expedition, we passed Loch a'Mhuirt, 'the murder loch', and Stan explained how it got its name. In the Middle Ages, a man and his wife lived on an island in the loch and Lord Reay took a fancy to the man's wife. His interest was not returned and she said that she would never leave her husband as long as he lived. Reay despatched archers to the loch, who shot the man and cut off his head, which Lord Reay then showed to the woman. 'Your man no longer lives,' he said, 'come with me.' She did, and as a reward was given a nearby loch known to this day as Loch na Mratha, 'the woman's loch'.

Stan also explained how, for many years, anglers fishing lochs, such as Loch a'Mhuirt, used to take small fish and bucket them over to a lochan close by and release them there. Thus, in time, these small fish grew to a considerable size and the location of the angler's private larder was a closely guarded secret. I have seen a 3lb 8oz trout come from one of the small waters in the vicinity of the murder loch, a tiny pond that you would hardly cast a glance at, let alone bother to cast a fly.

Another near-murder almost took place at Loch a'Mhuirt when Ann and I, and Blair and his wife Barbara fished it. Ann's terrier Heathcliff, who was still a puppy at the time, set off after a mallard. The bird flapped across the heather, apparently distraught, injured and in a panic, towards the loch, whilst its chicks settled safely to the ground. Heathcliff, intent upon catching their mother, dashed past. The mallard dived into the loch and Heathcliff followed. It was a windy day and the dog was soon in trouble, weighed down by his thick coat, his front paws splashing the surface as he was being blown further from the shore. I struggled to get my boots off to go after him, but Blair beat me to it. Half-naked, he waded out, grabbed Heathcliff by the scruff of his neck and tossed him ashore. With rather less than a friendly feeling, I stuffed the shivering dog into my poacher's pocket. That evening before we went down for dinner, we left Heathcliff, still sulking, on top of the hot water bottle placed in our bed, courtesy of the Scourie Hotel.

Walking on with Stan from Loch a'Mhuirt, we came to the southern end of the Gorm Loch, two sizable waters joined by narrows. It is easy to become disoriented here and, should a mist come down, finding your way out of the northern section and back into the southern part, where the boat is moored, can be very difficult. I know this from personal, embarrassing experience. Here again, it is worth a cast or three in the surrounding lochans. However, our primary objective then was Lochain Doimhain, two and half miles into the hills from the A894 Laxford Bridge/Scourie road. Doimhain is a narrow affair; to me, at first sight, deep and intimidating. However, we tackled up and Stan told me about Pennell Point.

'The first person each season to stand on the point and cast a Black Pennell slightly to the right of centre will hook a trout of about 1lb 8oz,' he announced, confidently.

Stan walked down to the point and did so and, almost immediately, was rewarded with a fine trout that did indeed weigh around 1lb 8oz. A few years later, with Ann and my son Blair, we arrived at Loch Doimhain and, to impress Blair with my local knowledge, I explained to him the significance of Pennell Point. 'I'm watching,' he said, sceptically. I cast my Black Pennell exactly as I had watched Stan do. Nothing moved, not a fin showed. I cast again, and again, and, muttering some entirely unintelligible excuse, invited Blair to try. First cast, a trout rose and took his Black Pennell and, yes, it weighed about 1lb 8oz. 'Thanks, Dad,' said Blair.

After Pennell Point, Ann and Stan and I climbed the slope at the east end of Doimhain, where we stopped for lunch, and then spent the rest of the day fishing a series of small lochans unnamed on the OS map but known locally as Aeroplane, Boot, Otter and Pound, and a few others that have not been given names. It was from one of the latter that, following Stan's advice, I had a lovely trout of 2lb 8oz. It was almost possible to cast across the loch, and Stan asked me cast out to the centre. The trout took instantly, was played and landed. I can't say which of these little waters impressed me most. The fish in the Pound Loch all weigh about 1lb, Aeroplane is scattered with tiny islands, Boot Loch is shaped like Italy, and Otter Loch is noted as a haunt of these most perfect of animals. On our way home we stopped to pay our respects to Ethel, a trout that Stan had stocked into a lochan five years before when it was a few inches in length and was now a grand old lady weighing several pounds. However, Ethel did not grace us with an audience, and, if she had, she would have been smartly returned safely to her abode. Arthur was another of Stan's 'children', estimated to be 6lb in weight. Arthur lived in a lochan close to Mrs Little's Loch, where our daughter, Lewis-Ann, caught her first trout when we fished there in 1974.

Some regular guests, such as Mrs Little, become associated with a particular loch, as is the case with Yeoman's Loch, a tiny Y-shaped lochan at the end of a long, hard trek. Roger Yeoman was passing one morning and happened to notice movement under the surface. He chanced a few casts and by the end of the season he had taken more than a dozen good trout from the loch. So, the Board Master, Stan Tuer, and the proprietor, Ian Hay, 'sitting in solemn conclave decree that, henceforth and forevermore the loch shall be known as Yeoman's Loch'. And it is. Another group of Scourie lochs have a delightful story to tell. They don't lie within the boundary of the hotel's fishings – nearly but not quite. So, when a guest comes back after a hard day in the hills with a beautiful basket of fish and is asked which loch they came from, they might be answered with a finger to the lips and a muttered, 'Shhhhh.' Thus, the lochs acquired the name, the Hush Lochs.

I suppose that even in the best regulated circles, people are at times tempted to stretch the rules; General Hugh Mackay, a soldier's soldier if ever there was one, would understand, as I'm sure a more modern major general such as Major General Osborne, who owned an estate that was adjacent to Scourie, which boasted a very good salmon and sea-trout loch. When news was brought to the Scourie Hotel that the general had passed on to that great loch in the sky, people were genuinely saddened because the general had been a highly respected member of the community. However, on the morning of his funeral, two senior Scourie guests, reading their papers after breakfast, raised quizzical eyebrows: 'Well, I don't think that the General will be needing his loch this morning,' said the one to the other. Newspapers were quietly folded; they headed for the hills. But the old soldier had the last laugh: in spite of their best efforts, the miscreants returned fishless.

I remember Ian telling me a story about another retired military gentleman, a colonel, and a regular visitor to Scourie. He arrived one year with his third wife, and the ashes of his late-lamented second wife tucked away in the boot of his car. Ian said, 'The lady's last wish had been that the colonel should scatter her ashes in the headwaters of the River Laxford. But, you see, his new young wife was not the sort of lady to enjoy much walking and the poor colonel just didn't know how he was going to get the job done. So I arranged for one of the estate stalkers to take the remains up the river, when the colonel and his lady were fishing.' Towards evening, Ian thought that he had better make certain that everything was in order before the colonel returned, and telephoned his friend: 'Now, Ian,' the stalker replied, 'don't you worry, everything is just as fine as it should be, and you can tell the colonel that his good lady will be well out to sea by now.'

In my days at Scourie, the most notable trout was Granddad, a legend. He had been seen and sometimes even tempted to splash at a fly. Once he had taken a Blue Zulu, but roared off and broke the cast. That was the first and only time that anyone had ever come near to catching him. With Stan's guidance, Ann and I set off one morning to see if we could see Granddad. We drove south from Scourie and parked at Geisgeil on the A894 by a shepherd's shelter hut close to Loch Bad nam Mult (*the place of the wedder*); the inlet stream at the north end of the loch tumbles down a sharp waterfall and we clambered to the top and followed the stream to the west end of a chain of interlinked lochs that stretch eastwards for nearly two miles: Loch nan Uidh, Loch Airigh na Beinne, Clar Loch Cnoc Thormaid and Clar Loch Mor.

Granddad's lair lay to the north of these waters.

We rested by the tiny lochan, drank coffee, and waited and watched expectantly. There was the rowan tree on the bank that marked where he was alleged to lurk, but I couldn't work out how I could get a fly to it. The solution I eventually arrived at was hardly artistic. Ann took my cast and, as I reeled out the line, she walked round the loch to a position where I judged my flies would pass close to the tree as I retrieved them. 'Thanks, Ann,' I called. 'Let go!'

I stripped the line whilst at the same time trying to keep the rod tip high so that the flies would be on the surface and, with luck, even 'bobbing' along. As my flies neared the tree, I tensed, certain that my moment of angling glory was upon me. The flies danced past the tree undisturbed by anything other than the wind and my pulling. As I sorted out the tangle of line at my feet, I felt ashamed at having stooped to such underhand tactics. After all, even if I had caught Granddad, he would have been put back. I am sure he died of old age, hopefully quietly, and in his sleep.

One memorable Scourie expedition took us five miles into the wilderness of hills and lochs to the north of Loch Stack. There were four of us in the party that morning, Blair and his wife, Barbara, Ann and me, and five if you include Heathcliff, Ann's Yorkshire terrier. Much of the way follows a good stalker's path that leads north-east from Stack Lodge to climb gently round the western skirts of the grey bulk of Arkle (2,852ft). After weathering Arkle, the path crosses the outlet burn that drains Loch an Easain and Loch na Tuadh into Loch an Tigh Sheilg. Blair and Barbara were intent on fishing Loch an Easain, two miles further east, so we parted company, and Ann and I walked down to explore Tigh Sheilg. Apart from the main water, there are a number of others to the south-west of Tigh Sheilg, all of which hold lively little trout and, I am sure, somebody's private larder, which I never discovered.

However, Stan had asked me to visit a loch to the north of Tigh Sheilg, which he said used to hold trout that were almost green in colour and I had promised to do so. I crossed the outlet burn and tramped the north shore until I found a little stream flowing into the loch. I followed it up a hill onto the lower slopes of Fionaven (2,999ft), one of Sutherland's most gracious mountains. I found the loch Stan had mentioned, Loch na Stioma Gile, overshadowed by the grey, ragged south face of Gaun Mor, the highest point on the Foinaven ridge. Resting my back against an accommodating rock, I poured myself a cup of coffee. The day was fine, warm and bright, and the view south was breathtaking: wave after wave of cumulous-caped peaks to Assynt; blue and silver lochs shining on a carpet of gold. I tied up a three-fly cast, Ke-He on the 'bob', Grouse and Claret in the middle, and a Silver Invicta on the tail, all size 14. There had been no sign of any fish moving and I was beginning to wonder if the loch held any trout. Keeping well back from the bank I cast a long line towards the middle and, raising the point of the rod, began drawing the flies across the surface towards me. With a sudden splash, two fish attacked the flies. Both were landed. They were about nine inches in length, in good condition, darkly spotted and, yes, they seemed to have a greenish tinge. Every time I cast, I caught a trout, more often than not two, and, once, three. I returned them all bar one, which I took back to show Stan.

At the end of the day we met up again with Blair and Barbara on a small sandy beach at the head of Loch na Tigh Sheilg, tired but happy with our expedition. We walked home in early evening sunlight passing between Loch Airigh a'Bhaird and Loch an Nighe Leathaid, both of which were stippled with rising trout. A buzzard circled lazily, a red deer stag haughtily marked our passage, the sentinel cone of Ben Stack (2,366ft) lay ahead. A hot bath before supper beckoned. Scourie will always hold a special place in my heart: watching Blair and Lewis-Ann fishing and the excitement they showed when their efforts were rewarded; Ann, map-reading me through the maze of lochs and lochans to our chosen destination, Heathcliff at her heel; the company of our fellow guests and of Ian and Mary Hay's endless courtesy; and our friend, Stanley Tuer.

Elphin is a scattered community of a few houses on the eastern edge of Assynt in north-west Sutherland. It lies across the A835 road between Ledmore Junction and the busy fishing town of Ullapool. When the village school closed, the building became an adventure centre used by groups of children, accompanied by their teachers, to kayak in Loch Veyatie and hillwalk, and to go on trout-fishing expeditions. In this manner, in 1976, I discovered Assynt. Our daughter, Lewis-Ann, was a pupil at Wick High School in Caithness and the school had arranged an outing to Elphin. They couldn't find a woman to watch over the girls, so my wife Ann agreed to go along, and because Ann was going I volunteered to help out with trout fishing. It was dark when we reached Elphin, and by the time everyone had been fed and chased off to bed, Ann and I were happy to do likewise.

I was last down for breakfast the following morning and, seeing the teachers all eating up their porridge, I realised why: I was the only man present who was beardless: the others didn't need to spend time shaving. Whatever, after breakfast I went out-side to see what I could see and looked towards the west. What I saw almost drove the breath from my body: a magnificent, splen-did mountain wonderland. The grey shoulder of Canisp (2,776ft), Suilven (2,398ft); Cul Mor (2,786ft) and Cul Beag (2,228ft) in the Inverpolly Nature Reserve. The shock of that first glimpse of the broken lands of Assynt has remained with me ever since. Forty years on, crossing the watershed from Glen Oykel by roadside Loch Craggie, I still feel today that same sense of excitement that I felt when I first looked into Assynt.

That morning, whilst Ann and Lewis-Ann set off with the kayak group, I joined the trout-fishing expedition. There were fourteen in the party, three adults and eleven boys, and we followed the route of one of Assynt's most notable paths, a twelve-mile hike from the east end of the Cam Loch to Lochinver. Our destination was three miles along this track to explore Lochan Fada, but a few of us sidestepped east from the track to have two or three well-rewarded casts in little Loch a'Chroisg before re-joining the party at Lochan Fada. Both these waters are resplendent with wild brown trout that rise readily to the fly, just the level of fishing that is most encouraging to young anglers, and to some older ones too. Indeed, this is probably true of most of the lochs in Assynt, although, of course, there are many that contain much larger specimens. Part of the joy of fishing in Assynt is the constant uncertainty of the size of the trout that has risen to your carefully presented fly.

Cam Loch suitably illustrates this point, for not only does it hold good stocks of frying-pan-sized trout but also fish in the mid-teens of pounds (a trout of 16lb was caught a few years ago). Boat and bank fishing produces results on Cam, but using the boat allows you to more comfortably reach the trackless south and north-west shoreline. However, if fishing from a boat, particularly along the north-east shore, be aware that although the bow of the boat may be on the bank, the stern could be lying in water more than ten feet in depth. Thus, if you must land, always exit the boat from the bow. When Ann and I last fished Cam Loch, the boat was moored in the vicinity of the little cemetery in the south-west bay and we took the chance to have a look at the island that dominates that bay. It has been suggested the island might have been artificially made, a crannog, constructed around the first century AD. An unusual dry-stone wall, perhaps built in the late 1700s, encloses an area on the island that still shows signs of having been cultivated, possibly to keep sheep out of this 'garden', but the overwhelming memory that we have of this little island is the captivating scent of wild garlic.

Cam's neighbour, Veyatie, is a four-mile-long narrow water with a wild trout population similar to that which exists in Cam Loch; modest-sized brown trout and some monsters, particularly in the vicinity of Loch a'Mhadial, which abuts the north-east shore of Veyatie; in high water conditions, it is sometimes possible to take a boat into a'Mhadial. Veyatie fishes best in June, when it is blessed with a significant mayfly hatch, and then again in July and September. The catchment area of these waters is vast, born amongst the corries of the Cromalt Hills to the east, then flowing west through Loch Urigill and the Na Luirg burn into the Cam Loch. Cam Loch drains directly into Veyatie over a small waterfall at the south-east end. The Uidh Fhearna stream then empties Veyatie into Fionn Loch, the white loch, which is dominated to the north by the intimidating bulk of Suilven, the 'pillar mountain' of the Vikings. The collected waters of thousands of acres of mountain and moorland then cascade over sixty-foot-high falls into the River Kirkaig, reaching the sea in Kirkaig Bay after a journey of some seventeen miles.

Loch Ailsh is another of my special places. It lies on the course of the River Oykel, which is born in Dubh Loch Mor, nestling in a corrie below the southern face of mighty Ben More Assynt (3,274ft), the highest mountain in Assynt. The river flows south for four miles before resting in Loch Ailsh, then rushing east to join the Kyle of Sutherland. I was introduced to Loch Ailsh by an outstanding photographer, John Tarlton (1914–80); his black-and-white images were magical and one photograph, of two anglers dapping Loch Ailsh for sea-trout, captured my imagination. The original lodge at the head of the loch was burnt down and the estate replaced it in the 1980s with a modern and very comfortable alternative.

Peter Voy was the Assynt Estate factor when Ann and I had a few days at the lodge. Peter was a most hospitable host, which I fully appreciated when he led us on a hill-loch fishing expedition the 'morning after the night before'. Our destination took us deep into the Benmore Forest to fish Dubh Loch Beag, tucked into a corrie between a shoulder of the Ben and Eagle Rock on Meall an Aonaich (2,346ft). It was a dreich day and the fishing was challenging, but the majesty of the setting was completely incomparable. Prior to our setting off, Peter's wife had given instructions that we should return with trout for starters for dinner that evening and, after a couple of hours thrashing the water to foam, it was beginning to look as though this was going to be a command too far.

Which is when Ann hooked an excellent trout. I watched her play the fish carefully and land it by drawing it ashore. Starters for dinner, honour satisfied. As was usually the case, Ann was accompanied by her faithful Yorkshire terrier Heathcliff, a bad-tempered little fellow to everyone except his mistress. In horror, I saw Heathcliff dive on the fish. I lumbered over to help, but by the time I arrived the wretched brute had buried the fish far beyond our ken. He sat watching me, his hairy face twisted into a malicious white-toothed grin. Gathering together ourselves and the shreds of our badly shattered self-respect, we headed south down the hill for a mile or so to spend the last few hours of the day fishing another little corrie loch, Sail an Ruathair. The loch was enveloped in mist and, eventually, we surrendered and trudged home troutless. However, strange as it might seem and in spite of our lack of success, it was an entirely memorable day.

To the east of Dubh Loch Beag and Sail Ruathair, tucked into a corrie between Carn nan Conbhairean (2,848ft) and Meall an Aonaich (2,346ft), is Loch Carn nan Conbhairean, another special place. It can be accessed by taking the right-hand track on the way north from Benmore Lodge: a tough eight-mile round-trip, skirting the east shoulder of Meall an Aonaich. Ann and I came to the loch from Duchally in Glen Cassley, where we were staying near the head of the glen with friends in a small, amazingly well-furnished and equipped cottage that had been seriously extended and upgraded. Although less taxing than the approach from Benmore Lodge, it is still a three-mile tramp over boggy ground to reach the loch, made even more taxing by having with us two five-year-olds who had to be shoulder-borne for much of the way. It was one of those rare blistering midsummer days and the first thing we did on arrival was to cool off in shallow water by the shore. We didn't catch any trout. Yes, we saw fish rising, but not to our carefully presented flies.

Loch Ailsh has always been noted for the quality of the sea-trout that run the River Oykel to reach the loch. Sea-trout have been almost wiped out in the West Highlands and Islands because of disease and pollution from factory salmon farms, and though they have also declined in east coast rivers and lochs, good numbers are still present. The difference being, of course, that there are no fish farms on the east coast of Scotland. These iconic fish appear in Loch Ailsh in late June and July, along with salmon and grilse, and can offer spectacular sport. Loch Ailsh also holds excellent brown trout. The largest trout that I have seen taken from the loch weighed 3lb 8oz and was caught by a laconic visiting French journalist.

Lord Vesty owned the estate then and it was managed in a traditional manner: ponies to bring stags off the hill, not argocats; rowing on the loch, no outboard motors. When asked to allow outboards, the laird was alleged to have replied, 'What is wrong with people these days, they can't walk up the hill to stalk a stag and now they can't row a boat?' Ailsh can turn nasty in the wind, and that is when fishing is at its most exciting, particularly dapping, with silver sea-trout rocketing from the crest of a curling wave to take the fly. Therefore, it was always advisable when fishing the loch to have the services of a gillie, or at least to be accompanied by a strong young friend, otherwise you might spend more time rowing than fishing.

Returning from Loch Ailsh to Lochinver, you pass through the hamlet of Altnacealgach, close to the shores of Loch Borralan. A famous angling retreat once stood by the shores of the loch, the white-painted Altnacealgach Hotel; noted for food, wondrous Danish-style open sandwiches, and, of course, trout fishing. I called in one afternoon to have a look at the fishing logbook and was astonished at the number of trout being taken from Borralan and, to the south, Loch Urigill; often baskets of more than 100 trout to two rods. None of these fish appeared to breach the 1lb level in weight, apart from a few specimen trout from Urigill of up to and over 3lb in weight. Shortly after my visit, the hotel was destroyed in a fire and eventually replaced by a motel. Strangely, I pass that way often but have never once seen anybody fishing Borralan.

Altnacealgach is also notable because of its name, when translated from the Gaelic it means *'the burn of the cheats'*. Many years ago there was a heated dispute about where the boundary between Ross-shire and Sutherland lay. To resolve the dispute, two elderly men were asked to walk the boundary, as they knew it, then that would be fixed as the true boundary between the two counties. The local minister was present to ensure that everything was conducted in an orderly and fair fashion. Before the two old men set off, the minister warned them, 'Mind you both, your feet are on oath.' After several hours the new boundary had been established and the walkers solemnly swore that their feet had never once left Ross-shire soil. Which was nothing less than the truth, because they had filled their shoes with Ross-shire soil before they set out.

When married couples reach silver-wedding status, many arrange to celebrate the event with a second honeymoon in exotic climes. Ann and I married in April 1961 and when our silver wedding came round we decided to go to Assynt. But spring came late that year so our outdoor expeditions were challenging. On the day of our anniversary, with my golden retriever Breac and Ann's Yorkshire terrier Heathcliff, we walked up the track overlooking Kirkaig River and picnicked in the shelter of a peat bank by the shores of the Fionn Loch, glowered over by a snow-scattered Suilven and clutching cups of hot coffee. On our return we stopped to view the sixty-foot-high Kirkaig Falls. The wind was so strong that it was blowing the water back up the falls.

The pool at the foot of Kirkaig Falls is difficult to fish, never mind the clamber down to reach the only fishing stance. There is room for only one person to cast from this rock slab. The other's task is to land any fish caught – lowering him or herself down to the water's edge whilst clinging onto a rope. The fish is then handed up to the angler on the stance. Savage entertainment. The trees on the cliff face at the other side of the pool are festooned with salmon flies, snagged by anglers struggling to land their fly in the right place and failing to do so. I remember once fishing this pool with a friend, Adrian Latimer. When we had struggled, fishless, back up the cliff to the track, carrying landing net and salmon rods, we found a young man and his girlfriend sitting on a rock, watching us. 'Been fishing, then, boys?' the girl asked in an unmistakably Australian accent. Nobody should call themselves a salmon angler until they have fished the Kirkaig, from Falls Pool to the sea.

Back down the track at Inverkirkaig, we stopped at Achins Bookshop, the remotest bookshop on mainland Scotland, to say hello to Alex and Agnes Dixon. The bookshop was established in 1963 and the Dixons had owned it since 1983. It is an Aladdin's cave of books, maps, gifts and clothing, and a warm, welcoming coffee shop. Alex told me that one of his best-selling authors was the poet Norman MacCaig. He is also one of my poetic heroes. MacCaig was an angler and acquaint with my own work. He was born in Edinburgh in 1910 and lived all his life in Auld Reekie, apart, that is, from his regular visits to Assnyt, which he loved beyond measure.

Alex Dickson told me a story and I think that Norman MacCaig had something to do with it. Apparently a huge salmon was caught at the mouth of either the Kirkaig or Inver and not, I understand, by the mouth. The fish was so large that there were not scales available sufficient to weigh it. When laid out on the table in the kitchen of the crofter who caught it, the tail overlapped one end and the head the other. The problem he faced was what to do with it. So he and his friends set to and cleaned the monster, then cut it up into steaks. These were carefully wrapped and the following morning every pensioner in the vicinity found a salmon steak on his doorstep.

The morning after our hike up the Kirkaig River to the Fionn Loch was brighter, so we decided to have a look at Canisp (2,777ft) and some of its hill lochs. We parked by little Loch Awe on the A837 Ledmore to Lochinver road. Loch Awe is very beautiful, although a bit too close to the road for us. It's a great trout loch and the ideal place to introduce beginners to the gentle art of fly-fishing. The trout are not large but very accommodating, and there is always the prospect, towards the end of the season, of encountering salmon – the loch is drained by the River Loanan into Loch Assynt and the River Assynt, a noted salmon stream. Canisp is not a taxing walk in normal conditions, a couple of hours to the top, but that day the weather deteriorated and after an hour we found ourselves struggling through knee-high snow in a growing blizzard. We abandoned our walk and hurried off the hill as quickly as we could. Discretion, rather than valour.

In fine weather, the view from the summit of Canisp is one of the most dramatic in Scotland: south across the mountains of the Inverpolly Nature Reserve, Cam Loch and Veyatie, Urigill and Borrlan to the Coigach peaks in Wester Ross; you feel as though you could reach out a hand and stroke nearby Caisteal Liath (2,398ft), the high point on Suilven; to the north runs a ridge that never falls below 2,000 feet over a distance of eleven miles – the triple peaks of Quinag (2,301ft), Glas Bheinn (2,546) and Conival (3,238ft), and mighty Ben More Assynt (3,274ft); on the horizon,

146

the long ridge of Foinaven; look westwards over a shattered landscape of lochs and lochans to catch a glimpse of the long islands of the Outer Hebrides: Lewis, Harris, North Uist, Benbecula and South Uist.

There are a number of trout lochs on the north shoulder of Canisp that might well reward a visit and all are visible from the top of the mountain: Loch Dubh Meallan Mhurchaidh, Loch Meallan Liatha and Loch na Faoileige. There is also a little loch, unnamed on the OS Map (Loch Assynt, Lochinver & Kylesku, Landranger Series), and as you descend from the mountain, you will find it easily near Meall Diamhain. Don't pass by without a cast. However, what makes Canisp a special place for me is the stream that flows out of the unnamed loch and broadens to become the Allt Mhic Mhurchaidh Gheir burn.

Ann and I always follow this burn on its journey down the hill to Loch na Gruagaich and the bridge over the River Loanan to where our car is parked. The stream must lie on a limestone base because it has cut a considerable gorge along its way; crystal clear water tumbling over grey and black boulders into deep pots where, on a hot day, you can strip off and cool off. In autumn the banks are heater-clad, rowans red-berried. Yes, there are trout, but we never disturb them. It seems wrong to do so. I think that God must have been in a very good mood the day he created this small piece of paradise. It is just about perfect.

Loch Assynt is the largest loch in the area, six miles long by up to three-quarters of a mile wide, often windy, unforgiving and surrounded by mountains. The Inchnadamph Hotel is the principal venue for visiting anglers, and for many years it was owned and run by the indomitable Willie Morrison. When I wrote regular angling reports for *Trout & Salmon*, I used to phone Willie each month to find out how the fishing was going.

'Well, not very much, Bruce,' he would invariably say. 'Very quiet.'

'Any salmon from the loch, Willie?'

'Oh, just a few, about a dozen, and, oh, a couple from the Loanan.'

'Brown trout, Willie?'

'We got a nice basket from Assynt the other day, three fish weighing 20lb, and the corrie lochans have given some nice fish over 2lb.'

In truth, the Assynt waters rarely send visitors away empty-handed and offer a vast range of sport to suit all levels of angling skill, from beginner to hardened expert. It is also true to say that the best of the fishing generally lies at the end of an invigorating walk, including to Loch Mhaolach-coire, known locally as the Gillaroo Loch because in days past the loch contained trout that closely resembled the fabled Irish trout of the same name that exist in Lough Melvin.

Part of the pleasure of fishing the Gillaroo Loch is in the walk out from Inchnadamph to reach it. The track follows the line of the River Trailigill – a Norse name meaning troll, or giant's burn – in Gleann Dubh, past the Inchnadamph limestone caves; the caves here are amongst the earliest archaeological sites in Scotland, where animal remains dating back to 8,000 years BC were discovered. The track divides near the caves, the right-hand branch leading to the Gillaroo. The noise of rumbling under-ground streams cutting through the limestone will accompany you. Look out also for the plants for which this area is justly famous: mountain aven, the rare Don's twitch grass, frog orchard and holly fern.

The setting of the Gillaroo Loch is dramatic in the extreme: Beinn nan Cnaimhseag (1,870ft) to the south, Braebag (2,356ft) and Conival (3,238ft) to the east. The loch covers an area of some thirty acres and is most effectively fished from the boat, although in stormy conditions good sport may also be had from the bank. Whatever the day holds, believe me, it will be a day to remember. Some years ago, after Ann and I fished Gillaroo, we decided that it was time to say hello to the summit of Ben More Assynt. We followed the Trailigill track north past the caves and then branched right to find Loch nan Curan and its satellite waters, little Loch nan Caorach and Loch Meall nan Caorach, all of which lie at about 2,000 feet.

As we passed, trout stippled the surface of the lochs, and we pressed on along the ridge to Conival. Mist came down, reducing visibility to a few yards, and because I had made a serious map-reading error on the way up the day was fast ending. So we left Conival and started for home. As we did so, we heard voices ahead and Ann's terrier barked loudly. A man appeared through the mist, firmly holding a lead to which was attached, in a harness, his young daughter. As he passed he gave us a cheery wave and said, 'Mine doesn't bark!'

A less taxing walk than clambering up Conival is a glorious round-trip south from Loch Assynt to visit a series of five lochs in the Glencanisp Forrest. Ann and I first made the journey one warm September day when we were staying with a party at Inver Lodge Hotel in Lochinver. The hotel was managed by Nicholas Gorton, endlessly courteous, efficient and a good friend. In my view Inver Lodge is probably the finest fishing hotel in the Highlands; the rooms are superbly comfortable and the food excellent, which is understandable given that the restaurant is under the care of the legendary chef Albert Roux. Before the Inver Lodge Hotel was built, the principal fishing hotel in Lochinver was the Culag Hotel, a gaunt, intimidating building near the harbour. Nicholas Gorton was the manager there and Charles McLaren ran fishing courses from the hotel; Charles earned his place in angling history with the wonderful fly, the Kate McLaren.

I sometimes think that the artificial flies we anglers use are designed not so much to catch fish as to catch us. Hundreds of patterns have been produced over the years and hardly a month passes without the introduction of yet another, always guaranteed to attract salmon, sea-trout or wild brown trout whatever the weather conditions. I have been fishing for more years now than I care to remember and I limit my angling armoury to a few well-trusted standard Scottish patterns. I make no apologies for doing so because they have been good friends to me for several decades.

Amongst my standard patterns is the Kate McLaren, a fly for all seasons and particularly excellent for sea-trout; indeed, to go fishing for sea-trout without a few Kate McLarens in your box is to be improperly dressed.

However, there has often been debate about how the fly got its name, so a few years ago I decided to establish the truth; not difficult for me to do because the person who could supply the answer was Charles's widow, Lily McLaren. Lily lives in the village of Altnaharra in north Sutherland where Charles, after relocating from the Culag Hotel, ran fishing courses from the Altnaharra Hotel. Given that I live in Tongue, only seventeen miles distant from Altnaharra, I arranged to visit Lily to ask about the birth of the fly and for details of the original dressing. Lily McLaren is a happy, smiling woman with a warm nature and ready laugh. She has a wealth of stories and knowledge about salmon and sea-trout fishing, and was taught to fish by her husband. Lily gave me an account of the naming of the fly and of the dressing:

'The Kate McLaren was first tied by William Robertson, a tackle dealer in Glasgow. The Robertsons were friends of Charles's father, John McLaren, and it was designed by John and named after his wife, Kate. The dressing is Tail: golden pheasant crest; Body: black-ribbed flat silver; Hackles: black tied down the body and at the head a natural red hen, one tied over the black – must be hen so as to work properly in the water.'

Charles's parents had the Kinlochewe Hotel in Wester Ross for many years, but when restrictions were placed upon access to certain areas of the West Highlands during the Second World War they moved to Blair Atholl. After the war the family returned

150

to Kinlochewe and it was there that Charles learned many of his fishing skills.

A few days after my meeting with Lily an envelope from Altnaharra arrived on my desk. Attached to the front of the card was a Kate McLaren taken from Charles's own fly box and, written on the back of the card, 'With best wishes – Lily McL'. If ever a fly was designed to catch an angler, that Kate McLaren certainly caught me.

Our start point for the expedition following our assault on Conival was at Little Inver, where a bridge crosses the river to the south bank. A track passes the shore of Lochan an-Iasgaich, an extension of the river, and then heads south towards the intimidating bulk of Suilven. Most of the names of places and mountains in the far north that can be easily reached and seen from the sea have names derived from the Norse language, whereas deeper into the heartland the names are invariably entirely Gaelic in origin.

The track leading south from the River Inver is easy-going, rising gently to round the east shoulder of Cnoc a' Leothaid (886ft) before descending to the first loch, island-clad Loch a' Leothaid, which produced lovely trout, fat and fighting fit. Loch Bad ant-Sluic is next, on the east side of the track, and we fished the bays adjacent to the island near the outlet burn, which flows into an Leothaid. A further half-mile brought us to Suileag Bothy, where we met the track out from Lochinver and Glencanisp Lodge – the most popular access route for climbers intent upon scaling Suilven. This track continues eastwards to Elphin and is a spectacular walk through the heartland of Assynt. We lunched by the banks of the Abhainn na Clach Airigh, which gathers in all the waters from the lochs to the east – Loch na Gainimh and Lochan Fada, which I had fished with the Wick High School boys back in 1976. The water in the stream is crystal clear and along its journey it broadens into inviting, attractive lochans where salmon lie, the largest being Loch Druim Suardalain and Loch Culag, before charging down the hill to enter the sea by Lochinver harbour.

After lunch, shadowed by a circling golden eagle, Ann and I and her faithful hound Heathcliff walked east from the bothy round the south shore of Bad an t-Sluic to the end of the track and onto the hill. Tramping over the rough ground, I had to admit to a grudging respect for Heathcliff; he dogged Ann's heel, with my bringing up the rear, and no matter how hard the going, his steps never faltered. We followed the inlet stream of Bad an t-Sluic to its source in Loch Coire na Creige, which lay on the lower skirts of Sron a Bhuic (1,217ft). Another mile north-east brought us to the west shore of the largest loch of the day, Loch Feith an Leothaid, three-quarters of a mile long by half a mile wide.

The wind had risen considerably since the morning, making casting difficult, and the trout were not in the mood, so we rapidly fished down the shore to the north end to where they tumbled out into a stream cascading rapidly over a pavement of bare rock. Thankfully, downhill and half a mile later, we came to our last loch of the day, Loch a' Ghlinnein, tucked into a corrie below Cnoc Ghlinnien (1,116ft), providing welcome shelter from the unrelenting wind. Everything about the loch pleased us. The force of the flow of water from the inlet burn had carved a deep channel, banked on either side by shallow water. It was impossible not to catch fish by casting into the flow and letting the stream work the flies. Again, the fish were not large but very pretty and strong. However, as I worked along the south bank, I had one or two offers that convinced me that the loch contained much larger specimens as well. I comforted myself with the thought that they would still be there another day.

It is always hard leaving a loch that you love. The last few casts, and then another few. Reeling in and securing the flies. Turning away and tramping home. It was about a mile and a half back to Little Assynt, where we had parked the car, but it was a stunning walk. The outlet flow from Loch a' Ghlinnien streamed white and sparkling down a deep glen, and we watched in delight from the side of the hill. The ground beneath our feet was well drained and made for easy walking. A few rowan trees clung to the hill-side, their red berries dancing in the breeze. Afternoon sunlight warmed our backs. It was one of these moments you wished would never end. Contentment and happy memories.

A principal means of maintaining said content and happiness has, to me, always been encapsulated in the lines:

> To keep the marriage happy
> And fill the loving cup
> Whenever you're wrong admit it
> And whenever you're right shut up.

I learned this the hard way. For instance, when I said 'I do', nobody told me I would spend the rest of my life sharing a bed not only with my wife, Ann, but also with a succession of Yorkshire terriers. However, I discovered that we shared a love of other things, such as fishing and hillwalking. The discovery that Ann was an angler came as a bit of a shock; I had been boasting about my piscatorial skills when she produced a photograph of a brown trout caught in a Cairngorm stream, the Allt Druidh in the Lairig Ghru. 'Two and a half pounds, it was,' she said, smiling.

I was not really a hillwalker either until I met Ann, when I sensibly realised that I would quickly have to become one. Serious hillwalking came as a bit of a shock to me, and also to Heathcliff. During his time with us, Heathcliff has scaled more than his fair share of Munros, Corbetts and MacDonalds, always positioning himself behind Ann, with me bringing up the rear. His worst moment, and mine, came when we were climbing Quinag (2,656ft) in Assynt on a windy September day. There is a narrow ridge on the descent from Spiedean Coinich, the most southern of the three peaks that form the mountain, and for safety's sake we decided to traverse it on hands and knees, rather than upright. Ann went first, then her faithful hound, then me. In the middle of the ridge, Heathcliff stopped, turned and came back towards me. I knew exactly what was going on in his furry mind: he had decided enough was enough and was heading for the car. I grabbed him as he tried to slink past and stuffed him unceremoniously up my jumper.

When I reached Ann, she cried out, 'Where's Heathcliff, what's happened to him?'

'Safe, Ann, safe and sound,' I replied, as I laid the tattered, ragged bundle of brown and gold into her arms, his hairy face twisted into a hideous, white-toothed grin.

The only other time the little dog 'baulked' at the prospect of a long walk was when he was sixteen years old. We were all set to climb to the high point of the Foinaven ridge, Ganu Mor (2,999ft) in north-west Sutherland, but Heathcliff, on the lead, refused to move. Ann guessed what the matter was, opened the car door and slipped the lead. Heathcliff shot back into the car and purposefully snuggled down on his rug. Point taken. Meall nan Tarmachan, Creag Meagaidh, Ben Hope, Carn Ghluasaid, Sgurr nan Conbhairean, Ben More Mull, Ben More Assunt and many more were all 'ticked off' Heathcliff's list before he slipped his lead for the final time. Appropriately, he lies buried on the slopes of Ben More Assynt, his last Munro, but lives on in our memories.

If it is possible to fall in love with a mountain, then I am in love with Quinag. The name derives from the Gaelic *water stoup* or *milk bucket* and it towers over Loch Assynt. The full glory of the three peaks of the mountain, over a distance of two and a half miles, south to north, is best exposed from the south, by Little Assynt: Spidean Coinich, the 'mossy peak'; Sail Ghbarbh, 'rough heel'; and Sail Gorm, 'blue heel'. Approaching from the north, after crossing the new bridge over the Kylesku narrows, the road twists up the hill with the buttress of Sail Gharbh, the highest point on the mountain thrusting aggressively towards the road. A traverse of the ridge involves a round-trip of some ten miles, with joy in every step.

There is a parking place on the A848 Kylesku shortly after you begin to descend to Skiag Bridge on the north shore of Loch Assynt. Cross the road and get onto the slow, grass- and rock-covered rising shoulder leading to the summit of Spidean Coinich. The vista from the top is mind-blowingly stunning, as it is indeed from all three peaks, and in my opinion amongst the finest views in Scotland. We had coffee on the top, looking south over a breathtaking landscape that had lain largely unchanged since the end of the last Ice Age. Finding the way off the top was confusing, the first time, but it descends to what we now call Heathcliff's Ridge from the west side of the summit. Quinag, unlike most Highland mountains, is surprisingly green and there are small pockets of weathered sandstone amongst the tangled rocks.

When we reached Bealach a'Chornaidh and were preparing to scramble up the cliff to the knoll at the top, we stopped to watch a man and woman already on the face. The woman appeared to be in some difficulty, unsure of whether to continue the climb or try to get back down. Her husband was close by, talking to her, trying to calm her and encourage her to continue. Suddenly, she seemed to find renewed resolve and shot up the remaining few yards as though she had been doing it all her life. We met the couple later on and stopped to speak. I asked the man how he managed to galvanise his wife into action. 'Simple,' he replied, 'I promised that if she got on with it, I would make supper tonight.'

There is a special trout loch up there, Lochan Bealach Cornaidh, tucked into the coire between Spidean Coinich and Sail Gharbh. It is nearly a quarter of a mile long by a few hundred yards wide. The loch contains perfect wild brown trout and there are few more dramatic places to fish. At the east end of the loch it is shallow and there is a sandy bottom, which makes wading comfortable. The south shore is overhung by the cliffs of Spidean Coinich, whilst the north shore is the best for bank fishing, although wading is not really advisable. Wind direction permitting, fish right round to the outlet burn.

Ann and I were coming down from the Bealach one afternoon when we found a friend, Derek Fothergill, busy fishing the north bank of Bealach Cornaidh. Derek is very much a traditional angler and he had an ancient wicker fishing creel, his grandfather's, bumping at his side. Derek gave me one of my most treasured rods, a fourteen-foot Hardy cane-built rod with a steel centre. It was built in 1895 and owned by Wilson Wordsell, chief engineer for London & North East Railways. No doubt, on his train journeys, he stopped off to fish Tyne, Tweed, Tay and Dee along the way, sensibly mixing business with pleasure. The rod had been refurbished by R. James of Shilbottle, near Alnwick, formerly a rod builder for Hardy's; it is a delight to cast with and as good today as it must have been when Wilson Wordsell first used it.

An excellent and very welcome stalker's track leads back to the car park from Lochan Bealach Cornaidh, but before leaving Quinag there are two other little lochs that may be interesting to those with a sense of adventure. They are very special and infrequently visited and lie on the skirts of Sail Gharbh. I shan't tell you the names, but if you are interested I'm sure you will find them. I was introduced to them by a friend, the late Angus MacArthur. Angus and his wife fished them many years ago and he told me, 'Bruce, I had the fish on for a minute before it broke me and, believe me, it was the size of a small battleship.'

Several well-known and notable lochs lie on the other side of the Kylesku to Skiag Bridge road, particularly the famous 'Corrie Lochans', scattered between Cnoc na Creige (1,946ft) and Glass Bheinn (2,546ft), always dour but reputed to hold specimen trout. To reach them, park by Loch na Gainmhich as you come up the hill from Kylesku. A track leads round the south shore of the loch, then up into the hills; not a walk for the faint-hearted and very much a question of pain before pleasure. This is also the route to the UK's highest waterfall, Eas a'Chual Aluinn (658ft), 'the maiden's tresses'. When in full flow, it is three times higher than the Niagara Falls. This is very much compass-and-map country, so be well prepared for a serious navigational exercise should a mist descend.

Having said which, as I write, a political mist seems to have descended over whether or not the UK should stay in Europe and it reminds me of the few days I spent showing a multi-cultural group of journalists the wonder that is Assynt; two Spaniards, two Germans and two French anglers. They represented three European fishing magazines, *Trofeo de Pesca*, *Der Fliegenfischer* and *La Pêche*, a journalist and photographer from each. I arranged the visit and acted as their host and guide, and Nicholas Gorton agreed to accommodate them at Inver Lodge Hotel. We spent our first day together, courtesy of Edmund Vesty, fishing the Middle Beat of the River Inver. The water level was perfect and fish were showing almost continuously. By lunchtime there were four fresh-run salmon on the bank: two to the Germans and two to the Spaniards. My French companions said nothing, but were seriously glum. I sensed an international incident brewing. Happily, the afternoon proved to be kind to the French, albeit with only one fish between them. But honour had been satisfied.

I had asked them to be back at the car for 5.30 p.m., leaving plenty of time to relax and freshen up before dinner. As I waited patiently to collect my little flock, I watched them coming down the riverbank. The track they had to follow divided just before a fishing hut. One branch, the correct route home, angled away from the river, round a small hillock to a bridge across the stream. The other branch led to a dead end and a precipitous drop into a deep pool. At 5.25 p.m. the Germans hove into view, their fish slung on designer ropes fitted with wooden carrying handles. At the junction they unhesitatingly followed the correct path and arrived at my side at 5.30 p.m. precisely. At 5.45 p.m., the Spaniards appeared, talking earnestly together; looking at the river, pausing to inspect pools and to point at splashing salmon. Their fish were slung casually over their backs. At the junction, they started down the wrong track, then, realising their mistake, they retraced their steps and rounded the hillock.

By 6.00 p.m. the Frenchmen had yet to appear and the Germans were agitated, worrying about dinner. 'We must go. We will be late. Leave them a note saying you will come back for them.' We heard the Frenchmen before we saw them, when they were some distance off, talking at the top of their voices. Then we saw them, gesticulating down the track, arms flying, the air blue with tobacco smoke. Without pause they took the wrong turning and arrived at the side of the river. Their salmon fell to the ground, almost into the stream. After a heated argument about what to do next, they walked back to the junction and continued the debate over another cigarette. I roared across the river and waved directions. Eventually they found the route and tramped over the bridge to where we were waiting. Full of courteous apologies for being late, they said, 'It is so beautiful, we just forgot about the time.' I walked back across the river to retrieve their salmon, which, in the white heat of argument, they had forgotten to pick up.

At dinner on the last night, the Germans, by way of a 'thank you', gave me a book. For the first time since leaving home, I reached for my spectacles. I put them on and gasped in fright. I had suddenly gone blind in one eye. Then I remembered my son Charles and daughter Lewis-Ann being particularly solicitous before I left: 'Here, Dad,' Charles said, 'you almost forgot your glasses.' The blighters had pasted a black patch over the port lens. I peeled off the patch, much to the amusement of the assembled company, and grabbed the cloth from inside the case to wipe the lens clean. As I did so, I exposed a neatly printed note, stuck firmly in place in the case, upon which was written Basil Fawlty's classic line: 'Don't mention the war!' Maybe if our political leaders spent more time fishing and less time gabbing they would get on better and perhaps make the world a happier place.

There are a number of trout lochs in Scotland named Meadie. I have fished three of them, one in Caithness and two in Sutherland. My favourite is the Sutherland Loch Meadie. It lies close to the narrow, tortuous track running north-west from Altnaharra through green Strathmore to reach the A838 road from Tongue to Durness on the north coast. I discovered it more years ago than I care to remember and it remains close to my heart – and even closer to my front stoop, it being only a forty-minute drive from Hysbackie.

From the road, Meadie looks to be a modest affair but, in fact, once out of the boat mooring-bay, the loch extends northwards for a distance of nearly four miles. It is a predominately shallow loch, at its widest part about half a mile across and at the north end a couple of hundred yards.

I was not the first member of Clan Sandison to visit the loch; that honour fell to my manager – my wife, Ann – who, after a horrifically fishless day on nearby Loch Hope, decided to have a day on her own. She chose Loch Meadie as the venue. The day turned out to be perfect for the job in hand, a gentle south-west breeze, sunny but not too bright. I was unconcerned about Ann being alone because she is competent in the use of an outboard motor and skilled on the oars; Ann used to row for the Edinburgh University Ladies' Rowing Club and could teach me a thing or six about feathering.

We were staying at the Altnaharra Hotel and, in the evening, before dinner, I asked Ann how she had faired.

'Not bad, really, Bruce,' she replied.

'Well,' I said, 'did you manage to catch anything?'

Ann smiled. 'I think it was about forty, but after that I stopped counting.'

I spluttered into my beer. 'Are you sure?'

'Oh, yes, I brought two back for our breakfast.'

'How big were the fish?' I enquired.

'Not very, about three to the pound, with the occasional fish of 10oz, but they are very pretty and fight hard. Why don't you come with me tomorrow and see for yourself?'

My efforts that day, again on Loch Hope, had been somewhat less than fruitful – two more sea-trout and I would have had a brace – so I agreed.

Weather conditions the following morning were a mirror image of the previous day and we set out full of confidence, certain in the belief that it was going to be a memorable day. It was. Although, for me, for entirely unexpected reasons. The total catch that day was a couple dozen trout: Ann caught twenty-four of them and I caught the rest. This happens to the best of us from time to time, at least it does to me when Ann is my fishing part-ner, but for the first time in my angling life I began to realise that there is no such thing as 'easy fishing' or, indeed, 'free-rising' fish; and that it was just as challenging and exciting to fish for small wild brown trout as it was trying to catch their larger brethren.

In later expeditions to the loch I have caught my fair share and, yes, they are very pretty trout and they do fight well above their weight. However, this is not the principal reason that I love fish-ing Loch Meadie. I go there because it is, quite simply, one of the most beautiful lochs in all of Scotland. The majesty of the loch is disclosed only when you pass through the narrows from the mooring-bay and are confronted by the full extent of the loch; scattered with small islands, fingering northwards in a sparkling, incandescent sheet; narrowing northwards by endless little bays, headlands and fishy corners; and then, finally, past the island guarding the waist of the loch, opening out again into the long north bay where a spider web of burns tumbles into Meadie from Creag Riabhach and Cnoc an Daimh Mor.

The tiny island, at the narrows, is the perfect place for lunch. That first time, when Ann and I fished the loch, we lunched on the island. It is scrub-and-tree covered, with a rocky margin. We lazed and talked and ate amidst the scent of wildflowers, bird-song and the flutter of moths and butterflies. These islands in Loch Meadie are very precious because they are protected from serious depredation by sheep and deer, and retain much of the characteristics that must have pertained for thousands of years. To the north, Ben Loyal crowned the horizon; to the north-west, the long ridge of Ben Hope. It was easy to rest there, lulled by the soft sound of loch water lapping the shore.

Some of the most memorable days fishing that I have ever enjoyed have been spent at Durness, in north-west Sutherland. There are four classic trout lochs here: Caladail, Borralie, Croispol and Lanlish, limestone-based and holding wild brown trout of outstanding quality. These waters are crystal clear and their fish fight harder than you could possibly imagine. Because of the limestone, the lochs have a high pH value and the limestone out-crop that feeds them first surfaces on the Trotternish Ridge in the island of Skye, then the south skirts of Ben More Assynt by Inchnadmph, followed by Durness and, lastly, it appears again in Shetland at West Mainland lochs and the Loch of Funzie on the island of Fetlar. The wildflowers surrounding these lochs are out-standing and, in many cases, of international importance.

Borralie is the largest and deepest of the Durness limestone waters, 100 feet towards the north end. For many years Borralie held the UK record for the heaviest Arctic char, a modest fish just under 2lb in weight, caught before char began feeding on pellets at fish farms. But according to divers who, a few years ago, car-ried out biological studies of the bed of the loch, huge fish were glimpsed, ghosting by, some of them estimated to be most cer-tainly double-figure trout. Another delight of Borralie is bank

161

fishing along the north-west shore in the evening, when large trout sometimes glide up from the depths to feed in the shallows.

The south end of the loch is shallow and I have found that a drift down the east shoreline, a few yards out from the bank, can be rewarding. It is surprising just how close to the bank fish lie; I have caught trout that were in danger of landing on the bank when they leapt from the water whilst being played. There is a substantial island here and you should engineer a drift through the narrows, fishing as you go, to reach the north end of Borralie.

I remember one fine day fishing Borralie with Ann and my son, Blair. We stopped for lunch on the west shore, across from the island. Ann set off to look at wildflowers, Blair to collect the mushrooms that grow prolifically in the cattle-manured, lime-rich soil. Later, with sandwich in one hand and cup of coffee in the other, I saw good trout rise within easy casting distance from the shore. Unceremoniously abandoning both sandwich and coffee I grabbed my rod and set a fly directly over the expanding rings of where the trout rose. Instantly, my tail fly, a Silver Butcher, was taken with a force that almost pulled the rod from my hand. I saw its dorsal fin as it roared off for the middle of the loch, breaking my cast. Dejected, I slumped to the ground.

'Did you see that fish?' I said to Ann and Blair. 'It must have been at least 5lb.'

Of sympathy came there none. 'Yes, Father, and no doubt by this time next week it will have been at least 9lb,' Blair quipped.

Loch Croispol is a smaller affair and has smaller fish, averaging 12oz to 1lb in weight, but here also there are surprises: the largest trout to come from Croispol weighed 4lb 8oz and was caught by the late Professor Norman Simmonds, author of one of my most treasured angling books, *Early Scottish Angling Literature*. Croispol is also one of the few lochs in Scotland that has a natural population of freshwater crayfish.

Little Loch Lanlish is fished from the bank and at times you would swear that it was fishless. But on mild June evenings I have seen the whole surface alive with feeding fish, including some of the largest wild brown trout found anywhere on Planet Earth. The Cape Wrath Hotel (now a private house) used to have a remarkable collection of glass-case specimens, many of which came from Lanlish and weighed in the teens of pounds. In recent years, I have seen two Lanlish trout that weighed 8lb and 8lb 8oz respectively.

However, I confess that Loch Caladail is perhaps my favourite Durness loch. It can be dour and unforgiving, but hooking, playing and landing a Caladail trout is, for me, one of the special joys of angling. Just being there is another. I have fished Caladail in all conditions: howling gales, rain, mist, dead-flat calms, blazing sun and finger-freezing chills. I have had blank days without number and, happily, a few red-letter days, but I never tire of going back for more. A day on Caladail has always been one of the highlights of my angling year.

The loch is also dear to me for other reasons: I have had the pleasure of fishing there with every member of my family: my wife, Ann, who invariably manages to out-fish me; my big son Blair, an expert angler, at least that is what he tells me; my daughter Lewis-Ann rarely goes home trout-less; second son Charles, strong and fearless, is as great on the oars as he is with rod; and my second daughter, Jean, always 'looks after me' splendidly.

Last season Blair and I shared a boat on Caladail with another great oarsman, my grandson Brodie, who has grown into a really competent and assured angler who seems to have a touch of magic when it comes to persuading trout to rise. I constantly remind him of who taught him to fish, but he just smiles and mutters, 'Aye, right, Granddad.'

Caladail is not a large loch. It measures half a mile north/south by some 600 yards wide at the north end, tapering to about 200 yards in the south. Boats are moored at the bay in the north-west corner, a few minutes' walk from where you park your car by the roadside cottage on the A838 from Durness to Rhiconich. The loch is larger now than it was in the early years of the twentieth century. In the 1920s it was decided to use Caladail as the water supply for the surrounding community and a dam was built across the outlet burn to raise the water level.

This resulted in a number of existing dry-stone walls being partly flooded, particularly down the west shoreline; the incongruous remains of the parts left above the raised water level are still visible today and make this shore very awkward to fish from the bank. The east shoreline can be easily fished from the bank, a 'lifesaver' when high winds make it impossible to launch the boat, providing that the wind is from the east. In truth, however, best results on Caladail come when fishing from the boat.

Caladail trout average around 1lb 8oz in weight, but good numbers of fish of up to 6lb are taken most seasons. I invariably fish a team of three wet flies on a long cast; indeed, as long as I can manage, which is generally twelve to fourteen feet in length. Forgive me, please, but I am too fixed in my ways to use the term 'leader'. My preferred flies are something bushy on the 'bob' – Loch Ordie, Ke-He or Coch-y-Bonddu; middle is always dun-coloured – March Brown, Greenwell's Glory, Wickham's Fancy; and the tail fly an 'attractor' – Silver Butcher, Silver Invicta, Dunkeld.

Most of my fishing is done with a floating line, always has been and, I suppose, always will; on Caladail, a longish cast and a quick retrieve, pulling the line down with my left as I simultaneously raise the point of the rod with my right. Caladail trout most often 'take' either as soon as the cast lands on the surface or close to the boat, as I prepare to cast again. However, some of my friends only fish a single small dry fly, a black pattern, and this method can also be very successful.

I have caught fish all over the loch, but two areas have produced most of them: a drift from the north-east corner of the loch, from the shallows following an angle towards the south-west; then, and perhaps the most productive drift, from the north bank straight down the middle of the loch towards the small island at the south end. The 'hot-spot', I think, is the area about 50 yards before the island. As the season advances, weed patches appear: learn to live with them, they often shelter good fish.

These are just my 'ramblings' and, of course, others might disagree, but I have been fishing Caladail for thirty years now and that which is described above has always worked for me. What I can't fully describe for you, however, is the special sense of magic that this loch arouses in me every time I go afloat. This is something that you will have to discover for yourself. But believe me, please, you will not regret doing so.

North Sutherland is a broken coastline that faces the full force of the Atlantic and is the least populated part of the UK. Since 1990 Ann and I have lived in Tongue, a community of some 150 souls on the east side of the Kyle of Tongue. The village is dominated by the ruins of Castle Varrich, a Clan Mackay stronghold dramatically perched on a cliff edge overlooking the shallow waters of the Kyle. Ann and I first visited Tongue from Caithness in the late 1970s, when the MacSob Log chose Loch Loyal and Loch Craggie for their annual fishing outing. We stayed at the Ben Loyal Hotel. The name 'MacSob' is made up from the initials of the four men who set up the event: Donnie Mackay, Bruce Sandison, Harry Officer and Adam Black. Our fishing partners were our sons, except for Donnie, a childless Church of Scotland Elder. Thus, we were Father-Son, Father-Son, Father-Son and Holy Ghost. The Sandisons were awarded the log that year, roundly celebrated amidst good company, not too few drams and enormous fishing lies.

After dinner, Ann and I walked through the village towards Ben Loyal (2,510ft), 'the Queen of Scottish Mountains'. In the twilight shadows the crenelated peaks of the Ben looked magnificent; a sweet scent of peat drifted lazily from smoking chimneys;

evening birdsong filled the air. On a hill to our left was a white cottage and we wondered who lived there and how they earned a living. It was such a contrast to our work-a-day Caithness lives, where I looked after an agricultural land drainage company, and Ann and a colleague ran busy dental surgeries in Wick and Thurso. In 1990, Ann retired and went back to her first love, painting, and by that time I was working as a writer and journalist (although people used to stop Ann in the street in Wick and enquire, solicitously, 'Oh, Mrs Sandison, has your man got a job yet, or is he still writing?') One morning, we noticed an advert in the paper for a property for sale in Tongue. We decided to have a look. It was the same house that we had pondered over as we walked through the village twenty years before, so we bought the cottage on the hill, Hysbackie.

The fact that Tongue is surrounded by wonderful trout, sea-trout and salmon fishing did not really influence our decision to move out 'beyond the Split Stane' – well, not much – but the position of the cottage and the views were irresistible. Hysbackie faces south, looking directly onto Ben Loyal. In the distance is Ben Hee (2,570ft), the 'Fairy Hill', and to the west Ben Hope (3,041ft), the 'Hill of the Bay' – the most northerly Munro on the Scottish mainland. A track twists up to our cottage from the minor road round the Kyle of Tongue, through a wood of silver birch, rowan and hazel, always loud with birdsong and the soft murmur of a tiny stream. Wildflowers carpet the forest: wood sorrel, violet, primrose, bluebell, orchids, lesser celandine and yellow pimpernel.

Ten minutes from our front door is Loch Hakel, full of accommodating wild brown trout. The fishing is organised by the Tongue and District Angling Club and visitors are always welcome. Permits are issued by the Ben Loyal Hotel, where outboard motors may also be hired. Hakel is one of my special places, not only because of the fishing but also because of the history and wildlife surrounding the loch. I once watched a pair of red-throated divers there, introducing their youngster to the art of diving. The youth was trying to persuade its parents that it urgently required food. With neck outstretched, the little one, begging, swam between an apparently indifferent mum and dad. The adults would dive, leaving their distraught infant on the calm surface. When they resurfaced, their offspring swam to them with renewed cries for breakfast. Suddenly, it seemed to get the message. In perfect unison, the three birds disappeared below the peat-stained waters of the loch.

Our ancestors, Neolithic men and women who lived here 4,500 years ago, would have been familiar with such a sight. Their descendants, Bronze Age people, Celts, Picts, Viking raiders and Clan Mackay, would also have noted similar annual events. In this moment, as I watched, I was inextricably linked to a part of their existence. I saw this magical display as through their eyes. I felt the same certainty which they must have felt in the orderly progression and pilgrimage of life, for both humans and animals.

At the south shore of Loch Hakel, on a small tree- and bramble-covered island, are the ruins of an Iron Age fort (500 BC–AD 500). Wade across and say hello to your ancestors. On the shore immediately adjacent to the island is a large, moss-covered boulder displaying one of the most remarkable and least known examples of Neolithic cup-and-ring markings in Europe, dating back to the Bronze Age and inscribed on the rock some 4,000 years ago; thirty 'cups' surrounded by eleven 'rings'. It is not known what they mean, although it is probable that they were of religious significance to the people who carved them. On a plateau a few hundred yards to the south and overlooking Loch Hakel is Druim na Coub, the site of one of the last clan battles fought in Sutherland, in 1431, between Clan Mackay and Clan Sutherland; a bloody broad-sword-and-axe affair, when Clan Mackay, led by their chief, Angus Du Mackay, won the field. A further step south from the battlefield brings you to the remains of a Bronze Age hut circle with associated burial chambers, one of which, marked by a cairn, has been excavated.

Another famous fight ended in March 1746 on the shores of Loch Hakel. A French ship the *Hazard* was bringing supplies, arms and money to support Jacobite forces led by Charles Edward Louis Casimir Sylvester Severnio Maria Stuart – Bonnie Prince Charlie, to you and me – who were camped on Drumossie Moor to the east of Inverness. The government frigate the *Sheerness* spotted the French ship in the Moray Firth and set off in pursuit. Passing through the Pentland Firth, aided by a north-east wind, the *Hazard* attempted to escape by sailing into the shallow Kyle of Tongue in the belief that the *Sheerness*, a heavier vessel, would be unable to follow. The *Hazard* ran aground near Midtown on the west shore. The *Sheerness*, however, followed and stopped within cannon distance of the *Hazard*. Hopelessly outgunned, the *Hazard* was soon reduced to wreck, leaving fifty of its crew dead and many others seriously wounded. The captain, George Talbot, determined to try to get some of the supplies, gold coins packed in barrels, by road to the Jacobite army in Inverness.

That night, 29 March, Talbot and those who had survived the carnage on the Kyle, unloaded the supplies and marched off along the west shore of the Kyle, where they were given comfort and shelter by sympathisers near present-day Kinloch Lodge. As they passed Loch Hakel, to lighten their load, they threw hundreds of gold coins into the water and shortly thereafter were ambushed by government forces on Cnoc Fada and forced to surrender. As for the gold, well, I guess that most of it somehow found its way into local sporrans. However, in the 1920s one gold coin was recovered from the hoof of a cow that had been grazing by the shores of the loch. Thus, when I am fishing Hakel, I always keep a sharp eye open for any golden glint.

Even the trout in the loch seem to be golden – not large, but fine fighters and perfectly shaped. I invariably open my fishing season with an hour or so on Hakel. The loch is largely circular in shape and ideal when it is windy; no matter from which direction it blows, or how strongly, there is always a sheltered part of the bank from which to fish. Another favourite of mine is little Loch Craisg, *'the loch of the crossing'*, in a hollow between Ben Tongue (990ft) to the north and Meall nan Clach Ruadha (1,102ft) in the south. Like Hakel, it is circular and the ideal fishing location in stormy conditions. The loch used to be the main water supply for the village and the water is crystal clear. The southern end is shallow, where the bottom is sandy and wading safe and easy. However, I believe that the west bank offers the best chance of sport. Don't be tempted to wade here because it is uncomfortable and dangerous to do so. In any case, the fish lie close to the bank; keep a few paces back from the edge to avoid scaring them out into deeper water. There is a sense of ease and peace about Craisg that is wonderfully calming. I always return from the loch feeling happy and refreshed.

A year ago, I spent a memorable afternoon with our youngest grandchildren, both aged ten, Pollaidh, Blair's daughter, and Jake, Jean's daughter. We fished Plantation Loch, by the road between Tongue and Altnaharra. As its name implies, the loch is surrounded by a conifer plantation and I first fished it in the early 1980s with Allan Finch, then owner of the Altnaharra Hotel, who leased the fishing from the Ben Loyal Estate. At that time the Plantation Loch was the premier trout-fishing water in the area, with fish averaging 1lb 8oz, with 3lb-plus specimens not uncommon. However, over the years the trout population in the loch expanded enormously and, consequently, the size of the fish fell dramatically – perhaps because of too many mouths depending on a finite food resource. Whatever the reason, trout in the loch now average around three-to-the-pound. But they are not shy about rising to the fly, whether from boat or bank, and, as such, it is a good place to take aspiring young anglers to fish.

Pollaidh and Jake have always been friends. Even before they could talk they seemed to find an affinity and this has remained constant. Jake is the more experienced angler, as is to be expected, given that his father is a skilled angler, shooter and stalker, and that his mother is a Sandison. It was a calm, cloudy day and I decided that the far bank and the head of the loch were the most likely to produce results. The loch was low and the walk round the bank was awkward and difficult. Jake, always the perfect gentleman, helped Pollaidh over the stones, taking her hand and carrying her rod when we had to wade round overhanging branches.

Half an hour later the midges arrived, in droves, and I stumbled about issuing midge nets. But they didn't complain, just kept on fishing, and missing fish after fish after fish. There came a roar of thunder, followed a few minutes later by the first drops of rain. Still they fished on. Then the skies opened and it poured stair-rods – vertical, torrential, neck-chilling rain. We were quickly soaked to the skin. And they still fished on. I called them ashore and suggested that we beat a hasty retreat to the car, which was parked some distance away, around the loch. I took their rods. They walked together, Jake, head up and shoulders back, with a firm grasp of Pollaidh's hand, keeping her safe. For me, watching them, it was a quite unforgettable and emotional moment. I felt proud and privileged to be their granddad.

Loch Loyal is the largest loch in the area, four miles long by up to half a mile wide, and dropping to a depth of 200 feet at the north-east corner by Bein Stumanadh (1,729ft). Ben Loyal towers over the west shore and the loch lies on the course of the Borgie River. The river is born amidst the streams that flow down from Cnoc an Daimh Mor (1,171ft) into the Allt Dionach-caraidh burn to Loch Coulside and feed into Loyal at Inchkinloch. Loyal then exits north through Loch Craggie and Loch Slaim to form the Borgie River. There is a lifetime's fishing here, in the main lochs and in the surrounding satellite lochans. Loyal and Craggie have large populations of small trout, as well as some surprises: the largest trout caught in Craggie weighed 11lb and a dozen or so salmon are taken most seasons, whilst Loyal also is capable of producing specimen trout. Which is part of the pleasure of fishing here: you are never quite sure if the fish rising to your fly is just another half-pounder or a potential occupant of the glass case of your angling dreams. The lochs can be wild and windy, and it is often impossible to launch a boat, but bank fishing can be just as productive.

We have had some famous days on Loyal and I remember one particularly when I fished with my younger brother, Fergus. Fergus lives in Northumberland and often makes a royal 'annual progress' round Scotland to spend time with my elder brother, Ian, and with us at Hysbackie. I introduced Fergus to fishing more years ago than I really care to remember, so we always have a couple of days out when he comes to the far north. The Loyal boats are moored halfway down the west shore, where a burn flows in at Lettermore, and the mooring-bay has been deepened to facilitate launching the boat. I carried the outboard motor down, whilst Fergus brought the fuel, fishing bags and rods. I had the key for the boat and, as Fergus was busy loading our gear aboard, I, with my back to him, was unlocking the padlock.

'Fergus,' I said, over my shoulder, 'do be careful here, the mooring-bay is quite . . .'

I heard a splash and a shout of alarm and looked round to see my brother up to his waist in the water. 'What were you saying, Bruce?' he replied, gasping for breath. I hauled him ashore, dripping, and suggested that we go home so that he could change. 'I'll wring them out,' he said. 'They will soon dry in the sun. Can't waste good fishing time, can we?'

That's my boy, I thought. That day we didn't encounter anything that was going to break the scales, but we had good sport and, as is always the case fishing with Fergus, lots of laughter.

There are a series of five interlinked named and unnamed waters to the south-east of Loyal on the northern skirts of Cnoc Bad na Gallaig (909ft). They drain into Loch Loyal and the most

171

productive is Loch nam Breac Buidhe. Spend the day fishing and exploring them all. At the north end of Loyal, and accessed by a track between Loyal and Craggie, is an enigmatic little loch where I once lost one of the largest trout that I have ever hooked. Bank fishing, the trout ran three times, almost taking my line down to the backing, leaping spectacularly at the end of each run. I eventually brought it to net, already reciting the tales I would tell about its capture. As I put the net in the water, the trout awoke again and ran, but this time between my legs. Instead of just letting it run, I tried to step over the line and, in doing so, fell backwards into the loch, losing both my dignity and the fish in the process. But it was a beautiful fish, wondrously marked and, in my estimation, close to 10lb in weight.

North from Craggie, on the moor above Loch Slaim, are two tiny lochans, again unnamed on the OS Map. It appears that they may have been occasionally stocked with trout from Loch Slaim, which is redolent with small trout. Perhaps worth a cast or three?

There are some lochs which, regardless of the fish, are simply enchanting. I have already mentioned Loch Craisg and Loch Hakel. They fall into this category. Across the Kyle of Tongue is another, Loch a'Bhualaidh, a small loch at the end of a two-mile tramp from the narrow road that runs south from the causeway towards Kinloch. You will find a parking area in an old quarry just before the bridge over a tiny stream. Walk back up the road and, by the first passing-place signpost, you should make out a faint track that seems to be heading north. Take this track, which soon turns west, and follow it up to the loch. Attempting the approach to the loch in any other way will lead you into some really tough tramping. After a few minutes you will find Loch Fhoinnaich on your left, a lovely water in its own right and full of freely rising small trout, an ideal beginner's loch. Loch a'Bhualiadh is made of sterner stuff and contains specimen trout. I have seen a basket of five trout from a'Bhualiadh the smallest of which weighed 3lb and the largest 5lb 8oz. However, and you will not be surprised to hear, they are dour, dour, dour. Indeed, I would not need all of the fingers on one hand to count the number of trout that I have been able to tempt to rise to my flies, no matter how carefully presented. And yet I keep going back because it is such a magical place to be. On a warm day, lying back in the heather with a sandwich and a cup of coffee, I forget all about fish and, truthfully, about anything. Unless, of course, I hear the sound of a rising trout.

Sometimes I'm asked which my favourite loch is and I find it almost impossible to answer. Most anglers will be familiar with this dilemma, and I suppose the most accurate answer is to respond by saying, 'My favourite loch is the loch I am fishing when I'm fishing it.' But, secretly, we all know that some lochs are more favourite than others, like Loch Haluim. It lies like a silver-and-blue butterfly on the southern skirts of Ben Loyal, sur-rounded by about a dozen other lochs and lochans, named and unnamed. The tramp out from the A836 road at Inchkinloch is not for the faint-hearted, nearly three miles over broken ground. But the rewards for effort are huge: utter solitude, majestic scenery, red deer, otters, red-throated divers, golden eagle, golden plover and greenshank; and an amazingly prolific loch, which has a vast population of wild brown trout. They may not be large in size, but, as is the case with so many of the lochs I have talked about here, the residents rise readily and fight fiercely.

Ann and I have had many wonderful days on Haluim, alone and with other members of Clan Sandison; long days of fun and laughter, when everyone caught trout. Fishing Haluim with my son-in-law, Ian Smart, and grandson, Brodie, we once had more than 100 trout between us. Even in the early months of the season, fish rise, and they do so almost regardless of weather conditions. Whether from boat or bank, blank days are unheard of on Haluim, but the boat makes it easier to explore all the bays and corners of this lovely loch. There is generally only one boat on the loch, so while it is in use is the time to set off in search of further sport amongst the surrounding waters. To the north, Loch a'Mhadaidh-ruaidh and Loch an Aon-bhrid, and to the south, An Coal-loch, Loch nan Elachan and Lochan Sgeireach. Some of these waters hold trout of considerable size. Catching them, however, means being in the right place at the right time with the right fly. Crossing the fingers on your right hand could help as well.

My thoughts on Sutherland, its hills, mountains, moorlands, lochs and rivers, are dedicated to our son-in-law, Ian MacLeod Smart, head keeper on the Ben Loyal Estate, the best of friends.

BENBECULA AND UISTS

The earth belongs unto the Lord
And all that it contains,
Except the Kyles and Western Isles,
They're Caledonian MacBraynes
          – Adapted from Psalm 24, Scottish Psalter, 1650

BENBECULA

In August 1977, when we were living in Caithness, I arranged a family fishing holiday to North Uist and Benbecula in the Outer Hebrides. A few days prior to departure a strike disrupted my carefully laid plans: Caledonian MacBrayne employees had begun a work-to-rule stoppage and the ferry service between Kyle of Lochalsh and Skye was closed. Eventually, I devised an alternative route to Skye, but it meant sailing from Mallaig, which was, in those days, a wearisome five-hour drive from Caithness; particularly for eight-year-old Charles and little Jean, who was only three at the time. Stirred and shaken by the long journey and a bumpy sail from Uig on Skye to Lochmaddy, we arrived in North Uist and set off to find the caravan we had booked in Benbecula, a mile or so from the principal town on the island, Balivanich.

175

We had all been amazed by the number of lochs and lochans we'd passed along the way. Well, in truth, not all of us: Jean was asleep on Ann's knee and Charles was dozing in the back between Blair and Lewis-Ann. North Uist and Benbecula seemed to be more water than land and everywhere we looked the moorlands sparkled with silver and blue waters; some of the lochs were scattered with islands, many of which had their own lochs. Crossing the causeway from North Uist to Benbecula, the sea was emerald green, stippled with white-crested waves. I think the sudden shock of this enchanted landscape raised all our spirits. That was nearly forty years ago, but I can see it as clearly today as I did then. With the car unloaded and everything stowed away, Ann made supper and we were all soon slumbering soundly, dreaming, on my part, at least, of two weeks fishing and exploring this exciting new world.

Of all the Outer Hebridean islands, Benbecula, 'the hill of the fords', shows greatest sign of change. Balivanich is the administrative centre for the Uists and for the southern islands of Eriskay and Barra. In the late 1950s the Royal Artillery established headquarters in Balivanich to service their rocket range on South Uist and this military presence has grown steadily until the present day, when its future remains uncertain.

The airport, which is both military and civil, lies to the north of Balivanich, with connecting flights to Stornoway and Barra, Inverness and Glasgow; a constant, modern bustle that has brought a considerable degree of prosperity and comfort to the local community, including an excellent and much patronised shopping centre. Although the military presence is very obvious and not entirely welcomed by all, Benbecula still retains its individuality, culture and charm. The western shoreline is fringed with fertile, productive machair lands, extensively farmed and drained, and edged by golden beaches. Moorlands sweep eastwards towards the stormy waters of the Little Minch, deeply cut by fjord-like inlets and scattered with the ruined shielings of former days.

Benbecula is linked to its neighbours, North Uist and South Uist, by causeways and access is easy today. But before 1960, when the late HM Queen Mother opened the causeway across the North Ford, getting onto Benbecula from North Uist was not so simple. The only way in or out was by means of a dangerous passage across the soft sand flats of the North Ford, five difficult miles over constantly shifting sands. A traveller in the 1890s gave this account of his journey:

Heading due north, we came at last to the north coast of Benbecula and the entrance to the North Ford. Never before had I seen a more forbidding looking spot: before us lay many miles of mud and water, interspersed with islets and black rocks and dark tangles of seaweed clinging to them. My companion, a priest, pointed northeast and indicated the line of the path across the perilous ford. 'Do you see those two high rocks out there looking like two sentinels?' said he. 'Well, the path lies in a straight line between here and there. It is about two miles, and a yard or two on either side of it means that you are in quick sands which immediately swallow any man, horse, cart, or trap that deviates from that path. From those two rocks out there you have to pick up a mark to the northwest and proceed straight for that mark which stands at the other extremity of the ford.'

Turning to my companion I said: 'Father, have you ever crossed this ford?' 'Often,' was the reply. 'I was lost in it one night as I was returning from a sick call on the other side. It was a wild night and I mistook my bearings in the darkness. While I was trying to correct them, I lost my horse and trap in the quick sands. The tide overtook me and washed me away; but in the end I reached an islet out west there, and so remained until two men in a boat found me the next evening.' Then removing his hat, he patted his snow white hair, and smiled whimsically as he said: 'It gave me this.'

Wrecked and rusting cars are a feature of the Hebridean landscape. They appear in the most unlikely places: in fields as make-do hen houses; as half-sunken hulks, poking awkwardly from the shores of lochs. It is not easy to dispose of old cars on an island, although it is said that a newly arrived army officer once tried to help solve the problem. The story is told that he decided to establish a good reputation with the islanders by organising a weekend wreck collecting as an exercise for his men. After successfully retrieving a number of apparently abandoned vehicles from various unlikely locations, on the Monday morning, when he arrived at his office, he found it besieged by outraged islanders demanding to know who had 'stolen' their property – cars that had been kept for use as spare parts – and who was going to compensate them for their loss.

A short walk from our caravan, across mushroom-studded, cowpat-caked fields, lay Loch Dun Mhurchaidh, one of the best trout lochs on the island, known locally, appropriately, as the Caravan Loch. Not only does this loch contain excellent, and allegedly huge wild brown trout, but it is also noted for Dun Buidhe; a prehistoric fortified dwelling occupied at the time of the birth of Christ and sited at the tip of a narrow promontory fingering southwards from the north shore. The loch is three-quarters of a mile north to south by up to a quarter of a mile wide. Key to success here is to avoid wading; the loch is shallow and trout tend to lie close to the shore – wading only chases them out into deeper water. Keep a step or two back from the bank and cast a shortish line, smartly drawing the flies back towards you. Blair and I fished the loch early in the morning and invariably returned to the caravan with trout and mushrooms for breakfast.

We also spent a day exploring the lochs to the south of Dun

Mhurchaidh, between Pennylodden in the west and Market Stances in the east; ten waters, named and unnamed on the OS Map (Sheet 22, Benbecula, scale 1:50,000). We had great sport with trout that weighed between 8oz and 1lb, particularly in the long, narrow loch between Loch Bail'-fhionnlaidh and Loch Eilean Iain. At the end of the day, we stopped at the Bay of Culla, on the west coast, where Jean and Charles splashed in shallow, crystal-clear waters. Another convenient track begins at the burial ground at Nunton on the B892 road and takes you easily to another half-dozen named and unnamed lochs, which will also guarantee success and pleasure. Indeed, within the bounds of the B892 to the west and the A865 to the east there is sufficient fishing to keep you busy for weeks, let alone for a few days.

Prior to our first expedition to these airts, I had the great good fortune of meeting a retired army officer, Colonel Fraser, who had spent his last years in service stationed at Balivanich. He very kindly gave me a copy of a map upon which he had marked a number of lochs on Benbecula and North Uist that were his special places. Thus armed, we found Loch Ba Alasdair, a series of interlinked lochs that seemed to be a part of paradise. I set off to circle all of the waters, stopping on the way to give special attention to two tiny, unnamed lochans that the Colonel told me held specimen trout. They were, of course, dour, but the largest trout he had encountered there weighed over 4lb.

The headwater loch of the system lies on a hill above the main water and, for obvious reasons, is known locally as Bluebell Loch. It is probably one of the loveliest lochs that I know; all bank fishing and an endless delight of corners and fishy points. The time I spent there is indelibly stamped into my mind. I followed the outlet stream down from Bluebell Loch to the narrows, where Ba Alasdair enters the sea at Oban nan Forsanan, and found shoals of sea-trout swarming amidst the rocky spread of seaweed along the shore.

Another of my special places on Benbecula is somewhat more

distant: Loch Scarilode. It is in the east, beyond the gentle slopes of Rueval, where Prince Charles Edward Stuart waited impatiently in 1746 for Flora MacDonald and his escape to Skye disguised as her maid, Betty Burke. The track to the loch was originally a Clanranald kelp road and starts from Market Stance, the old centre of agricultural trading and cattle dealing on Benbecula. It winds past Loch Ba Una's shallow, sandy north shore, where we stopped for a picnic. Blair and I then left Ann, Charles and Jean to fish Ba Una, and continued eastwards. The track twists through the moors north of Loch Hermidale, then between Loch na Deighe fo Dheas and Loch na Deighe fo Thuath, swinging south-east over the hill and down to the shores of Loch Scarilode, where the remains of an old shieling stands above the sea at Oban Haka.

High banks surrounded Scarilode's deep blue waters. A red-decked rowan clung to a small promontory on the south bank. Heather covered the hillside and the emerald green of former cultivation brightened the bleached yellow of sedge and deer grass. Bank fishing was made awkward by the steep sides of the loch and the depth of the water close to the shore, but halfway down the north shore we discovered a flat, extensive ledge covered by a foot or so of water, which allowed easy and safe wading.

The trout we caught were not large but were wonderfully marked and spotted with red as red as rowan berries. More so, about the loch, there was a serenity that defies description, a sense of timelessness. In the 1940s the croft at Scarilode was still worked, children trekking hard miles north to school at Rossinish each day. The last family left Scarilode in the early 1970s, just before Blair and I first walked down that narrow Clanranald track. I was sorry to have missed them, but happy to have found a small piece of heaven at Scarilode.

NORTH UIST

A flight of shearwaters overtook us, hurrying low over the waves to some urgent appointment in North Uist. September showers swept in and I edged into a sheltered corner. A startlingly white wake flowed astern as our propellers churned through the green waters. Red buoys marking lobster pots bobbed by the rocky shore. As we approached the island, the way ahead seemed to present an unbroken, impenetrable wall, with the hills of North Lee (860ft) and South Lee (921ft), and Eaval (1,138ft) to the south, leaping from the grey waters of the Minch. Madha Beag and Madha Mor, the Gaelic for 'big dog' and 'little dog', twin islets, guard the narrow entrance to Loch Madha.

The ferry threaded its way past Glas Eilean Mor, Faihore and Ruigh Liath, bringing welcome respite from our stormy journey. Matchstick figures grew into sweater-clad seamen and the bustle of berthing and landing began; a gentle, ship side graze of steel against timber, a diminishing throb of engines, thick male ropes looped over dark iron bollards, cars and lorries key-twisted to life. Except one car, mine. I searched furiously through my pockets. No car keys. My blood pressure rose. I dashed back to the lounge and hunted under various tables. No keys. I explained to the crew member directing offloading what had happened and he said, 'Have you tried the boot?' The miscreant keys were there, where I had covered them with bits of jackets and fishing gear after boarding.

North Uist is seventeen miles long by twelve miles wide, but time and tide have shattered the island into a thousand pieces. Sea and freshwater lochs twist and intermingle in a mad maze through peat-covered moorlands surrounded by gently rounded hills and, on the west coast, fertile machair grasslands that blaze with wild-flowers in the soft Atlantic spring. Loch Madha itself wanders round a coastline of nearly 200 miles, scattered with hundreds of little islands, the most significant of which are Flodday, Hamersay, Ferramas, Cliasay Beg and Chasay Mor, Keallasay Beg, Keallasay

Mor, Minish and Cnap Ruigh Dubh. Headlands finger the bay, probing east, begging the sea to keep its distance.

I bumped down onto the pier and drove up to the white-fronted Lochmaddy Hotel, which dominates the harbour. I remember a previous owner of the hotel, George Peart, telling me of his introduction to one of Lochmaddy's many characters. One morning, soon after George had arrived, a small, weather-beaten figure appeared at the door.

'Good morning, Mr Peart, I'm your dustbin man.'

George shook his hand and asked, 'Oh, is that so, and exactly what is it that you do for me?'

'Well, you see,' came the reply, 'every Thursday morning I take the dustbins from behind the hotel and place them by the road. When they have been emptied, I take them back.'

George thought for a moment and then asked how much this service cost. 'No more than ten pound a week and very good value it is too.'

On further investigation, it transpired that the old rogue had never in his life lifted anything heavier than a pint mug or a dram to his mouth. George politely declined the offer and said he would do the job himself.

Lochmaddy is a tiny cluster of neat houses clinging precariously to the bay, as though constantly surprised at having successfully survived centuries of turbulent Scottish history. Its people are courteous and welcoming, as Dr Samuel Johnson experienced and described during his Highland tours with Boswell in 1773: 'Civility seems a part of the national character of the Highlands,' he said. The harbour was once busy with upwards of 300 vessels during the herring fishing season. Vikings called the village home; stroking their dragon-headed, shield-sparkling longships through the broken Hebridean waters to shores crowded with waiting women and ragged, cheering children. Medieval pirates sought shelter and provisions at Lochmaddy during murderous forays in the Minch.

The village is a quieter place today and is the main population centre of the island's 1,700 inhabitants. A primary school serves the needs of little ones before they are thrust into the world of secondary education at the senior school on Benbecula. There is a single church, the Free Church, a courthouse, a tourist information centre by the ferry terminal and the village store, run for many years by a Mrs Morrison. The first time I called at the shop, in 1979, I noticed an antique glass display case on the counter, filled with cakes and Bibles. God is alive and well on North Uist, and has been for more than 1,000 years.

One of the most important religious sites in the Outer Hebrides was in the south-west of North Uist, close to the village of Carinish and just before the start of the causeway across the sands of the North Ford to Benbecula. Teampull na Tnonad, Trinity Church, built by Bertrice, Prioress of Iona in the early years of the thirteenth century; an important university for priests. Teampull na Trionad's most famous scholar was Johannes Duns Scotus (1265–1308). Duns Scotus also studied and lectured at Oxford and in Paris, where he argued against the Christian theology propounded by Thomas Aquinas. Duns maintained that theology was built upon faith, not upon theory. A practical man. A Scot. The ruins of the Teampull, where Duns Scotus spent his youth, still watch over the tides that race to cover the shifting sands between Baleshare Island and Carinish.

Nearby is a small graveyard where the remains of many of Clan MacDonald lie asleep in peace. This is more than can be said for the unfortunate victims of the last great clan battle in the Hebrides. This was fought in 1601 between the ever-fractious MacDonalds of North Uist and the Harris Macleods. The fight took place near Carinish, close to Johannes Duns Scotus' church. The bodies were dumped unceremoniously in a burn known to this day as 'the ditch of blood'.

North Uist is circled by the A865, which has one spur northwards to Newtonferry, the stepping-off place to the island of

Berneray, which lies a few miles over a seal-bobbing sound and now linked to North Uist by a causeway. Although there is no record of Prince Charles Edward Stuart ever hiding on Berneray after Culloden, a more modern Prince Charles 'hid' there a few years ago, living the crofter's life and planting his potatoes along with the rest of the islanders. The only difference with Prince Charlie's tatties and those of his neighbours was that when news leaked out a clamour of London journalists descended upon Berneray offering a king's ransom in cash for our future monarch's spuds. They should have known better. Two hundred and fifty years ago the people of the Hebrides refused a reward of £30,000 to hand over the earlier Prince Charles and were hardly likely to accept modern blandishments of cash for the hard work of another.

Berneray's links with royalty go even further back than Bonnie Prince Charlie. The island is the birthplace of Sir Norman Macleod of Berneray, a supporter of King Charles I during the English civil war. Macleod led a group of his clansmen in the Royalist forces at the Battle of Worcester in 1651. When the Royalists were defeated, Norman Macleod and his brother had to flee for their lives. After the Restoration in 1660, King Charles II repaid the Macleods' loyalty by granting them knighthoods. Berneray is a lovely island, quiet and peaceful, with splendid beaches along the west coast.

Just as splendid are Berneray's only two lochs, Loch Bhruist and Little Loch Borve, not only because of the trout they hold but also because of the supreme beauty of their surroundings. They lie on the edge of the machair, which in spring and summer is a vast, coloured carpet of wildflowers, loud with the cry of the resident and visiting birds that nest there. Bhruist is a shallow loch, about three-quarters of a mile long by some 400 yards wide. Trout average around 1lb in weight, with good numbers of fish up to and over 2lb. It is easily fished from the bank and wading is comfortable, although a boat is sometimes available. Bhruist drains south into tiny Little Loch Borve. Little Borve is so small that the whole loch can be covered from the shore. Don't wade. Keep well back from the bank to avoid alerting the inhabitants of your evil intent. The Berneray lochs are not over-fished, since relatively few anglers are aware of their existence. Hurry along and make their acquaintance.

Back on North Uist, I fondly remember a day we spent on Loch Eashader with our children. The loch lies to the south of Middlequarter, in the north of the island, and is accessed from the A865 by a rough track after a seriously bumpy mile. As is the case with so many waters in the Hebrides, the setting is spectacular: Ben Aulasary (712ft) and Marrival (755ft) to the south, and Sgurr an Duin (367ft) and Beinn Dubh Shollais (301ft) to the north. We set up camp at the east end of the loch and fished down the south bank, where it was safe to wade and there were little headlands and bays to explore. The fish were not large, but they rose readily to the fly and fought splendidly. There are a number of other small waters, named and unnamed on the OS map, and they all drain to the east into their large neighbour, Loch nan Geireann, two miles distant over the moor. Eashader is a special place. The day was warm, with only a gentle breeze. The picnic was excellent and the fishing rewarding. What angler could ask for more?

Loch nan Geireann is one of North Uist's finest lochs, more commonly known as Geireann Mill because of the old watermill that lies close to where anglers park their cars, off the A865. The loch is two miles long and up to three-quarters of a mile wide across the bay that is divided by Aird Reamhar, a long and narrow island, where the remains of drinking vessels and plates dating from prehistoric times suggest that this could have been the site of a pottery factory for the whole of North Uist. I have no doubt that those so engaged also fished that loch. They would have found then, as anglers do today, that Geireann Mill had salmon, sea-trout and a huge stock of brown trout. Bank fishing is possible, but get afloat to more readily explore that large water. Treat every rise with caution. It could be just another small trout, or it could be something much larger. This is the special joy of fishing Geireann.

Further joy may be found where the flow from Geireann winds across shining white sands to reach the sea past the island of Oronsay and the long finger of Corran Aird a' Mhorain. With care, at low tide, it is possible to walk over these sands to a wonderful sea pool, where Clett and Rubha Glas form a barrier to the returning Atlantic. A rocky breakwater holds back the foam-flecked breakers, forming a sheltered seaweed-fringed pool. Crystal-clear waters reflect the colours of sands, clouds and sky – green, emerald, silver, blue and gold; salmon and sea-trout, shining bars of silver, surge in with the tide, leaping and splashing in a heart-stopping display. If North Uist means anything to me, then the evening view of the Geireann sea pool is my dearest thought; a memory that brightens the darkest hour, filling my mind and heart with hope and beauty.

This area of North Uist suffered dreadfully during the dark days of the Highland Clearances, when Lord Macdonald, the laird, decided to evict his tenants so that their land could be let out more profitably to sheep farmers. Alexander Mackenzie, in his masterly history of the Highland Clearances, written in 1883, described the plight of the people of Sollas:

> Notices of ejectment were served to take effect on the 15th May, 1849. When the people refused to move Mr Colquhoun, the Sheriff Substitute, arrived at Sollas with a force of thirty three policemen from Inverness and brutally evicted the families. There was considerable resistance, principally from the women of Sollas, but to little avail.

In 1850, the other villages on the north coast were also cleared: Malaclete, Middlequarter, Dunskellor and Grenitote, amounting to 603 people. Macdonald's factor defended his actions concerning the evictions from his Hebridean estates claiming that he had been 'prompted by motives of benevolence, piety and humanity, because the people were too far from church'.

Alexander Mackenzie gave the laird and his henchmen a proper blessing: 'Oh God! what crimes have been committed in Thy name, and in that of religion? Preserve us from such piety and humanity as were exhibited by Lord Macdonald and his factor on this and other occasions.'

There are several hundred freshwater lochs on North Uist, a lifetime's fishing, but before leaving, come with me to another special place: Oban Sponish, an inlet on the long fjord on the north shore of Loch Eport. As the crow flies, it is two miles south from the A867 Lochmaddy to Clachan road. However, being unable to fly, the way across the moor to Oban Sponish is a taxing journey, as the unmarked route twists and turns round the myriad shores of Loch Scadavay and its satellite waters. If you are unfamiliar with the route, take a compass. I was, however, lucky in that my son, Blair, who was then living and working in the islands, led the way.

A bar of rock across the mouth of the inlet holds back the rising tide until it is covered, and sea-trout flood in on the flow. Casting to them is challenging because of the rocky nature of the banks and the fronds of seaweed, but few angling experiences, in my view, can match the thrill of hooking and playing a sea-trout in these conditions. Their strength is quite remarkable. The best time to fish is about two hours before low tide and two hours as the tide turns. It might seem a long way to tramp for four hours' fishing, but it is worth every step of the way, believe me.

SOUTH UIST

Before the present-day causeways were built, the ford between Benbecula and South Uist was shorter than its meandering northern neighbour between Benbecula and North Uist. Because of this, the South Ford crossing was always the most dangerous;

people tended to take chances with the tide, dashing across the sands at the last minute and some paid with their lives for this indiscretion. The Creagorry Hotel, on the north shore, in Benbecula, was a busy and well-patronised place by those waiting to cross the white sands. John Francis Campbell, a Gaelic scholar who stayed there in 1859, wrote, 'A general air of listlessness lay about the whole establishment. Breakfast, ordered at 8 and no sign of it until 10, but a capital place for stories.' When my wife Ann and I paid our first visit to the hotel in 1977, there was little evidence of any 'general air of listlessness'; the bar was brim-full of laughing people, all telling capital stories, in Gaelic. Not being blessed with the Gaelic, the stories remained the property of the tellers and of their listeners. Other potential items of portable property lined the shelves behind the bar: neat rows of brown paper bags, each containing a half bottle of whisky and two cans of export, pre-packed carry-outs to save serving time when 'Last Orders!' was called. The hotel was noted in the *Guinness Book of Records* for the vast amount of 'water of life' consumed there, and this tradition is alive and well today.

The causeway over the South Ford was completed in 1942 and is still known as O'Regan's Bridge, named after the priest who was most active in encouraging its construction. It transformed life on the islands, and during the war provided a vital military link with the airfield at Balivanich. The original single-track road was replaced in 1982 by a two-lane highway across the shifting sands of the South Ford, which were, and still are, a popular place for gathering cockles and other shellfish. To the west, a long line of Atlantic waves whiten the horizon, rushing towards the black ribbon of the causeway.

When I last crossed the ford, I felt the customary nerve-tingle of excitement that I always feel arriving on South Uist. The island is about twenty-two miles in length by up to eight miles wide and my old friend, the A865 road, runs the line of the west coast, from Lochmaddy in North Uist to Lochboisdale in South Uist.

Lochboisdale is the principal town on the island, established in the eighteenth century. In the mid-nineteenth century Gordon of Cluny, then the laird, evicted most of his tenants and packed them off to Canada.

The South Uist mountains of Hecla (1,988ft), Corodale (1,729ft) and Beinn Mhor (2,034ft) dominate the eastern horizon and, shortly after crossing the South Ford, another causeway crosses the emerald and green waters between Loch Bee and East Loch Bee. East Bee is a huge expanse of shallow and brackish water, almost a mile long by half a mile wide. It has several 'arms' that narrow and nearly cut the northern part of South Uist in half. The Atlantic just about meets the Minch through the narrows at Clachan and is only prevented from doing so by floodgates at the head of Loch Skipport. East Loch is considered to be one of the best trout lochs in South Uist.

When my granddaughter Jessica was little, and staying with us, Ann used to put her to bed and say her prayers: 'This night when I lie down to sleep, I pray the Lord my soul to keep . . .' and so on. One evening, Ann had got to the blessing bit – 'Mummy and Daddy . . . and everyone else' – but when Ann said, 'and bless all my friends at school,' Jessica's eye opened and she said, 'Not all of them, Granny, not all of them.' I confess that I feel the same way about East Loch Bee.

I have never caught a significantly large trout there and I have thrashed it, unsuccessfully, to a foam on many occasions. Yet I cannot deny its attraction, and thus I keep going back for more, in the firm belief that the longer I remain fishless, the sooner my day will come.

My son Blair was secretary of the South Uist Angling Club and used to send me regular updates of fishing the loch, along with photographs of the trout he caught there. Indeed, I have seen a wonderful fish, taken by young Jeremy Paterson from where the tide from West Loch Bee flows through the culvert under the causeway into East Loch Bee. It weighed over 4lb. Blair and one of his chums, Ian Jack, used to compete to see who would say 'stop' as their boat drifted ever further into shallow water, barely two feet deep, and invariably caught splendid trout as they did so. Bee is very lovely and part of this delight is exploring the long 'arms' that lead off from the main body. The Shell Loch, unnamed on the OS map, is approached down the section of Bee that leads to the Flood Gate. Shell Loch, in itself, is a substantial water, reputed to hold excellent trout. Getting to it, however, can be difficult. I remember upon one occasion, when water levels were low, having to get out of the boat and drag it over a sand bar whilst being watched by about two dozen highly suspicious mute swans.

Whilst I can't recount any personal piscatorial triumphs, I can, however, tell of a moment that has always remained with me. It was at the end of the day, when Ann and I were mooring the boat. Evening gathered round us. As we watched the changing colours, a dark shape flung itself from Hecla's high corries: a golden eagle, soaring in the mountain thermals, its vast, dark wings seemingly motionless, pitch-black against the gold and white sky. A second bird majestically appeared, and the two turned, wheeled and twisted in an amazing display. We held our breath, speechess in wonderment. It was a moment of complete beauty and certainty. I think that these moments shape our lives and define that which we understand, and what we believe. Perhaps this is why we fish and why we know that catching trout is but a small part of being an angler, and why we are blessed.

Another gem in the northern part of South Uist is Loch Druidibeg, a National Nature Reserve cared for by Scottish Natural Heritage and covering more than 3,500 acres. The reserve was established in 1958 and is considered to be an outstanding example of the gradual change from heather-clad peat moorlands to the gentle, fertile coastal machair plain that fringes the western shores of South Uist. The loch is a wild scattering of small islands, secret bays and promontories, drawing its strength from the heights of Hecla, a mighty monument of Lewisian gneiss, the oldest rocks in Britain. The islands in Druidibeg preserve ancient, native woodlands, protected from the ungentle administration of men, sheep and cattle by the dark, acid waters of the loch.

Willow, rowan, birch and juniper grow in profusion on these islands; wild hyacinth, angelica, meadowsweet and royal fern abound. Greylag geese call Druidibeg home, living there throughout the year. Those most lovely of all Highland birds, black-throated divers, nest on the islands and by the shores. But the reserve is not a museum; it is a modern, working entity, demonstrating that man and nature can live in beneficial harmony. Druidibeg's moor and machair blossom into glorious colour in spring and summer, with bluebell, yellow bird's-foot-trefoil, purple harebell, red clover, daisy, orchids, eyebright, lady's bed-straw and wild thyme.

The lime-rich machair is used for crofting in the traditional way: livestock graze the machair during winter months and are taken out to the hills in summer. Consequently, plant life flourishes, and the lochs provide an ideal habitat for waders: dunlin, redshank, snipe, ringed plover, oystercatcher and lapwing. Heron and otter hunt the lochs; corncrake grate from shoreline reeds and marshy tussocks; corn bunting and twite nibble heads of ripening oats and barley; hen harrier, kestrel, peregrine, merlin and short-eared owl sweep over the silent lands in search of prey.

Until recently, fishing was prohibited on the loch, but is now available. My information is that, like many of the South Uist hill lochs, the trout are small and in the order of three-to-the-pound, but I have no doubt that much larger specimens are present. However, and unquestionably, it is a wonderful place to fish.

South from Hecla, the island rears heavenwards in a wild range of dramatic peaks, formed by the force of the massive geological thrust plane that created the Hebrides millions of years ago. Ben Corodale, breached by Bealach Hellisdale, leads down to the remote cave on the cliffs overlooking the sea where Prince Charles

Edward Stewart hid in 1746. To the west, roads lead out into the machair and the village of Howbeg. One of South Uist's most famous sons, Neil MacEachan, a school teacher, was born in the village. He was one of Prince Charlie's most loyal and devoted supporters. After the disaster of the Battle of Culloden, MacEachan travelled with his fugitive would-be king during all his long Highland and island journeys, and was with the prince when he was rowed to safety over the sea to Skye.

MacEachan eventually arrived in France, where he married and settled in Sedan, and in 1765 had a son, Jacques Etienne Joseph MacDonald. Jacques joined the French army in 1785 and quickly gained fame during the turbulent years of the French Revolution. In 1798, he was made Governor of Rome and, in 1809, after the Battle of Wagram, Napoleon elevated this Celtic soldier to the rank of general and made him a Marshall of France and Duke of Taranto. But Etienne never forgot his Hebridean origins and in 1826 he made the long journey back to South Uist. He visited his father's home at Howbeg and gathered up a box of earth and stones from his father's land, which he carried back to France. When Jacques died at Courcelles le Roi in 1840, the soft machair soil joined him in his grave.

Less easy to remove from the South Uist environment are the inhabitants of its superb freshwater lochs, which are home to some of the finest quality wild brown trout in Europe, as well as salmon and sea-trout. For a number of years Ann and I took the rental of Gorgarry Lodge for two weeks in June, which is perhaps the best time for fishing the machair lochs, as some tend to become weedy as the season advances. Grogarry Loch itself was only minutes away from the lodge. The loch has a well-deserved reputation of being home to specimen trout and I always enjoyed being there. Boat fishing brings the best results and although, in truth, there is no one area of the loch better than another, most of the action I had seemed to occur at the west side, where the water shallows onto a sandy bottom. Just where the water begins to shallow, there the trout would rise. Fishing the south end, where there are a number of little islets, was also a favourite area.

However, I often found myself bank fishing the loch immediately to the north of Grogarry, Loch nam Balgan. The trout there average around three-quarters of a pound, with a few larger fish as well, although I rarely caught anything over 1lb in weight. But they were extremely beautiful trout and nam Blagan really was a splendid little loch to fish, with comfortable wading all round. In high winds, when launching a boat was impossible, nam Balgan was always welcoming.

To the east of nam Blagan and joined to it by a small stream, there is an unnamed loch that is infrequently fished. I decided to explore it one evening after supper. I found the south bank to be virtually impossible to fish from, but the north bank was ideal, provided, of course, the wind was right. I stayed on the bank because wading looked uninviting and cast a short line armed with three flies, traditional Scottish patterns and old friends of mine: Messrs Ke-He, March Brown and Silver Butcher. I caught only one fish, but it was the largest brown trout that I have taken from South Uist waters and weighed just under 4lb.

Loch Stilligarry, to the south of Grogarry, also holds notoriously large trout, although they can be hard to tempt to the fly. I have never had much success on Stilligarry, except for one memorable occasion some years ago in April. We were staying with Blair and his wife, Barbara. Although probably too early in the season, it was decided that we should have a walk on the beach and, thereafter, picnic at Stilligarry and maybe have a cast or two or three, just to show willing. After a fishless half-hour, I found that I was the only angler left and, glancing over my shoulder, I noticed Blair with his hip-flask at the ready, to warm the inner man.

That was when I heard the trout rise, just a bit too far out for me to reach. I was not wearing waders, only boots, but I was determined to cover the rise and waded in, catching my breath as the cold water engulfed my legs. I managed to cast over the spot where the fish had risen and he took my tail fly. That trout fought furiously, but I managed to beach him after what was only a few minutes, although to me it seemed like a lifetime. Triumphantly, I marched back to the car with my prize and announced, 'Is there a dram spare amongst you fair-weather fishers for a real angler?'

Blair always showed his worth as an angler, and as a gentleman. He was with us one week at Grogarry when fishing was difficult and our companions were becoming increasingly unhappy about the lack of fish. At the end of the day Blair returned from Stilligarry with a brace of the most perfect trout you could ever wish to see, each weighing 2lb 8oz. Everybody's spirits were lifted and they all began to catch fish. Blair's success reminded me of a similar incident, told to me by one of South Uist's legendary gillies, the late Charlie MacLean, who I had the privilege of meeting in the 1980s. Charlie was born on the island of Tiree and was a gentle, soft-spoken man with an accent redolent of heather and hills. We sat before a blazing peat fire, an April gale howling outside and a good dram inside, whilst we talked.

Charlie told me, 'Some years ago a party of sportsmen were staying at Greagory Lodge. Twelve of the guests fished, so every evening names were drawn from a hat to decide who should have which loch the following day and I had to gillie for the folk who drew West Loch Ollay. Now this is a very good loch, a machair loch, near Ormiclate Castle, about three-quarters of a mile long by half-a-mile wide, and with trout that average more than 2lb. Well, I fished that loch all week, each day with a different gentleman, and no matter how hard we tried we never touched a fish. You can imagine, come Friday evening, that no one was anxious to fish "that" loch again.

'The gentleman who drew West Loch Ollay arrived at the lochside on the Saturday morning looking very despondent. But by the end of the day it was an entirely different matter: eighteen beautiful fish were in the boat, not one less than 2lb. We took trout from all over the loch: by the islands, in the shallows, along the weed-beds, in the deep – as perfect a basket of trout I have never seen before or since. Nor have I ever seen such a happy smile on a man's face. My gentleman could hardly wait to show off his catch at the lodge.

'What a commotion there was, then, and it was mostly coming in my direction: I hadn't taken them to the right places; I'd put up the wrong flies; it was all my fault that they hadn't got good baskets as well. So I asked my gentleman to show his friends exactly where we'd been fishing. They trooped through to the big map on the wall and my gentleman pointed out exactly where we'd taken the fish – and weren't they the very same places where we'd been fishing all week! But the fish were on their tails that day and no mistake. We were just lucky to be in the right place at the right time, for no matter how well you know a loch, if the fish aren't in the mood, there's nothing you can do about it other than to keep on trying and trusting to luck.'

This leads me to recount another story that Charlie told, and one that has become a significant part of my angling armory, particularly when the fish are being dour. Two gentlemen were in the boat with Charlie at the time: Ian Christie, a solicitor from the island of Skye, and a local man, Kenny McKinnon.

Charlie said, 'It had been a long day, with not much doing, and hope of a good basket fading fast. Now, Ian had a small cassette player with him and a tape of Gaelic melodies sung by Callum Kennedy. So, to pass the time, he turned on the recorder. There was still no sign of fish. But then, as the beautiful song, "My brown-haired girl", was playing, up came as beautiful a trout and grabbed Ian's fly. No further fish rose, so when the tape was finished, they played it again and the moment the strains of "My brown-haired girl" floated over the loch, up came another trout. Now this seemed to be too much of a coincidence, so they rewound the tape and stopped it just before the magic melody. No sign of a trout. But as soon as "My brown-haired girl" was sung, up came another trout and took Ian's fly. During the course of the afternoon they tried several other tunes on the fish, but they liked nothing other than "My brown-haired girl". It was played again and again, and each time it produced a fish, until they called it a day.'

After hearing Charlie's story, I did feel doubt, and he sensed that, and gave me Ian Christie's telephone number. I phoned Ian, and he confirmed that what Charlie had said was entirely true, and that Kenny McKinnon would also verify the facts. Ian was an innovative fly-tier and said that he would send me a copy of the fly he had designed and named the Charlie MacLean, in honour of that memorable event. I have fished with a Charlie MacLean ever since and sung to trout. Believe me, it does work. How, I know not, but it does.

I find it difficult to say which my favourite machair loch is because they are all very special places to fish: West Loch Ollay, mid Loch Ollay and east Loch Ollay – until we got to know them better, Ann and I cruelly dubbed them bugger Ollay, sugar Ollay and damn Ollay. I should confess, however, that the only salmon I have caught on the Uists was taken on a Charlie MacLean when I was bank fishing along the rocky north shore of East Loch Ollay with John Kennedy, then fishery manager for the South Uist Estate. John took a 3lb trout that must have migrated through the system from West Loch Ollay. Other machair lochs I know well include Altaburg, Bornish, Upper Loch Bornish, Upper Loch Kildonan and Loch Hallan.

Then, of course, there are the sea-trout and salmon waters. I don't know them well, other than that they can produce out-standing sport: Schoolhouse, Roag and Fada, which drain through the Howmore River to the sea. The Howmore is the only significant river in the Uists and Benbecula. The other sea-trout and salmon systems are Loch Kildonan and the Mill Loch, and the Barph system, which drains into the sea near the township of Lochboisdale.

I remember an unforgettable day on Upper Kildonon with a friend, the late Alistair Grunert. I used to fish with Alistair at Altnaharra in north Sutherland, where he acquired the nickname 'Five Salmon Grunert', for his expertise on Loch Naver. Alistair was always prepared to adapt his technique to suit prevailing conditions, but he really excelled himself that day on Upper Kidonon. The wind was blowing hard and I doubted that we would be able to launch the boat and would have to bank fish. I glanced round to see that Alistair was not putting up his rod but assembling a large and colourful kite. Astonished, I asked, 'What on earth are you doing? We are here to fish, not to fool around with kites.'

'Bruce, I just wanted to see if I could hook a trout using the kite,' Alistair explained.

'And exactly how do you intend to do that?' I enquired, suspiciously.

Alistair showed me. He attached a length of nylon to the tail of the kite and then tied on a large, bushy dapping fly. 'This way I will be able to stand on the bank and fly the kite out over the water, I will work the kite so that dap dances along the surface and attracts a fish. Now, Bruce, stop arguing and help me launch the kite.'

'You must be joking,' I replied. 'What if someone comes along and catches us at it?'

'As far as I am aware there is no law that says we can't fish with a kite. After all, in the Far East they use cormorants, so what's the problem?'

I confess that I was intrigued, and held the kite aloft whilst Alistair backed away, letting out line. 'Now,' he shouted, and I let go, and the kite immediately took off in the strong breeze and swooped over the loch. Clearly, Alistair had been practising somewhere because he so skilfully controlled the gaudy kite that the dapping fly began dancing along the waves in a most enticing manner and, a few moments later, sure enough, a trout rose and took the fly. Alistair jerked hard on the control strings and the trout was lifted into the air. This is exactly when I noticed an angler who had been bank fishing further up the loch coming towards us.

He was concentrating, watching where he was putting his feet rather than looking up in the air, where Alistair's trout was directly above his head. He walked by, completely unaware of what was happening, placed his rod in the boot of his car and drove off. Alistair brought the trout to the ground, a fish of about 1lb in weight and none the worse for its brief experience of flying. It was unhooked and restored to the loch.

Thinking that our controversial act had gone unnoticed, I breathed a sigh of relief, only to see an estate Land Rover heading our way.

'For goodness sake, Alistair, get that damned kite in the car, now,' I said.

The Land Rover stopped and Big Alastair's head appeared. Alastair was one of the keepers and was big, very big, but a gentle giant. 'How's it going, boys?' he asked. 'Any luck?'

'Not much,' Alastair I replied. 'What would you suggest?

Big Alastair thought for a moment, then said, 'Well, really, it is a choice between two alternatives. You can go south to Lochboisdale or north to Grogarry. But you will find that both the pubs there are open. Good luck.' He gave us a cheery wave and drove off.

Alistair immediately brightened. 'That's great, Bruce, I'll get the kite out again.'

'Alastair, never in a million years. Which way do you want to go, north or south?'

I also always enjoyed fishing Altabrug, a loch of two parts: the larger western section is on the machair, whilst its eastern part is more peaty and dark in nature. If you are new to these airts, as I once was, finding your way to the boat mooring-bay is a bit of a challenge. So many narrow roads head west from the A865 that it can be confusing finding the right one. Having done so, you will find that the boat is conveniently moored roughly midway between the two sections of the loch. Thus, if it is windy, you can find shelter in the east part, whilst if it is calm, then you may attack the machair section.

There is a small island just offshore at the mooring-bay that was probably artificially made in prehistoric times. A Dun, a fortified dwelling house, would have been built on it, the oldest example of which is in North Uist and thought to have been built between 3,200 BC and 2,800 BC. I was fishing Altaburg one day with Ian Alison, an Edinburgh doctor, and Tom Rochford, a barrister from the south of England who was exactly the opposite to Big Alasdair, noted above. Tom always had a little nap after lunch. That day, he had settled himself in the bow of the boat to do so, as I rowed upwind into the machair part of Altaburg. It was a hard row and I was trying to get up to begin the drift as quickly as possible. Missing a stroke completely, I toppled backwards at speed, landing on top of Tom, much to his alarm and discomfort. When he had recovered, I suggested, rather unkindly, that rather than sleeping perhaps he would like to row, thus avoiding a similar accident. This suggestion was politely refused, but Tom remained cautiously alert for the rest of the journey.

However, my favourite machair loch would probably be Bornish, which is, in my opinion, one of the UK's premier trout lochs: shallow, lime-rich, three-quarters of a mile from north to south, by up to a quarter of a mile across. The trout are outstandingly lovely and average in the order of 12oz to 1lb in weight, although larger fish of up to and over 3lb are not uncommon. Fish rise and can be taken through the length and breadth of the loch, although I have always found the south end, below the island close to where the boats are moored, to be the most productive area. The trout rise readily, even when the wind is blowing hard. I once had two visitors with me who were desperate to fish the loch, as they were leaving the island the following day.

The wind was really hard and I knew that it would be impossible to handle the boat in these conditions. However, I decided there was one chance. We roped the boat up to the shore near the west end of the loch, where I explained my plan. We should get the boat out from the edge as far as we could, then, with a drogue forward and aft, ready to chuck in the loch, allow the wind to take us down the loch in one long drift. Any fish taken would have to be landed by the angler who caught them, alone, and as quickly as possible. I am quite sure that to this day these guys regularly dine out on their account of that wild, mad drift down Loch Bornish. We bumped ashore, wet and shaken, in a bit of a heap at the east end, but with, remarkably, four fish in the boat, then roped it back to the mooring-bay.

But I love Bornish for other reasons as well as for the quality of its inhabitants. And particularly for the wildflowers that surround its shores. It is not difficult to find thirty different species within a few square yards, including magnificent orchids. On a soft evening touched by a whisper of sea scent, oystercatchers chatter and curlews call. Otters have fished beside my boat.

All that fishing means to me seems to live peacefully at Bornish.

These pages are dedicated to James Paterson, the complete angler, and to his wife and 'minder', Rosalyn, who have been our wonderful friends for many years. Also to their sons, Jonathan and Jeremy, with happy memories of times we have shared together fishing.

ADDENDUM

Ad rud bhois na do bhroin, cha bhi e na do thiomhnadh
(That which you have wasted will not be there for
future generations)

– Gaelic saying

MACHAIR

The word 'machair' is used extensively in the section of this book
about North Uist, Benbecula and South Uist. Machair is a Gaelic
word meaning grasslands and the most extensive areas of
machair are to be found on the west coasts of the Uists and
Benbecula. For those who may not be familiar with the name I
thought that it might be useful to give a description of the
machair, how it was formed and of its importance as a breeding
site for native and visiting birds, invertebrates and for the astonishing array of wildflowers that flourish there. The machair is
unique in Europe and is only found in the western and northern
isles.

The machair has developed over thousands of years, through
wave action and wind. Creatures living in the shallows, and
shells, are ground down and washed towards the shore. The
wind then picks them up and blows them inland, covering the

soil in the immediate vicinity of the coastal plain. Thus, this land becomes enormously fertile and made even more so by traditional farming methods; primarily seasonal grazing by cattle and the cultivation of crops such as potatoes, oats and rye. Late June is perhaps the most rewarding time to see the machair, when, on South Uist, for instance, a twenty-mile-long wildflower carpet extends from Rubha Aird na Machrach in the north to Ceann a' Gharaidh in the south.

When Ann and I think of the island, in our mind's eye we see this wonderful wildlife garden. Ann's primary interest is wildflowers, whilst I have always had a love affair with birds. Within a small space, it is possible to find more than three dozen different species of wild flower, including purple, spotted and butterfly orchid. In spring the machair is bright with the colours of different species of wildflower; bluebells, yellow birds foot trefoil, harebell corn marigold, buttercup and daisies. At the RSPB nature reserve at Balranald in North Uist, rare red-necked phalarope breed. The machair hosts 25 per cent of the UK's breeding population of dunlin and ringed-plover, along with redshank, lapwing, snipe and oystercatcher. The numbers of corncrake, with their 'rusty-engine', grating call is increasing. In winter, the machair welcomes twite, corn bunting and white clouds of snow bunting.

Get there if you can and experience one of the most remarkable sights on planet earth.

THE BATTLE OF THE FLOWS

The Flow Country of Caithness and East Sutherland is a vast area of more than 1,500 square miles and it played a pivotal role in my life, and in that of my wife, Ann, and our children. When we lived in Caithness from 1975 until 1990, the Flow Country became our playground. As a family, we tramped miles there, fishing; a landscape of peat moorlands scattered with blue lochs and lochans, peopled by red deer, wildcat and otters, greenshank, golden plover and dunlin. Hen harriers quartered these open lands, hunting for prey amidst red-tinged sphagnum tussocks, bog asphodel, milkwort, sundew and spotted orchids. The Flow Country had lain largely untouched by the hand of man since the end of the last Ice Age and was widely recognised as being the finest remaining example of blanket bog in the world. Today, it is being proposed as a UNESCO World Heritage Site.

Some of this precious landscape was severely damaged during the 1980s by inappropriate factory tree-farming, entirely driven by wealthy investors to avoid paying tax, including Dame Shirley Potter, a former leader of Westminster Council, TV personality Terry Wogan, singer Cliff Richard and snooker star Alex 'Hurricane' Higgins. The company at the centre of the system was Fountain Forestry Limited; they bought the land from local lairds and then sold it on to private investors on the basis that Fountain Forestry would plant and manage the trees on their behalf; at its height, if I remember correctly, there were 147 investors, all with either London or Home County addresses, none of whom, to my knowledge, ever visited their land or their trees.

At that time Fountain Forestry's managing director in the north of Scotland was Michael Ashmole. Mr Ashmole, in defending his company against criticism that the planting was destroying the habitat of greenshank, famously replied '. . . if the bird can't survive on the land we leave unplanted then it doesn't bloody-well deserve to survive.' He and his fellow directors managed to survive quite well on salaries in the order of £80,000 to £100,000 a year (in today's terms, nearer £1 million), but the greenshank were not so lucky. Greenshank are summer visitors who return to the same nesting sites each year, generally close to a large rock for ease of recognition, and adjacent to a source of water. When the chicks hatch and can see and walk, the parent birds take them to drink. But after the forestry ploughs had done their work, the birds were faced with ridges four feet in depth, which they were unable to negotiate.

Ann and I had seen for ourselves what was happening in the Flow Country during our walks there, so we decided that we would try to do something to stop the destruction. Thus, from 1985 until 1988, when the planting stopped, we devoted ourselves to that task. I wrote about what was happening, arranged radio and television coverage of the planting, and contributed to a seemingly endless number of radio and television programmes. I remember working with a team from News at 10, headed by Lawrence McGinty, ITV science editor. I took the team to the deserted village of Broubster, cleared of its population during the nineteenth century, and suggested to Lawrence that the camera should focus through a broken window of a croft house onto the rows of conifers behind.

'Why?' he asked.

'Because,' I replied, 'those trees belong to Terry Wogan.'

I also engineered an extraordinary annual general meeting of the Caithness Tourist Board to debate the motion that Lord Thurso, Robin Sinclair, chairman of the board, should be removed from that office because of his involvement in the Flow Country forestry and his support for the disposal of nuclear waste in the Flow Country. A public meeting was held in Watten Village Hall where Lord Thurso and I were each given ten minutes to present our case. When I stood up to speak, I saw before me a sea of scowling, unfriendly faces. Councillor John Green was, I think, chairing the meeting and whilst I was speaking he suddenly snapped at me, 'Just a minute!' Confused, I asked why he had interrupted. 'Just a minute,' he said, 'and then your time is up.' I finished speaking and sat down to complete silence.

When Robin Sinclair stood up to speak, the hall erupted in loud cheers, people standing and clapping their hands. Towards the end of his allotted time I noticed John Green, his hand below the desk where we were all sitting, tugging at Robin's coat and whispering, 'My lord, my lord, your time is up.' Thurso ignored him and carried on talking for another few minutes. A vote was taken and the result announced: for the motion, three votes; against the motion, 102. Once more the hall erupted in loud cheering and waving of hands. I have never felt so isolated in my life. But I had achieved my objective: local and national press, radio and television snapped up the story and the plight of the Flow County was once more in the news.

But Ann and I and our children paid a heavy price for our involvement. I was accused of damaging job prospects by my opposition to the planting. Highland Regional Council even went to the length of issuing a press release advising that my views were not to be trusted, as they failed to appreciate the economic benefits, both nationally and locally, that the planting would bring; allegedly, the council and the tree-planters claimed, more than 2,000 jobs. Anonymous and obscene letters and telephone calls began to arrive. At school, our children were bullied. A Wick shopkeeper refused to serve Ann because of the damage I was doing to employment prospects in the county. A passing van slowed to hurl a sack into our garden. It contained a large and very angry adder. People whom I had counted as friends crossed to the other side of the street when they saw me coming.

The end came in February 1988 when *The Observer* exposed exactly what had been happening in the Flow Country and the names of the investors involved. The Chancellor at the time, Nigel Lawson, closed the tax loophole that had fuelled the frenzy and the planting stopped. It has been estimated that the financial loss to the Treasury was allegedly in the order of £40 million. The largest number of people employed in the planting never amounted to more than 100, and most of them worked on a self-employed basis. But the trees remain, constantly battered by northern winds, and when harvested leave a wasteland behind them – hundreds of acres of tree stumps and ploughed moorlands.

In recent years, the RSPB has purchased a large area of the plantings in east Sutherland and is trying to restore the area to its

former glory by cutting down trees, blocking drains and attracting thousands of visitors to their interpretive centre at Forsinard
in Strath Halladale. I am, however, saddened by the fact that the
RSPB claim to have been responsible for 'saving' the Flows by
mounting a campaign, 'just in time' to do so.

In my honest opinion, nothing could be further from the truth.
I was there then and can't recall seeing much involvement from
the RSPB, apart from a few comments from Roy Dennis, their
man in the north. I do, however, remember seeing, on prime-time
television, Prince Charles up to his knees in the Flow Country,
telling viewers why it was so precious. But I can't remember the
RSPB being involved. If they were – if they did run a campaign –
it failed miserably: nearly 200,000 acres were ploughed and
planted.

In 1990, we moved from Caithness to Tongue in Sutherland,
when school pupils, preparing for exams or work projects, would
come to see me to talk about what had happened during the
Battle of the Flows and why it had happened. It hurt to do so,
and it still hurts, particularly when I see a lot of the people who
wouldn't give me or my views the time of day jumping on the
bandwagon of preserving the Flow Country and enjoying the
millions of taxpayers' pounds being provided to do so, trying to
undo the damage that their indifference helped create. I make no
apology whatsoever if I sound bitter. I am. Ann and I suffered
financially and emotionally because we believed that what was
happening was wrong, and because we were prepared, against
all the odds, to stand up and say so. And, yes, we would do the
same again today.

THE HIGHLAND CLEARANCES

There is still considerable controversy today over the Highland
Clearances of the nineteenth century, when thousands of people
were forced off their land by their lairds to make way for more
profitable sheep farming. Some allege that extreme brutality was

used upon an essentially defenseless population; others, that because of overcrowding the lairds were acting in the best interests of their tenants.

To better understand what happened, read the available material that records these events, including the Sutherland Papers; Alexander Mackenzie's *History of the Highland Clearances*; Donald Macleod's *Gloomy Memories*; John Prebble, *A History of the Highland Clearances*; and perhaps the most valuable source, the findings of the Napier Commission set up in the later years of the century to establish the facts, the precursor of the Crofters Holdings (Scotland) Act 1886, which created legal definitions of crofting and gave crofters protection against any such action taking place in the future.

However, because I have mentioned the Clearances in my text, I have included here a transcript of letters in connection with the Clearances that occurred in the Uists and Barra, taken from Alexander Mackenzie's magisterial volume, which, I suggest, shows beyond reasonable doubt the horror of what happened to these people.

In order to persuade them to go, in August 1851, Cluny's factor, Mr Fleming, commanded everyone to attend a meeting at Lochboisdale, warning that anyone failing to do so would be fined a sum of £2. He promised them, if they agreed to go, that they would be well taken care of in Canada: an agent would meet them at Quebec, they would be provided with food, shelter, clothing and money, and a guide would take them on, into Upper Canada, where there was land and work waiting.

A report in the *Quebec Times* gave the facts:

We noticed in our last [edition] the deplorable condition of the 600 paupers who were sent to this country from the Kilrush Unions. We have today a still more dismal picture to draw. Many of our readers may not be aware that there lives such a personage as Colonel Cordon, proprietor of large estates in South Uist and Barra, in the Highlands of Scotland; we are sorry to be obliged to introduce him to their notice, under circumstances which will not give them a very favourable opinion of his character and heart.

It appears that his tenants on the above mentioned estates were on the verge of starvation, and had probably become an eyesore to the gallant Colonel! What they were to do there? was a question he never put to his conscience. Once landed in Canada, he had no further concern about them. Up to last week, some 1,100 souls from his estates had landed at Quebec, and begged their way to Upper Canada; when in the summer season, having only a daily morsel of food to procure, they probably escaped the extreme misery which seems to be the lot of those who followed them.

On their arrival here, they voluntarily made and signed the following statement: 'We the undersigned passengers per Admiral, from Stornoway, in the Highlands of Scotland do solemnly depose to the following facts: that Colonel Gordon is proprietor of estates in South Uist and Barra; that among many hundreds of tenants and cottars whom he has sent this season from his estates to Canada, he gave directions to his factor, Mr Fleming of Cluny Castle Aberdeenshire, to ship on board of the above named vessel a number of nearly 450 of said tenants and cottars, from the estate in Barra; that accordingly, a great majority of these people, among whom were the undersigned, proceed voluntarily to embark on board the Admiral, at Loch Boisdale, on or about the 11th August, 1851.

'But that several of the people who were intended to

be shipped for this port, Quebec, refused to proceed on board, and, in fact, absconded from their homes to avoid the embarkation. Whereupon Mr Fleming gave orders to a policeman, who was accompanied by the ground officer of the estate in Barra, and some constables, to pursue the people who had run away, among the mountains; which they did, and succeeded in capturing about twenty from the mountains and islands in the neighbourhood.

'But they only came with the officers on an attempt being made on handcuffing them; and that some who ran away were not brought back, in consequence of which four families at least have been divided, some having come in ships to Quebec, while the other members of the same families are left in the Highlands.

'The undersigned further declare, that those who voluntarily embarked, did so under promise to the effect, that Colonel Gordon would defray their passage to Quebec; that the Government Emigration Agent there would send the whole party free to Upper Canada, where, upon arrival, the Government agents would give them work, and furthermore, grant them land on certain conditions.

'The undersigned finally declare, that they are now landed in Quebec so destitute, that if immediate relief be not afforded them, and continued until they are settled in employment, the whole will be liable to perish with want.

'SIGNED: *Hector Lamont and 70 others.*'

The *Quebec Times* report continued:

This is a beautiful picture! Had the scene been laid in Russia or Turkey, the barbarity of the proceeding would have shocked the nerves of the reader; but when it happens in Britain, emphatically the land of liberty, where every man's house, even of but the poorest, is said to be his castle, the expulsion of these unfortunate creatures from their homes – the manhunt with policemen and bailiffs – the violent separation of families – the parent torn from the child, the mother from her daughter, the infamous trickery practised on those who did embark – the abandonment of the aged, the infirm, women, and tender children, in a foreign land – forms a tableau which cannot be dwelt on for an instant without horror.

Words cannot depict the atrocity of the deed. For cruelty less savage, the slave dealers of the south have been held up to execration. And if, as men, the sufferings of these our fellow creatures find sympathy in our hearts, as Canadians their wrongs concern us more dearly.

The fifteen hundred souls whom Colonel Gordon has sent to Quebec this season, have all been supported for the past week at least, and conveyed to Upper Canada at the expense of the colony; and on their arrival in Toronto and Hamilton, the greater number have been dependent on the charity of the benevolent for a morsel of bread.

Four hundred are in the river at present, and will arrive in a day or two, making a total of nearly 2,000 of Colonel Gordon's tenants and cottars whom the province will have to support. The winter is at hand, work is becoming scarce in Upper Canada. Where are these people to find food?

FARMING – FANTASTIC OR FOLLY?

Salmon farming is alleged to be one of Scotland's most success-ful industries and is estimated to be worth upwards of £500 mil-lion pounds to the Scottish economy each year. The industry also claims to support 6,500 jobs, many of which are in remote rural areas where other employment opportunities are limited. Scottish farmed salmon is one of Scotland's biggest export earners, second only to whisky in value. What could there possibly be to dislike about such a clearly valuable adjunct to the Scottish economy?

Farming salmon seemed like a good idea at the time, back in 1965, and a perfect enhancement to subsistence crofting in remote rural areas of the West Highlands and Islands. It was believed that the industry could provide much-needed employment by attracting young families to the area who would then sustain and expand every aspect of community life; new faces and new ideas, a bustling economy and busy shops, more children at local schools, a golden age of growth and prosperity.

Others were less sanguine and predicted that the end result would most likely be tears, acrimony and pollution on an unpre-cedented scale. They claimed that insufficient research had been carried out into the environmental impact of salmon farming and that to proceed without a sound scientific base would be irre-sponsible. This view was echoed in one of the last reports the Nature Conservancy Council, government advisors on environ-mental matters, delivered to the government prior to it being replaced by Scottish Natural Heritage.

Fifty years down the line the doubters seem to have been right: conflict and acrimony certainly surrounds the industry. Some communities in the West Highlands and Islands are mounting furious battles to try to keep the fish-farmers out of their back-yards; thousands of people sign petitions opposing the expan-sion of salmon farming into new areas; conservation groups are considering legal action, accusing fish farms of driving distinct populations of wild salmon and sea-trout to the verge of extinction. They allege that the sea lice that breed in their billions in the farmers' fish-packed cages attack not only farm salmon but also wild fish that pass by their cages.

These allegations have been vigorously denied by the industry. They say that there is not enough evidence to suggest that their sea lice are responsible for any declines in wild fish stocks. Dr Richard Shelton, Principal Officer at the government's Freshwater Fisheries Research Laboratory in Pitlochry, and now retired, and Professor David Mackay, the former North Region Director of the Scottish Environment Protection Agency (SEPA) don't seem to agree. BBC News reported on 13 June 2000: 'Professor David Mackay told a conference in Norway last year that intensive farming [of salmon] was distorting natural ecosystems. The SEPA northern regional director also said that evidence the sea lice from the caged fish were harming wild stocks was beyond reasonable doubt.'

In a letter to Andrew Thin, the Scottish Government's Freshwater Fisheries Review chairman, dated January 2014, Dr Shelton wrote: 'My colleagues and I at the Freshwater Laboratory and our opposite numbers in the Irish Republic have known since 1989 that the collapse of sea-trout populations in West Highland Scotland was being driven by the large number of sea lice associated with the cage rearing of salmon . . . Efforts to reduce sea louse numbers to a level which do not threaten the wild fish have failed dismally despite the large scale use of dangerous chemicals which do ultimately threaten the valuable lobster, prawn and crab fisheries in the Highlands and Islands.'

None of these claims and counter-claims is new: for more than twenty years the industry and those concerned about the adverse impact they say salmon farming is having on the marine and freshwater environment have been fighting over this same ground. All of the many attempts at finding common purpose through consultation have failed: meetings, joint committees, discussion papers, aquaculture framework strategies, codes of conduct, et al.

At the heart of this dispute are matters of importance, now, and to future generations: on the one hand, the perceived risk to the health and integrity of an irreplaceable part of Scotland's natural heritage, its wild salmonids; on the other, the economic wealth that the fish-farmers say they bring to the nation. However, the beauty of the Highlands and Islands of Scotland draw thousands of visitors each year to enjoy the majesty of its mountains, moorlands and myriad lochs and rivers.

Visiting yachts anchor in sheltered bays, crews coming ashore in the evening to local restaurants and hostelries to relish wonderful seafood; scallops, mussels, lobsters, crab and prawns, freshly delivered each day. Children splash in crystal-clear shallows and play on white-sand, near-deserted beaches. Local communities rely on income by providing visitors with bed-and-breakfast accommodation, self-catering cottages and caravan sites and other services. Guesthouses and hotels cater for all tastes and offer extensive employment opportunities.

Rod and line sport anglers have always prized the salmon, sea-trout and brown trout that thrived in this once-pristine, unpolluted environment. But now many lochs and rivers that once supported remarkable numbers of fish are virtually devoid of these species because, it is alleged, of the impact of fish-farm sea lice. The Loch Maree Hotel in Wester Ross, where some 1,500 sea-trout could be caught each season, and which employed eleven gillies to guide anglers to the best fishing spots, has closed its doors. Other West Highland and Islands fisheries that enjoyed a worldwide reputation for the quality of sport have suffered a similar fate, including Stack, More, Shiel and Eilt, and the rivers Dionard, Laxford, Inver, Kirkaig and Ailort, where the fish-farming story began.

The late Mrs Pauline Cameron-Head of Inverailort House is credited with bringing the dubious benefits of salmon farming to Scotland. In 1965 she agreed to lease her land for use as a shore-base from which to service a fish farm in Loch Ailort, a sea loch on the famous 'Road to the Isles', close to where Bonnie Prince Charlie landed in 1745 to try to reclaim his father's lost kingship of the British Isles.

The fish-farm company involved in the deal was the precursor of the company we know today as Norwegian-owned Marine Harvest, the largest producer of farm salmon in the world. The company operates a fish farm in Loch Ailort to this day. Loch Eilt and the River Ailort, which drain into Loch Ailort, used to be counted as amongst the most prolific sea-trout systems in Scotland and could produce 1,000 sea-trout each season. A picture, taken in 1941 of Lochan Dubh, an extension of the river, shows just how many sea-trout used to run the system. It was sent to me by Iain Thornber – historian, archaeologist and author from Morvern. He explained that explosives were used to kill the fish in the picture, hence the soldier with the fishing rod strategically placed to try to suggest that the fish had been caught legally.

All of the fish were sea-trout and they were used to feed Special Operations Executive commandos stationed at nearby Inverailort Castle. Iain remembers Pauline Cameron-Head telling him that the number of sea-trout in the system was so great that the noise they made splashing upstream to spawning grounds could be heard from the castle. Now, the numbers of sea-trout caught may be counted on the fingers of one hand, with some fingers to spare.

The assumption that fish-farming would be initiated and carried out by crofters never materialised; capital costs were high, disease episodes and consequent loss of stock frequent, and the expertise required to successfully rear fish to slaughter-weight was woefully absent. This knowledge gap was eagerly filled by fishery scientists from government agencies, the Fisheries Research Services, now renamed as Marine Scotland, and by scientists from a number of universities, including Aberdeen and St Andrews, and the Department of Aquaculture at Stirling University. Funding grants for further research programmes into fish-farming came from the European Union, UK government and industry bodies.

Within a short time the industry began to consolidate into fewer and fewer farms owned and run by fewer and fewer multinational companies, the majority of which were Norwegian. In the 1980s, when 20,000 tonnes of farmed salmon were being produced annually, the industry directly employed in excess of 2,000 people on the farms, fulfilling the claim that jobs were being created. However, by the mid-1990s when production peaked at nearly 150,000 tonnes, employment figures, because of advances in technology – particularly automatic feeding systems – the number of jobs had fallen to below 1,000. Indirect employment, however, soared, reaching an alleged 7,000 people; but almost 50 per cent of these jobs were taken by immigrants from Europe and the Middle East, and some 25 per cent of those were illegal entrants to the UK. Indeed, it is not unreasonable to argue that if immigrant workers were not available, then the industry could face a huge crisis; witness to which statement is the fact that a few years ago Marine Harvest was advertising for Polish-speaking applicants to more effectively help train their Polish workers.

The industry claims that it is one of the most highly regulated businesses in the world and open to constant scrutiny and control. This is substantially true, but those worried by the fish-farmer's actions suggest that such scrutiny is poorly implemented and ineffective, one anomaly being that for most of its existence the Crown Estate had the sole right to issue sea-bed licences to operate fish farms and to issue planning permissions. The Crown Estate benefits to the tune of approximately £2 million a year from fish-farming and this suggested a clear conflict of interest. After more than seven years of government promises, the planning role was given to local authorities. SEPA also had to give its approval for operating cages in the sea and generally did. For instance, during the period 2008 to 2011, SEPA received more than 200 applications, all but fifteen of which were approved.

The problems for wild salmon and sea-trout from fish farms are, however, vividly illustrated by comparing wild fish numbers in east coast rivers, such as the Spey, Dee, Tay and Tweed, with those in the West Highlands and Islands: whilst there has been a total collapse of wild stocks in many of the latter, with few signs of recovery, there are currently significant numbers of fish returning to spawn in the former. There are no fish farms in east coast waters because, when fish-farming began, I believe that it was decided to adopt a precautionary principle to protect the east coast rivers and give the industry free reign to operate amongst the smaller rivers in the west. There was no public consultation in connection with this decision, but, in substance, this is the core of the present dispute: wild fish that have survived in these waters since the end of the last Ice Age seem to be being sacrificed for the financial benefit of a few.

There is a way out of this impasse that would, I believe, be of benefit to both sides of the argument: move the industry into land-based closed containment systems. There would be immense financial savings for the industry, including freedom from sea-lice attack and other sea-borne diseases, reduced expenditure on chemicals and medicines, no escapes from farms and a more secure work-platform for staff. For anglers, Scotland's wild salmon and sea-trout would have unhindered and safe access to their natal spawning grounds to get on with what they do best, the propagation of their species.

Such land-based closed containment systems already operate in Canada – Kuterra Salmon on Vancouver Island – and the Norwegians themselves are also showing interest in the project. It makes sense – at least it does to me, and it offers a realistic opportunity to bring this sad, sorry and unseemly conflict to an end. Realistically, only the Scottish Government can bring this about, but I have no confidence that they will do so now or in the future. For nearly three decades I have tried to do what I can to bring these matters to the attention of the public, in the belief that if they knew the real cost of the farm salmon they would not buy it. I don't, do you?

THE ANNUAL GENERAL MEETING

The Annual General Meeting of the Sandison Family Fishing Association was held in the Dining-Room, Louisburgh Street, Wick, Caithness, at 8 p.m. on 23 October 1977.

Members Present: Mr Bruce Sandison (Chairman) and Mrs Ann Sandison (Secretary and Treasurer), Mr Blair Sandison (Maintenance and Repairs Officer), Ms Lewis-Ann Sandison (Social Affairs Officer), Mr Charles Sandison (Catering Clerk), and Miss Jean Sandison.

Associate Member: Horace Cat.

The minutes of the last meeting having been read, the Chairman welcomed the members, including the newest, Miss Jean Sandison, aged three. He hoped Miss Sandison would enjoy her association with the Association and asked the Secretary to restrain the new member from eating the agenda papers.

The Chairman reported that the catch for the year showed a satisfactory increase on previous years, due largely to his personal skill and untiring efforts on behalf of the Association. He commented that perhaps, in future, other members of the Association should try harder.

Ms Lewis-Ann Sandison said that if other members fished as often as the Chairman did, then the figure would have been considerably higher – but someone had to wash dishes, cut lawns, do the ironing, cook meals, babysit and generally look after the house.

The Secretary thanked Ms Lewis-Ann Sandison for her kind remarks. She said that she felt it was her duty to ensure that all the members had as much opportunity as possible to go fishing and that she did not really mind, as long as everyone else enjoyed themselves.

Ms Lewis-Ann Sandison replied that she was talking about

herself, not the Secretary, who had been out fishing far more often than certain other members of the Association.

The Chairman called the meeting to order and thanked Ms Lewis-Ann Sandison for her work on behalf of the Association. He assured Ms Lewis-Ann Sandison that her remarks would be noted and appropriate action taken to ensure that other members shared her heavy burden.

Mr Charles Sandison pointed out that although he would be delighted to play a greater role in such matters, members should be aware that his time was strictly limited, due to the pressure of work at school.

Mr Blair Sandison said that he would like to raise the question of missed fish, and asked the Chairman what action he proposed to take, if any, to improve his casting technique.

The Chairman replied that he was far more concerned by the apparent difficulty some members had when trying to use a landing-net, particularly when landing the Chairman's trout.

Mr Blair Sandison commented that if members were expected to work with second-rate, worn-out equipment, accidents were bound to happen. Whilst he regretted losing the Chairman's 1lb trout, he felt bound to add that it was unreasonable to expect members to hang out of boats for hours in force-five gales whilst the Chairman allowed a small fish to run rings round him.

The Chairman said that the trout in question had weighed at least 41b and that Mr Blair Sandison's failure to land the fish was, to say the least, suspicious. It was agreed that the Secretary investigate the purchase of yet another landing-net for next season.

Miss Jean Sandison said that she wanted to go fishing. The Secretary explained that it was too dark and that all the fish had gone to their beds. Miss Jean Sandison began to cry and said that it was not fair.

Due to the rising cost of electricity and the expense of keeping the dining-room fire going, the Chairman proposed that the meeting be continued in the kitchen. Ms Lewis-Ann Sandison said that it was only because some people wanted to be nearer the drinks cupboard.

Mr Charles Sandison said that he would like some warm, sweet tea, chocolate biscuits, lemonade or anything else that happened to be going.

The Chairman said that he would prefer a large whisky with a little water and Mr Blair Sandison said that he would too.

Upon being put to the vote, the motion was carried and the meeting continued in the kitchen.

Mr Charles Sandison reminded the meeting that there were only fifty-one shopping days left until Christmas and please could he have a fishing-rod of his own. Miss Jean Sandison said that she wanted one too.

The Secretary was instructed to raise the matter with Mr Claus, but the Chairman reminded the meeting that funds were limited and that his rod would require refurbishing after falling into Loch Watten.

Mr Blair Sandison said that whilst he sympathised with the Chairman's predicament, he felt that this expense should be borne by the Chairman, personally, since it had been due to the Chairman's own stupidity that the rod had been lost.

Whilst agreeing with Mr Blair Sandison, the Chairman pointed out that the cost of hiring a frogman for a day had not been light and that he had hoped that the Association might agree to help with these costs.

Ms Lewis-Ann Sandison said that she agreed with Mr Blair Sandison and that people should pay for their own silliness. The Secretary reminded the members that it was customary to be polite to fellow members and asked Ms Lewis-Ann Sandison and Mr Blair Sandison to withdraw their remarks and apologise to the Chairman.

Ms Lewis-Ann Sandison and Mr Blair Sandison said that they were sorry. Mrs Ann Sandison said that the cost of recovering and repairing the Chairman's rod was far cheaper than the cost of buying a new rod, and members should be glad that the Chairman's rod had been found.

Upon being put to the vote, it was agreed that the Association pay 50 per cent of the cost of having the Chairman's rod refurbished, provided that he promised not to do it again, and agreed to stop hiding his fly boxes from other members.

At this point Horace Cat left the meeting to attend to urgent business in the garden.

The following year's holiday was discussed at length. Ms Lewis-Ann Sandison proposed that the 1978 venue should be the southwest of France, a Greek island, or at least somewhere where there was a beach and it was warm – like normal people enjoyed.

Mr Blair Sandison sympathised with Ms Lewis-Ann Sandison but pointed out that baking beaches and Greek islands were not noted for the excellence of their trout fishing. Upon being put to the vote it was agreed that the 1978 holiday should be a fishing holiday in the wilds of Sutherland.

It was proposed by Ms Lewis-Ann Sandison and seconded by Mr Blair Sandison that the Chairman and Secretary curtail their smoking and drinking in order to defray anticipated holiday costs and provide better equipment for other members with the money thus saved.

The Chairman and Secretary suggested that a sub-committee be formed to investigate this possibility, reporting back to the Association at their next Annual General Meeting.

Ms Lewis-Ann Sandison commented that such a solution seemed to her to be nothing other than an undignified attempt to delay making a decision and demanded a named vote on the subject.

Upon being put to the vote, three members, Mr Blair Sandison, Ms Lewis-Ann Sandison and Mr Charles Sandison, supported the motion. Mr Bruce Sandison, Mrs Ann Sandison and Miss Jean Sandison opposed the motion.

The Chairman then used his casting vote to decide the issue in favour of a sub-committee report, reminding Ms Lewis-Ann Sandison that this was simply another example of the democratic process in action.

The Sandison Cup for the heaviest trout of the season was then awarded to the Chairman, for a fish weighing 1lb 14oz from Loch Watten. There was some desultory clapping and Miss Jean Sandison said that she wanted one too.

Congratulating the Chairman, Mr Blair Sandison said that he had no doubt that he would win the Cup back next season, provided the Chairman stopped knocking his fish off while pretending to land them.

It was unanimously agreed that the Chairman and Secretary be reappointed for the following year.

In his closing remarks, the Chairman thanked the members of the Association for their continued support and said that he felt privileged to belong to one of the best angling clubs in the world.

Miss Jean Sandison having fallen asleep, and there being no further business, the meeting ended at 11 p.m.

Bruce Sandison (Chairman) SFFA